Social Studies and Social Sciences: A Fifty-Year Perspective

◆❖◆

Stanley P. Wronski
Donald H. Bragaw
Editors

National Council for the Social Studies

Bulletin No. 78
ISBN 0-87986-052-9

NATIONAL COUNCIL
FOR THE SOCIAL STUDIES

Library of Congress Catalog Card Number 86-61765
ISBN 0-87986-052-9
Copyright © 1986 by the
NATIONAL COUNCIL FOR THE SOCIAL STUDIES
3501 Newark Street N.W., Washington, DC 20016

TABLE OF CONTENTS

CONTRIBUTORS

Beverly J. Armento is an Associate Professor of Social Studies Education and the Director of the Center for Business and Economic Education at Georgia State University in Atlanta. She has held leadership positions in the National Council for the Social Studies, American Educational Research Association, and the National Association of Economic Educators. Her most recent publications include "Research on Teaching Social Studies" in AERA's *Handbook of Research on Teaching,* and various chapters on economic education in NEA and NCSS publications. Her research interests focus on the development of economic thought in children of various ages.

John K. Bare is a Professor Emeritus of Psychology at Carleton College, having taught there for 25 years, in addition to nine years at William and Mary and two at Brown University. He has been the chairperson of the Education and Training Board of the American Psychological Association, President of APA's Division of the Teaching of Psychology, and Director of the Human Behavior Curriculum Project from 1973 to 1977, which was funded by the National Science Foundation to APA.

William E. Becker, Jr., is a Professor of Economics at Indiana University. He has published numerous articles in the *American Economic Review, American Journal of Agricultural Economics, Journal of Finance, Journal of Human Resources,* and other refereed research journals. In addition to authoring several commissioned monographs and giving expert statistical and econometric testimony in Minnesota and Indiana courtrooms, he has written *A Complement to Choice* and coedited *Academic Rewards in Higher Education* Prior to joining Indiana University's faculty, he was a tenured faculty member at the University of Minnesota and a research fellow of the Federal Deposit Insurance Corporation. He received his Ph.D. in economics from the University of Pittsburgh in 1973.

Donald H. Bragaw, Chief of the Bureau of Social Studies at the New York State Education Department, has been involved with social studies education at all levels of schooling, elementary through graduate school, as both teacher and administrator. He is immediate past president of the National Council for the Social Studies. He has also served as president of the New York State and Long Island Councils for the Social Studies.

Thomas L. Dynneson is a Professor of Education and Anthropology. He is currently serving as Acting Coordinator of the Anthropology Department and also coordinates social studies education at the University of Texas of the Permian Basin. While he was a Visiting Scholar at Stanford University, several project and research studies resulted in grants and publications in cooperation with the two universities. Author of over 30 articles in addition to books, pamphlets, and chapters, he has applied anthropological concepts to the processes of learning and teaching. His current project is a joint project with Stanford University relating to culture and citizenship.

J. Ross Eshleman is a Professor of Sociology at Wayne State University. He chaired the department for 10 years prior to resigning in 1983 to devote full time to teaching and writing. He has written textbooks entitled *Sociology: An Introduction,* now in a second edition, and *The Family: An Introduction,* now in a fourth edition. He has served as director of seven summer institutes for high school teachers of sociology, has received two Fulbright teaching awards to the Philippines, and was employed in the education directorate of the National Science Foundation.

John G. Gunnell is a Professor of Political Science at the Nelson A. Rockefeller College of Public Affairs and Policy, State University of New York at Albany. He is the author of books and articles dealing with the history of political theory and problems of social scientific inquiry. His most recent work is *Between Philosophy and Politics: The Alienation of Political Theory.*

Joseph M. Kirman is Professor of Elementary Education, Social Studies Area, and Director of Project Omega for Research in Remote Sensing and Aerospace Education at the University of Alberta. He is a former member of the Province of Alberta's Social Studies Curriculum Committee and a former Chairperson of both the NCSS Curriculum Advisory Committee and Science and Society Advisory Committee.

Richard S. Knight is Associate Professor of Secondary Education at Utah State University. Formerly a high school social studies teacher, he now teaches classes in social studies curriculum and methods, values education, adult development and theories of teaching. He has written about students' rights, moral and values education, and teaching citizenship through high school psychology courses. He is currently interested in reconciling traditional values with modern values in social studies and in the entire secondary curriculum.

Salvatore J. Natoli is Deputy Executive Director of the Association of American Geographers as well as the Project Director for the Geographic Education National Implementation Project (GENIP), a joint project of the National Council for Geographic Education, the AAG, the National Geographic Society, and the American Geographical Society. He has taught geography in secondary schools, colleges and universities, and worked with the U.S. Office of Education before joining the AAG as its Educational Affairs Director in 1969. He is author or editor of over 60 publications in various fields of geography and geographic education. His most recent publication is *Geography in Internationalizing the Undergraduate Curriculum.*

Roger C. Owen is a Professor of Anthropology at Queens College, City University of New York, where he was elected Distinguished Teacher of the

Year, 1984–85. Owen's specialty is the study of American Indians and Mexican peasants, on which he has published over 30 articles and monographs. He also has done extensive work in social studies curriculum development and teacher training through National Science Foundation institutes. He is the author of *Inquiring about Culture: Studies in Anthropology and Sociology*, an elementary school social studies text.

Paul Robinson is an associate Professor and Head, Division of Teaching and Teacher Education, in the College of Education at the University of Arizona. He is a former secondary teacher, previous chair of the College and Faculty Assembly of NCSS and past president of the Arizona Council for the Social Studies. His publications focus on the history of the social studies curriculum. He is currently editing a volume of historical essays for Kappa Delta Pi, an International Honor Society in Education.

James P. Shaver is a Professor of Secondary Education and Associate Dean for Research in the College of Education at Utah State University. He has taught social studies at the junior and senior high school levels. He is a past president of NCSS and a recipient of the NCSS Citation for Exemplary Research in Social Studies Education. His publications include five books related to citizenship education, the Analysis of Public Issues Program for classroom use, and over 70 articles. A current research interest is the modification of attitudes toward disabled persons.

Thomas J. Switzer is the Associate Dean of the School of Education at the University of Michigan in Ann Arbor. A former high school teacher in Iowa, he came to Michigan as a curriculum writer for Sociological Resources for the Social Studies, a curriculum project of the American Sociological Association. At the University of Michigan, his teaching and research have focused on social studies education, the dissemination and utilization of new curricular materials, and the change process in education. He is currently completing a term on the curriculum committee of the National Council for the Social Studies.

David D. VanHoose is an Assistant Professor of Economics at Indiana University. He teaches courses in macroeconomics and monetary economics at the undergraduate and graduate levels and has authored recent articles in the *Journal of Banking and Finance,* the *Journal of Macroeconomics,* and the *Journal of Money, Credit, and Banking.* Before joining the faculty at Indiana University, he was an instructor at North Carolina State University and at East Carolina University.

David D. Van Tassel is the Elbert J. Benton Professor of History at Case Western Reserve University in Cleveland, Ohio, and is the founder and president of National History Day. He has served as vice-president of the American Historical Association, Teaching Division. He co-authored *Computer-Assisted Research in Educational History.* His other publications include *Recording America's Past: An Interpretation of the Development of Historical Studies in*

America, 1607–1884, and, most recently, an article, "From Learned Society to Professional Organization: The American Historical Association, 1884 to 1900," which appeared in the *American Historical Review,* and a volume of essays entitled *Cleveland: A Tradition of Reform.*

Barbara J. Winston is Professor of Geography and Environmental Studies at Northeastern Illinois University in Chicago. She is a former elementary and secondary teacher who now teaches in the geography, environmental studies, and social studies programs at Northeastern Illinois. Her most recent publication is *Map and Globe Skills: K–8 Teaching Guide,* published by the National Council for Geographic Education. She is currently working on a 4th grade social studies textbook; with a committee she is developing detailed K–6 curriculum guidelines in geography.

Michael Wertheimer is Professor of Psychology at the University of Colorado at Boulder. A generalist in a field that has many specialties, he has been president of the Rocky Mountain Psychological Association and of several divisions of the American Psychological Association: teaching of psychology, theoretical and philosophical psychology, general psychology, and the history of psychology. Among his recent books are *Fundamental Issues in Psychology, A Brief History of Psychology, Psychology: A Brief Introduction,* and *History of Psychology: A Guide to Information Sources.* He was the 1983 recipient of the American Psychological Foundation's Award for Distinguished Teaching in Psychology. James Brodie, David Fendrich, Suzanne Mannes and Matthew Sharps were graduate students in psychology, and Chie Okuda and James Weisberg undergraduates at the University of Colorado at the time Chapter 13 was drafted.

Stanley P. Wronski, Professor Emeritus of Education and Social Science at Michigan State University, is a past president of the National Council for the Social Studies, and also of a regional council and a state council. His publications include a social studies methods book, a social foundations book of readings, and a high school textbook. He was a member of the U.S. National Commission for UNESCO and spent two years as a consultant to the Ministry of Education in Thailand. He has taught inservice courses for teachers in international schools in Japan, Okinawa, the Philippines, Central America, Europe and Egypt.

NCSS Publications Staff for *Social Studies and Social Science:*
A Fifty-Year Perspective
Charles R. Rivera, *Editor and Director of Publications*
Anne Janney, *Associate Editor*
Mary Pat Doherty, *Art Director*
Mildred Edwards, *Indexer, Proofreader*
Margaret Cromartie, *Publications Assistant*

PREFACE

It was the worst of times. In 1935, the world was still mired in the deepest depression of the Industrial Age. Industries were operating at a fraction of their potential output. Unemployment in the western world was at a record high. In the United States, a new administration was proposing a New Deal that would fundamentally change relationships among government, industry and labor. In Europe, the rising surge of 19th-century nationalism that had given birth to two unified nations was now transforming these political entities into emerging totalitarian states.

It was the best of times. The field of the social studies was in ferment. In 1935 a distinguished group of historians, social scientists and educators, organized into a National Commission on the Social Studies, had just completed a five-year study that would have an impact on the curriculum for decades to come. Experimental and highly controversial social studies textbooks were being adopted in many schools, and the then revolutionary educational theories of John Dewey and his fellow progressives were being sparsely but significantly implemented in both U.S. and European schools.

This publication documents the development of the social studies during the past 50 years. Because the social studies do not exist in a social vacuum, the editors have also invited distinguished social scientists to chronicle developments in their respective disciplines during the same period. What emerges from these dual inputs is a composition depicting society and the social studies—sometimes blending harmoniously, at other times carrying complementary themes, and occasionally punctuated with contrapuntal rhythms and tunes.

One major motif occurs in a sometimes joyful and other times ominous key: the social studies reflect and are influenced by the social setting in which they exist. The social upheavals of the 1930s also saw the appearance of scattered radical social studies curricula. The McCarthyism of the 1950s stifled not only political dissent but also academic freedom—extending even into the secondary and elementary schools. The new Great Society of the 1960s also ushered in the New Social Studies. The return to conservatism of the 1970s and '80s was paralleled by a return to the basics—frequently with devastatingly negative impact on both the quantity and quality of social studies offerings in the schools.

If this publication gives the reader some greater insight and broader perspective on the evolving nature of the social studies, it will have served its purpose. And the editors will have mainly the various chapter contributors to thank for this accomplishment. The instruction to the social science authors was to give a panoramic view of their discipline stressing the persistent problems, issues and trends in the *study* of that subject from approximately 1935 to 1985. The parallel instruction to the social studies authors was to give an overview of the persistent problems, issues and trends in the *teaching* of that subject from 1935 to 1985.

The editors wish to acknowledge the invaluable assistance given to them by the Director of Publications of the National Council for the Social Studies, Charles Rivera, and his staff associates. And it is with a feeling that goes beyond fatherly pride and appreciation that we also recognize the many hours of editorial assistance volunteered by Linda Wronski, who has drawn upon considerable past experience as an editor of a professional journal.

Stanley P. Wronski
Donald H. Bragaw

INTRODUCTION

Donald H. Bragaw

This volume marks the third time that the National Council for the Social Studies has brought together a group of essays dealing with the social science disciplines and the major intellectual developments that have occurred within each field. In 1958, Roy Price edited the 28th yearbook entitled *New Viewpoints in the Social Sciences.* According to Price, the purpose of the National Council then was to "present new viewpoints in the several social science disciplines, to the end that such findings may be more extensively incorporated in addition to those which have already been utilized in American education." Jack Allen, president of the National Council that year, noted in his Preface that there was a "lag between the data provided by social science research and the information present in the mainstream of social studies teaching." Both Allen and Price saw this National Council publication as serving the profession by closing the gap between scholarship and school instruction.

The second effort to update information about the social sciences came as a result of a joint project conducted by the National Council for the Social Studies and the American Council of Learned Societies between 1958 and 1962. Harcourt, Brace published the *Social Studies and the Social Sciences,* a volume of essays whose express purpose was to provide a "cumulative picture of what the social studies curriculum might include." The key question posed to each of the symposium writers was: "What ought a high school graduate know about my field?" Each of the discipline scholars considered that his or her own area should receive a central position in the social studies curriculum and couched the recommendations accordingly. In his introduction to the symposium, Bernard Berelson, distinguished sociologist and then head of The Population Council, said that the relation of the social sciences to the social studies was to "give high school students the best introduction we can . . . to the best knowledge from the social science disciplines as a means to an end of producing responsible citizens." Such knowledge should make students aware of cultural diversity, the need for a wider perspective on society, and a knowledge of some research methods. Berelson saw these needs as especially important, considering that the secondary school social studies program would be the last exposure of many students to these fields of knowledge, and that such exposure would provide the intellectual base to prepare for the inevitable changes they would experience in the 21st century. Of course, the 1962 volume reflected the state of the art in the social science disciplines, but its primary purpose was to provide guidance for the selection of social sciences content for the elementary and secondary social studies program.

The editors of this present publication have chosen to peg the time span of these chapters at 50 years to approximate the time between the appearance of the 16 volumes that constituted the Report of the Commission on the Social

Studies of the American Historical Association (1932 to 1937), the first independent annual meeting of the National Council (1935), and the 50th anniversary of the latter event (1985). The editors have also followed the lead of those who edited previous volumes by including history as one of the social sciences, fully realizing that some readers may desire to classify that discipline as one of the humanitites. Any attempt to separate history and the social sciences when it comes to defining social studies is wasted energy for programs in schools, which, unlike many universities, do not force the unnatural separation of the disciplines. History and the social sciences have affected each other so significantly over the years that the strict lines of separation have become blurred. Geography, anthropology, sociology, political science and economics have strong historical bases, and history has been greatly enhanced by the use of social science concepts and research. Social studies, as a school subject, draws upon all the social science disciplines for its main strength, and occasionally incorporates materials from other areas including the natural sciences, mathematics and the humanities. The study of society would not permit a narrower focus.

The present volume retains one of the major features of the two previous ones. It updates the major trends in history, political science, sociology, economics, psychology, anthropology and geography. In doing so, it provides an intellectual history as a background check on the social sciences for curriculum writers, teachers, administrators, methods course instructors and other interested parties. Even within the relatively short span of 50 years, important changes have occurred in all the academic fields of study. Those changes have, in part, reflected the changing nature of our society (e.g., a growing awareness of both black and female roles), as well as changing perspectives as a result of basic research in each of the disciplines (e.g., greater emphasis on quantification of data).

Two new features distinguish this publication from its predecessors. The first is the emphasis on *continuing* problems, trends and issues in both the social sciences and social studies. That is, the social science authors were asked to answer not only the question "What's new?" but also "What's old—but still significant?" For example, the chapter on political science deals with the still unresolved problems of what should be the theoretical underpinnings of the discipline. The chapter on sociology deals with the continuing influence of three prominent 19th century "founding fathers" of the discipline, and the chapter on economics has as a recurring theme the proper mix between laissez faire economics and governmental intervention in the market place. In this respect the essays deal with the fundamental yin and yang themes in the study of any discipline—continuity and change.

The second new feature is the series of complementing essays describing what developments have occurred in the teaching of the discipline areas at the elementary and secondary levels. Each of these essays, written by a professional who both knows the academic field and has observed school practice, seeks to identify the major impacts that the disciplines have had upon the teaching of social studies. Each one of the authors has touched upon the dilemma of social studies as being a collection of discrete social science courses (the simplified university approach), or discrete courses with an overarching, but usually loose, thematic unity (i.e., citizenship education), or a program of study that integrates or synthesizes data from all of the disciplines around a notion—for example, social reconstruction. On the one hand, geographers decry poor student knowledge of basic political/physical geographic information; yet they still want students to be knowledgeable about the larger issues of the impact of geography on public policy. It is the balance of knowledge of the specific discipline and the usefulness to overall notions of citizen responsibility that has yet to be achieved in social studies education—and the search continues.

It was not the intention of this volume to attempt to solve such dilemmas; but the essays do, I believe, resharpen the arguments and provide a better basis upon which to renew the struggle. It may be my own predilection, but I feel that most of the essays reach a consensus—one that may not have previously existed—around the recognition that social science/social studies programs might more profitably be directed at educating a citizenry in how to deal with public policy issues. Sharpening the debate to that focus may promote a greater sense of the holistic mission of social studies education. While the Harvard public issues project of the 1960s accomplished that exact purpose, few of the other discipline-oriented projects of that time were really concerned with that potentially centralizing goal for school programs in social studies. The present essays suggest to me that the profession may well be on the verge of an intellectual breakthrough. We still need, as Wilma Longstreet has sought, a new research orientation toward citizenship as a discipline. Public policy notions and research may be a line into that goal. What was not programmatically "acceptable" in the 1960s may now be an idea whose time has come.

An important caveat to the reader should be made at this time. Despite the organization of the volume around discrete, separate subjects it should not be inferred that the editors are advocating a social studies curriculum based exclusively on separate subjects like history, geography or civics. Compelling arguments can still be made for a holistic, unified social studies curriculum or at least one that integrates two or more of the traditional subjects. The separate subject organization of this volume was dictated by limitations of space and time. However valid the rationale for an integrated social studies curriculum may be, it is beyond the scope of one volume.

Almost midway in the period under discussion in these essays, the social sciences and the social studies experienced major ferment. Readers who lived and taught in the halcyon days of the late 1950s and 1960s will recall the amazing intellectual and methodological strides that all of the social science fields made at that time. The post-World War II period had witnessed an upsurge in the popularity and development of social and behavioral science disciplines, and in the late '50s and '60s the impact of enormous federal funding brought about additional stimulation. That ferment reached into the elementary and secondary schools as well. Many of the "new social studies" educational projects that emerged during that period narrowed the intellectual gap between the university and the schools. Most of these projects involved one or more university scholars from both the social sciences and education in a collaboration with school teachers for at least part of the time. Indeed, the power of these projects was the substantial discipline (sometimes multidiscipline) base that each had. From that base innovative methodology emerged. Each of the pedagogically oriented essay writers in this present volume—some with nostalgia, and all with conscious recognition of achievement—mark out this period as one of great thinking and forward progress in attempting to reconcile the most recent social science research with equivalent research in how students learn. As a result of the work of Jerome Bruner, Ted Fenton, Fred Newmann and others, a very real effort was made to involve students as the key part of the learning process. The social—interactive—part of social studies education became a highly significant factor. All of the essay writers also recognize, however, that even with noble implementation efforts, the project's materials never found wide acceptance. That fact does not detract from the ultimate influence that these projects had, especially in the area of critical thinking skills. This impact can be seen today in textbooks and materials that have incorporated many of the project's innovative ideas.

Because social studies is the study of society in the past, present and future, it calls upon the information and methodologies of any and all disciplines— social sciences, physical and biological sciences, the humanities—to help students make sense of their world and encourage their participation in its development. Social studies obtains strength from its mission of empowering students to take masses of social science and other data to study, clarify and organize it to define or explain certain social interactions. It is important, then, that long-range continuity as well as short-range changes in social sciences and social studies be understood at this time when all education is undergoing reexamination.

School district personnel charged with looking at their social studies curriculum will find the essays helpful as gauges against which to measure the currency of this information and the conceptual and instructional bases of their programs. In part these essays constitute meta-research guides to help winnow the less significant from the more significant trends that should channel teacher reading and preparation. In an ideal scenario, school districts, in collaboration with local college and university personnel, would allow opportunities for the intellectual updating of their instructional staff. Research, reading and thinking time is not ordinarily provided to classroom teachers, and summer curriculum institutes frequently assume that a quick-fix substantive upgrading can be accomplished in the period between the closing of school and the beginning of the district's annual summer curriculum writing program. Only through providing such time can the heavy reliance upon textbooks be broken, and boards of education be confident that their staff is equipped to provide the best educational experiences for the students.

CHAPTER 1

TRIALS OF CLIO

David D. Van Tassel

During the past half century, as the world was torn by numerous revolutions and a world war, the discipline of history had its own revolution. Historians could point to appropriate theories to justify their view of themselves as objective scientists or moral judges or assume many roles in between. History has seen the breakdown of two powerful narrative syntheses: the Eurocentric "rise of Western Civilization" and with it the change from the expressive art of narrative to the explanatory prose of analysis.

The last two decades have also seen the proliferation of new methodologies: the rapid growth of quantification—cliometrics; the introduction of psychological method in the form of psychohistory; and sociological concepts, techniques and terminology in generational history and historical demography. In addition, the last two decades have seen the opening of new fields of study: African history, Asian history, Middle Eastern history, and Eastern European history. New groups have come within the purview of the historian: women, blacks, and ethnic groups of all kinds. The New History of the old progressives has evolved into the New Social History. And finally, what appears to be an impenetrable tangle in the web of history created from skeins of information produced by new and powerful analytical tools, new subject matter, sources, and interpretations may be unwinding into a new narrative synthesis emerging from historians' application of an anthropological concept of culture.

The sense of crisis and change is ever present among historians. In the 1930s, while the Depression loomed large in the minds of most historians, a still more pervasive crisis agitated the followers of Clio, the Muse of history. It was the "intellectual crisis which, so far as thinking goes, dwarfs the present economic unpleasantness into insignificance" (Nichols 1933). Old values seemed to be disappearing, ideas that were long hallowed by general acceptance were being discarded, and "the rarified air of the intellect resounded with the crash of falling idols" (Nichols 1935). But historian Roy Nichols predicted that the coming new synthesis in the teaching of history would make use of a principle akin to relativity. "It will," he said, "have as its core a theory of relative values—the complexity of life can be resolved only by sorting out some threads and analyzing and comparing them."

This was a characteristic statement of the painful awakening to uncertainty in the sciences as the historical profession groped for greater sophistication. The most dramatic aspect of this searching process was the attack upon and rapid decline of the long-held faith of historians in their own objectivity.

THE NEW HISTORY

Proponents of the New History, whose manifesto was published by James Harvey Robinson in 1912, had by implication supported a kind of historical relativism. However, their major concern was to broaden the scope of history by using the methods and concepts of the newer social sciences to develop a history more pertinent to the solution of present problems. The proponents of the New History for the most part still believed in the possibility of arriving at objective truth through the scientific method. They "did not believe that they were entering a realm in which the usual canons of scientific procedure no longer applied and in which the values of the historian precluded scientific objectivity" (White 1957). Their only acknowledged bond with relativism was that they emphasized the importance of each generation searching the past for knowledge pertinent to its own problems, and since these problems changed, the knowledge and views of the past would change.

A more recent approach to relativism emphasized the inability of the scientist-observer to determine any absolute truth that would transcend time and space. The position grew slowly from the pragmatism of William James, the instrumentalism of John Dewey, and the critiques of Theodore Lessing during World War I. Lessing pronounced history to be no science at all but a creative act that gave meaning to meaningless life. All views of the past, he argued, were created by people who wished to engender faith and hope in the future. The idea of the scientific history was just another such myth, since only the realm of nature yielded truth that could be expressed in firm propositions or even in numbers.

The critique of scientific history broadened in the 1920s when Einstein's theory of relativity was widely popularized and heatedly debated among intellectuals, casting widespread doubt about social scientists' and historians' ability to achieve the scientific objectivity that they claimed. It was the Italian philosopher-historian Benedetto Croce who appeared to supply an accommodation. Croce viewed human life as an on-rushing, ever-creative process, and within it stood the historian as full participant. Yet, Croce maintained, he could still be impartial through scholarly discipline, although not objective in the sense of having no views on the world. As Ernst Breisach recently pointed out, this "made all history contemporary history, because . . . the present and the past were linked inextricably—the past existed in the present reality."

The historical profession in the United States appeared to awaken to the implications of relativism with dramatic suddenness—shocked by the double-barrelled blast fired by two presidents of the American Historical Association (AHA)—Carl Becker in his 1931 address, "Everyman His Own Historian," and Charles Beard in his comments in 1933, "Written History as an Act of Faith." Actually, Becker, among others, had been prodding the profession with questions such as: "What is a historical fact?" and "Can the historian be 'detached' in writing history?"

The New History and the new approach to historical relativism quickly dominated the thinking and writing of most young historians during the latter part of the 1930s and in the 1940s. The leaders and initiators of the New History, or what has since been called progressive historiography, were mainly students of Charles Beard, Carl Becker, James Harvey Robinson and Frederick Jackson Turner. They published a series of propositions with which a majority of a representative sample of historians agreed, including one that focused on the Beard-Croce's happy accommodation on relativism. This appears in the proposition that written or spoken history is to be best understood not only by analysis of its structure and documentation, but also "by a study of the possible attitudes arising from the life and circumstances of the author," which is followed by the Crocian compromise that

> since every written history represents a selection of facts . . . , the clarification of thought and purpose is a necessary preliminary for all historians who desire to emancipate themselves from the bondage to the subconscious . . . and to seek the utmost impartiality possible to the human mind. (Social Science Research Council 1946, 135)

RETREAT FROM RELATIVISM

During the decade of the 1950s, the debate over theory became a pedagogical tool in seminars on historiography for graduate students. The practitioner was content to reveal his biases and go on with his work. Questions, however, never stay dormant for long. Questions of the philosophy and theory of history found a forum in a new journal, *History and Theory,* established in 1962. The revisionist critics of United States' participation in World War II, such as Charles Beard, Harry Elmer Barnes and Charles C. Tansill, fixed blame and launched bitter charges, accusing Franklin D. Roosevelt of conspiracy with interventionists to lead the country to war. These historians pronouncing moral judgments, however, went almost unnoticed in the celebration of the triumph of U.S. ideals in World War II and unheard amidst the din of subsequent "Cold War" rhetoric.

On a broader scale, however, there were growing indictments of historical relativism and increasing discomfort on the part of historical relativists who could find no solid ideological grounds for moral judgment. The international Nuremberg and Tokyo trials resurrected universal moral law and human rights as the ultimate yardstick for civilized human behavior. Anthropologists under the leadership of Clyde Kluckhohn, among others, focused their attention on cultural similarities rather than differences in the search for universals. German historians were expected to renounce their Nazi pasts with proper moral condemnation, which they obligingly did. In fact, they argued that the events of the 1930s represented a discontinuity in German tradition—the failure of a generation humiliated by defeat in World War I, which was brought on through outside forces and leadership of a few militarists (Gabriel 1957; Hamerow 1983).

In the 1960s, as college students and faculty members began participating actively in the civil rights movement in the South and the growing anti-Vietnam-War protests, historians were once again forced to reconsider their role. John Higham asserted that the historian's detachment could only go so far as to determine the viable alternatives to a choice of action known or knowable by the participants, but then the historian should become moral judge.

No sooner, however, had the discussion over this pronouncement waned than historians, dazzled by the potential of the new computer technology and techniques of quantification, revived the old vision of making history an objective science. The historian in this view acts as an objective observer, accumulating vast banks of data and testing verifiable propositions, such as the degree of social mobility in the 19th century or questions relating to voting behavior. This group of social science historians found its forum at first in the *Historical Methods Newsletter,* initiated in 1967, and then in *The Journal of Interdisciplinary History* and the Social Science History Association, begun in the early 1970s.

The issue of objectivity, which still persists, not only affected the way in which historians went about their work, but also the way they presented it, as a continuing story or as a series of snapshots. Another persistent issue revolves around the question of synthesis; or if historians are to present a story at all, what is the plot, the central story line?

The last 50 years have seen the rise, modification and disintegration of two powerful narrative syntheses: one was embodied in the popular introductory college course, Western Civilization, and the other was presented in Charles and Mary Beard's best-selling, massive, sweeping survey, *The Rise of American Civilization.* Both were products of progressive historiography, and both originated within the setting of Columbia University. The first, Western Civilization, was largely inspired by James Harvey Robinson and Carlton J.H. Hayes. Robinson and Beard sought to make explicable to students the day's newspaper. As Robinson put it, the central question was "How did we get this way?" The answer, he believed, came from "living history," the part of the past that continues to the present. Modeled on biological evolution, his

> central narrative excluded everything defunct, anomalous and sensational . . .
> eschewed all of the lost causes and dead ends. . . . Much that has been included in
> historical manuals would of necessity be left out as irrelevant or unimportant.
> (Quoted in Allardyce 1982, 705)

Historians would then deal only with the events, the individuals and the movements that marked the triumphs of the forces of light over the forces of darkness, moving western European man on in his steady progression towards modern democratic and industrial civilization. In England this would be dubbed the Whig interpretation by Herbert Butterfield.

DECLINE OF WESTERN CIVILIZATION COURSES

The Western Civilization synthesis began to erode in the 1950s and 1960s with the rise of Third World nationalism, presenting politicians, the public and scholars alike with an international environment of polycentrism and cultural diversity. As Gilbert Allardyce put it,

> emerging were other peoples, other histories, a globe of historic diversity beyond
> the imagination of earlier westerners, a cosmos where pluralism replaced the "one-
> ness" of history and where human experience could not be ordered into a unilineal
> pattern of development. (Allardyce 1982, 718)

The death knell was being sounded as early as 1976, at an AHA session on the Western Civilization course, when Frederick L. Chayett bid it a not very fond farewell "because despite its claim to being universal, . . . it was limited and provincial, . . . a history of those who were men, white, Christian and European" (Allardyce 1982, 719). In 1980 the American Historical Association brought together a wide range of college and university teachers of history to discuss six models of the "introductory history course" at a conference in Annapolis, Maryland. The conclusion of the conference, in the words of Warren Susman, its chair, was: "There can no longer be one introductory course for there is no one model possible to serve this function at all institutions for all students."

There had indeed been some early alternative scholarly syntheses, such as Oswald Spengler's disillusioned attack on Western faith in inevitable progress—*The Decline of the West* (1918; revised for English translation 1926–28).

In the early 1930s the classical scholar Arnold Toynbee launched a monumental attempt to survey the history of civilization, giving the Hegelian-Marxist dialectic a twist in which he argued that new civilizations arose out of a chrysalis of old civilizations and that they survived or fell according to their ability to respond to challenges both internal and external, natural and human. A more recent effort at synthesis was William H. McNeill's *The Rise of the West,* which smacked of the old progressive optimism but attempted to incorporate the western story as a phenomenon of world history. None of these, however, seriously influenced either scholarship or teaching of history.

The real dilemma of world history comes from two complementary pressures toward egalitarian treatment of all peoples: the first from the assumption of many recent historians that no culture is superior to any other and that one stage of a culture did not constitute progress beyond the preceding stages; and the second from the political need to respect the sensitivity of new, nonwestern nations. Therefore, how is the westernization of the world to be treated? Some historians condemn it as economic and cultural imperialism. Others, believers in progress, claim that Western culture has unified the world through advances in hygiene, education, science, self-government and individualism. The fact is that when historians have dropped westernization as an integrating theme for world history, the course has often become an unrelated parallel series of histories of world cultures.

TREATMENT OF UNITED STATES HISTORY

The progressive synthesis of United States history, which coupled economic motivation with faith in progress, produced a dramatic structure. It pitted the forces for democracy—the working class—against the forces for privilege—upper-class landholders and industrial capitalists—in a continuing struggle that inevitably resulted in better and ever broadening political, economic and cultural democracy. It was not only a history that had moved internally but was designed to give the society purpose, to hurry the process along and to hedge against backsliding. Historians trained in the late 1920s and 1930s began producing after the interregnum of World War II, and in the immediate post-war years they seemed to fully endorse the tradition of democratic reform and protest. Merrill Jensen's *The New Nation* (1950) recorded the advancing struggle of democracy in the 1780s. Arthur M. Schlesinger, Jr., in *The Age of Jackson* (1945) told the story for the 1830s. Eric Goldman, in *Rendezvous with Destiny* (1952), moved the story from the Gilded Age through the New Deal. C. Vann Woodward, in *The Origins of the New South, 1877–1913* (1951), told the story of the democratic movement and the impact of industrialism in the South. Henry Steele Commager continued Vernon Louis Parrington's unfinished story of modern thought in the United States.

In 1948, however, Richard Hofstadter sounded a note of dissent in the introduction to his iconoclastic work, *The American Political Tradition and the Men Who Made It.* The current "lack of confidence in the American future" and a "rudderless and demoralized state of American liberalism" he attributed in part to the absence of any real differences between liberal and conservative impulses throughout our national experience. The customary emphasis of our historians on conflict, Hofstadter said, has obscured the underlying agreement that major parties and movements have always shared. Ours has been "a democracy in cupidity," which offers no coherent guidance in a new, more dangerous era. This signaled the beginning of a major critique of the progressive synthesis, as monograph after monograph challenged the significance of the economic conflict.

John Higham pointed out that "one after another, the great crises, which progressive historians had depicted as turning points in the battle between democracy and privilege, came under fresh examination. In each case, the scale of conflict seemed to shrink. Sharp divisions between periods, sections, groups, and ideologies disappeared. Overall, the new digging amounted to a massive grading operation that smoothed and flattened the convulsive dialectic of progressive history." What appeared was a large degree of uniformity and agreement. Higham continued, "Instead of a polarized culture—a culture eternally divided between over- and under-privileged groups, between a party of the past and a party of the future, between noble ideals and ignoble interests—young scholars glimpsed an essentially homogeneous culture full of small impermanent variations."

A good example of this leveling process occurred first with the consideration of Schlesinger's *The Age of Jackson,* which posited an urban working class as the vanguard of the Jacksonian movement, that involved intellectuals, farmers and laboring men and epitomized the enduring struggle between the business community and the rest of society. Historians taking a new look at sources discovered that Jacksonians were as often merchants and professional people as "laboring men." Schlesinger's "working class" appeared to display no consistent political allegiance, and acquisitive business motives entered heavily into the Jacksonian program. The so-called "common man," it appeared, was a business man, and Jacksonianism represented a rising middle class (Sellers 1958).

No sooner had the consensus historians of the 1950s finished leveling the peaks and filling the valleys of progressive history than the classrooms were filled with anthologies organized around a debate—conflict or continuity—at each critical period of U.S. history, and a new fragmentation process began. New Left historians, neo-Marxists, began issuing a drum beat of critiques of our historiography from diplomatic to political and intellectual history. The real history of foreign policy, they asserted, was not to be found at the negotiating table but in the board rooms of U.S. business. The real history, in fact, had not yet been written. It was not of dominant elite groups but of the "people"—the "inarticulate masses." The civil rights movement of the late 1950s and early 1960s called attention to black history. Then one by one each ethnic group entered the fray as it found a champion among the new ethnic and urban historians. The feminist movement thrust the struggle for equal rights into colleges and universities, establishing Women's Studies programs, which set the agenda for a whole new subfield, women's history. Coincidental with the emergence of the New Left historians was the appearance of the social science historians whose subjects were the same, but their tools were statistical and their methods were those of the social sciences. They coalesced in 1974 in the Social Science History Association.

Radical historians, stimulated by the work of Fred Harvey Harrington and William Appleman Williams, rewrote almost every phase of the history of our foreign relations, unfolding a story of the growth of U.S. imperialism, inevitable and often conspiratorial. When Walter LaFeber wrote of *The New Empire: An Interpretation of American Expansion, 1860–1898,* he highlighted the motives and manipulations of steel, petroleum, textile, transportation and banking interests in using U.S. power to open and control new markets in Asia and South America. He next turned his attention to the "Cold War," which he saw as an inevitable product of our country's expansionism. He supported the then shocking indictments of Gar Alperowitz and Gabriel Kolko that the United States bore the burden of responsibility for the "Cold War" because of Truman's precipitous and aggressive policy and the inherent expansionist requirements of U.S. capitalism (Maier 1980; McCormick 1982).

Radicals, however, turned to every period in our history seeking to expose the story and the experiences of oppression to include the left-out people, to restore the people to history and history to the people. Black history, spurred by the civil rights movement, came in for heavy scholarly attention, particularly slavery: the institution, the experience and the consequences in modern racism and segregation. John Hope Franklin's standard progressive history *From Slavery to Freedom* appeared irrelevant as the newer historians sought to establish a separate black identity, contrary to the integrationist theme of Franklin's work (Blassingame 1972). This movement saw the development of Black and Afro-American Studies programs and centers, established on college and university campuses, not only to furnish social centers for black students but to bolster black identity with pride in past achievements and role models. Other area studies programs were stimulated by our nation's interest in the Far East, Southeast Asia, and the Middle East.

Like the new diplomatic history, black history and the new social history had both methodological and ideological origins. The methodological and conceptual inspiration came from Marc Bloch and the French *Annales* school with their admonition and example to study in great detail the economic and social patterns of life over a long period of time in a relatively small area.

Another stimulus came from the Cambridge school of population studies in England which sought to reconstitute pre-industrial English society—life in the 17th and 18th centuries, the study of households, families, and population movement. The first evidence of the new social history in America came with a spate of community studies concentrated in the New England colonial period, beginning with Sumner Chilton Powell's Pulitzer-prize winning *Puritan Village* (1963), and including studies by Bushman and others. The cumulative impact of these and other studies was to revise the view of the New England community as an open, democratic and frontier community to the picture of a closed community where land for newcomers was scarce, if available at all, and new ideas were treated as heretical; but above all, they focused on the family, its economy and the roles of women and children. The publication of the English translation of Philippe Ariès' *Centuries of Childhood: A Social History of Family Life* (1962) gave new impetus to the study of the family, coming at a time when the family seemed to be falling apart as the generation gap became a chasm, as children moved into the psychedelic world of the counterculture, while New Left historians embraced the study of all people, and particularly groups such as blacks, ethnics and women.

Thus, the new social history, beginning with the study of families and communities, branched out into the study of women, embraced by the feminist movement. A later subfield of family and women's history was the history of old age, a field in which some of the pioneers in family history, such as Peter Laslett, John Demos, Tamara Hareven and Daniel Scott Smith, also broke ground (Laslett 1979).

SOCIAL SCIENCE IMPACT

New methodologies and concepts were introduced from the social sciences, enabling historical scholars to ask wholly new questions in every field, questions so different as to create new economic history, new political history, new social history, new urban and rural histories, and new fields of history such as psychohistory, historical demography and comparative history. By far the most noticeable, if not the most important, methodological impact on history was the wholesale application of statistics made possible by the new technological breakthrough in electronic computers, allowing historians to handle vast aggregates of data in a relatively short period of time as never before. Thomas C. Cochran, Alfred D. Chandler and Robert W. Fogel led the way to redirecting U.S. economic history. Cochran challenged historians to look beyond the presidential synthesis and apply social science techniques to the economy. In a controversial paper, he argued that the Civil War, far from stimulating the economy and accelerating industrialism, inhibited that development. Chandler took as his task to relate the dynamic forces in the economy to the emerging innovations in the world of business (Chandler 1977). Fogel, dean of the cliometricians, first tested his counterfactual hypothesis when he questioned whether the railroads were really the central feature in U.S. economic development. Even more controversial was Fogel and Stanley L. Engerman's *Time on the Cross: The Economics of American Negro Slavery* (1974). In comparing the output of the midwestern small farmer with that of the slave economy, they found in essence that slavery was profitable.

This direction of the new economic history seemed to have its limitations, according to critics who rose up in force to demolish the statistical reliability, question the selection of data, and challenge the ability of cliometricians, through statistical correlations, equations and adherence to strictly theoretical concepts, ever to come to grips with human reality. The theoretical world in which market forces and rational human beings operate without friction bears little relation to the actual world in which rules and customs, as well as complex human motivations, interfere heavily in economic phenomena. While some true believers, such as J. Morgan Kousser, characterize the *Time on the Cross* episode as a "cockfight among cliometricians," proving the strength of social scientific history, it seems to have been more significant as an embarrassment that has led to questioning the assumptions and muting the claims for the new economic history (Kousser 1980).

The new labor, urban and rural histories proliferated in the 1960s and 1970s. Beginning in 1960 with the publication of a new journal, *Labor History,* a new emphasis began to emerge. It rejected the older unionization subject and themes as peripheral, if not irrelevant, and broadened the field to take in the entire working class and work itself. The new labor historians addressed such questions as: What was the nature of the workers' culture as opposed to middle-class culture and occupational mobility? And what was the worker's role in the particular industry's technological advance?

In 1974 supporters of the new urban history also established a journal. Eschewing the older urban biographical approach, it addressed such issues as social and geographical mobility, ethnicity and neighborhood structure (Conzen 1980). The new rural history is just beginning to emerge and has no new journal of its own, although it promises to take over the pages of *Agricultural History,* which began in 1927. It is essentially, according to Robert Swierenga, "the systematic study of human behavior over time in a rural environment," addressing such questions as: Did agriculture undergo a commercialization process comparable to industrialization? Did modernization of the countryside destroy rural values and family life? How did geographical mobility in the countryside compare to the rapid turnover of population in the city? Much of the new work stems from the pioneering efforts of Paul W. Gates and Allan G. Bogue, and of James C. Malin (Winkler 1985).

SPECIALIZED HISTORIES

Specialized histories such as legal history, church history, the history of education and of medicine, followed much the same pattern. The seminal work of James Willard Hurst has emphasized the impact of law on society, particularly on the economy. New legal historians are examining the ways in which the courts have reflected, or deflected, societal pressures, developing law, as it were, from the grass roots. Church history, too, abandoned the institutional approach to ask broader and more sociological questions extending from the work of H. Richard Niebuhr and Will Herberg.

The study of education tended to look beyond the institutional schoolhouse to examine other forms of education and other ways in which a society passes on its culture to younger generations. Educational history, like diplomatic, labor and black history in particular, became a weapon in the ideological warfare swirling around the school systems in the late 1960s (Ravitch 1983). The history of medicine was initially broadened by women's issues, with scholars like Carol Smith Rosenberg effectively demonstrating that male physicians' medical prescriptions and knowledge of women's ills and biological limitations were culturally defined. Others looked at the changing definitions and consequent treatments of the mentally ill.

In this massive development which has become known collectively as the New Social History, political history cannot be ignored, though many historians have tried. Politics in the 1960s and early 1970s were deemed superficial history by most of the new social historians, reflecting passing issues and those only with great distortion. New political historians, however, were quick in adapting the new quantitative methods to addressing questions of voting behavior and analysis of legislative groups, as well as of the population at large, and in asking questions as to how strong were party affiliations in determining voting patterns and what other allegiances were more powerful determinants. Gradually the world of the smoke-filled room, party bosses, machines and all the old trappings of political history disappeared. On the other hand, some historians, examining particular periods, began to evolve a concept of political culture constituted of a commonly held ideology and set of assumptions, reflected in behavior, rhetoric and institutions.

Three areas—psychohistory, comparative history and popular culture—emerged with some fanfare in the early 1970s, but they have yet to realize their promise. Psychohistory got its major impetus from the pioneering work of the neo-Freudian psychiatrist Erik H. Erikson with the publication of his *Young Man Luther: A Study in Psychoanalysis and History* (1958), and from William Langer's challenge in his 1957 presidential address to the American Historical Association, "The Next Assignment." While a great deal of good and interesting work has been produced by psychohistorians and all biographers are now constrained to examine carefully the childhood experiences of their subjects, the field still has to meet the criticisms that have been launched from the beginning. Critics have charged that psychobiographers often make inferential leaps from adult behavior to infantile experiences, ignoring intervening developments and variables, explaining political conduct from infantile trauma. On the more general level there has been a failure to make the link between the mode of parenting and a pattern of national or group behavior (Loewenberg 1980).

Comparative history had been called for by Marc Bloch in the 1930s but was not to find much of a following until the late 1950s with the establishment in 1958 of the journal *Comparative Studies in Society and History* and in 1968 the publication of C. Vann Woodward's and a group of leading U.S. historians' collections of essays. Most of the work in the field in the United States has concentrated on the institution of slavery, with increasing treatment of such disparate areas as the women's movement and Canadian-American studies. However, one of the proponents of comparative history notes that, "unless it becomes a recognized subdiscipline within history in the manner of comparative sociology, politics or literature, it is unlikely that it will become a major trend within the profession" (Fredrickson 1980).

Popular culture emerged as a field of study based on the 1960s' emphasis on the people and on scholars' efforts to deal with the production of mass media, from the dime novel to the soap opera. *The Journal of Popular Culture* was launched in 1967, publishing a good deal of interesting trivia without much analytic rigor or methodological framework. Borrowing from theories of folklorists has proved to be unsatisfactory. The most stimulating work has come from Neil Harris and the late Warren Susman.

A "NEW" NEW HISTORY

In short, the bewildering proliferation of new methodologies, new fields, and subfields during the last 50 years has constituted a revolution in historiography which has been dubbed the "New" New History. Some of this newer history may be characterized as emphasizing analysis over narrative; emphasizing thematic or topical treatment over chronological; and relying on statistics, oral interviews, sociological models and psychoanalytic theories, rather than on the more "impressionistic" critical analysis of public and private documents, legislative debates and administrative memos. The new history focuses on social groups—the family, social problems, factories and farms, work and play, birth and death, childhood and old age, crime and insanity—while the old history focused on "elites"; i.e., political, military and social leaders and their institutions.

The new history has now broached the tolerable limits of fragmentation. The criticism, always there, is reaching a crescendo and during the last five years has been met with a sweeping review, re-evaluation, and, if not retreat, retrenchment. It calls for a new narrative, a new synthesis, a new "more fruitful interaction" between fields.

There has also been at least one divisive split in the new history between the Marxist and the social scientific historians (Berkhofer 1983). The same sort of split has divided women's history among the original feminist historians and the social science historians (Smith 1983). The political historians are debating the need to restore politics to political history (Hayes 1985).

In economic history, the split between the cliometricians and economic historians has nearly driven historians from the pages of the *Journal of Economic History*. The new urban historians, according to David C. Hammack, have begun to "return to the old-fashioned questions of politics, policy and power that fascinated the first generation of workers in the field." The new military historians, late emerging on the scholarly horizon, are already cognizant of the internal and external criticisms and are admonishing themselves "to join the historical mainstream," not to become "too fragmented," and to restore the "military" to military history (Winkler 1985).

Besides the general impression that the new histories have fallen short of their original promise, although contributing much new data and many new insights, there is a general feeling of need, not only for synthesis within the specialties but for an overriding narrative theme. Lawrence Stone, one of the outstanding U.S. practitioners of the new social history, has called for a revival of narrative, as have Bernard Bailyn and C. Vann Woodward and, most recently, Gertrude Himmelfarb, who argues persuasively that if we do not return to narrative, "we will lose not only the unifying theme that has given coherence to history, . . . not only narrative that has made history readable and memorable, but also a conception of man as a rational political animal" (Himmelfarb 1984).

Meanwhile a new synthesis and potential for narrative theme has been growing by accretion in unrelated areas of U.S. history. It has come from an unlikely combination of anthropological theory and intellectual, political, social and economic history. The initial stimulus seems to have come from the work of anthropologist Clifford Geertz. Ideology, instead of a doctrine or system of consciously held ideas, is viewed instead as a very complex array of symbols, values and beliefs by which members of a society order and give meaning to their political and social lives. Thus, ideology reflects the entire way of life prevalent in a society. Ideology changes with shifts in the entire social and economic order. It is now possible to "discern a general pattern of five major ideologies arranged in a cyclical fashion that constitute the basis for this new interpretive synthesis" (Singal 1984). First is the Puritan ideology, which emerges out of the work of the community studies of the new social historians. Emerging out of the decline of Puritanism is republicanism, and emerging from the republican ideology were two new ones, the slave ideology of the South and the "Free Labor" ideology in the North. The clash between the two resulted in the Civil War, out of which emerged the final ideological synthesis which Louis Galambos has characterized as "the organizational synthesis." An ideology once formed and dominant survives unchallenged only until social and economic conditions change, which, in turn, brings new ideology that replaces the old. It is a variation of the Hegelian–Marxist dialectic. It is similar to Toynbee's analysis of the rise and fall of civilizations, albeit over much shorter periods of time (Galambos 1970; Kelly 1978).

While this is too brief and oversimplified an account of the intellectual history of historiography in America, it is safe to say that history in America and American History have undergone enormous changes in the past 50 years. It is also safe to predict that specialization and fragmentation will continue, although at a slower, less assured pace, while new narratives will appear in the next few years and the ideological synthesis will prevail in United States history. In world history, the rise of the West will have to be taken into account. While the returns are not nearly as fully in as in U.S. history, the indications are that modernization may be the unifying theme.

REFERENCES

Allardyce, Gilbert. "The Rise and Fall of the Western Civilization Course." *American Historical Review* 87(June 1982): 695–725.

Beard, Charles A. "Written History as an Act of Faith." *American Historical Review* 37(January 1932): 221–236.

Beard, Charles A., and Mary R. Beard. *The Rise of American Civilization,* 4 vols. New York: Macmillan, 1927–42.

Becker, Carl. "Everyman His Own Historian." *American Historical Review* 39(January 1934): 219–229.

Berkhofer, Robert F., Jr. "The Two New Histories: Competing Paradigms for Interpreting the American Past." Organization of American Historians. *OAH Newsletter* (May 1983): 9–12.

Blassingame, John W. *The Slave Community.* New York: Oxford University Press, 1972.

Breisach, Ernst. *Historiography: Ancient, Medieval, and Modern.* Chicago: University of Chicago Press, 1983.

Bushman, Richard L. *From Puritan to Yankee: Character in the Social Order in Connecticut, 1690–1765.* Cambridge, MA: Harvard University Press, 1967.

Butterfield, Herbert. *The Whig Interpretation of History.* London: G. Bell & Sons, 1931.

Chandler, Alfred D. *The Visible Hand: The Managerial Revolution in Business.* Cambridge, MA: Belknap Press, 1977.

Conzen, Kathleen Neils. "Community Studies, Urban History, and American Local History." In *The Past Before Us: Contemporary Historical Writing in the United States,* edited by Michael Kammen. Ithaca, NY: Cornell University Press, 1980, 270–291.

Franklin, John Hope. *From Slavery to Freedom: A History of American Negroes.* New York: Knopf, 1947.

Fredrickson, George M. "Comparative History." In *The Past Before Us: Contemporary Historical Writing in the United States,* edited by Michael Kammen. Ithaca, NY: Cornell University Press, 1980, 457–473.

Gabriel, Ralph. *The Course of American Democratic Thought,* 2nd ed. New York: Ronald Press, 1956.

Galambos, Louis. "The Emerging Organizational Synthesis in Modern American History." *Business History Review* 44(Autumn 1970): 279–290.

Geertz, Clifford. "Ideology as a Cultural System." In *Ideology and Discontent,* edited by David E. Apter. New York: The Free Press, 1964, 62–72.

Hamerow, Theodore S. "Guilt, Redemption and Writing German History." *American Historical Review* 88(February 1983): 53–72.

Hammack, David C. "Patrician Elitism as History: The First Generation of Urban Historians." Paper delivered at the annual meeting of the Organization of American Historians, Minneapolis, April 1985.

Harris, Neil. "Iconography and Intellectual History: The Half-Tone Effect." In *New Directions in American Intellectual History,* edited by John Higham and Paul Conkin. Baltimore: Johns Hopkins Press, 1979, 196–211.

Hayes, Samuel P. "Society and Politics: Politics and Society." *Journal of Interdisciplinary History* 15(Winter 1985): 481–491.

Higham, John. "Beyond Consensus: The Historian as Moral Critic." *American Historical Review* 67(April 1962): 609–625.

Higham, John, et al. *History.* Englewood Cliffs, NJ: Prentice-Hall, 1965.

Himmelfarb, Gertrude. "Denigrating the Role of Reason: The New History Goes Bottom Up." *Harper's Magazine* 268(April 1984): 84–90.

Hofstadter, Richard. *The American Political Tradition and the Men Who Made It.* New York: Knopf, 1947.

Kelly, Robert. *The Cultural Pattern in American Politics: The First Century.* New York: Knopf, 1979.

Kousser, J. Morgan. "Quantitative Social-Scientific History." In *The Past Before Us: Contemporary Historical Writing in the United States,* edited by Michael Kammen. Ithaca, NY: Cornell University Press, 1980, 433–456.

LaFeber, Walter. *The New Empire: An Interpretation of American Expansion, 1860–1898.* Ithaca, NY: Cornell University Press, 1963.

Langer, William L. "The Next Assignment." *American Historical Review* 63(January 1958): 283–304.

Laslett, Peter. "The Traditional English Family and the Aged in Our Society." In *Aging, Death and the Completion of Being,* edited by David D. Van Tassel. Philadelphia: University of Pennsylvania Press, 1979.

Loewenberg, Peter. "Psychohistory." In *The Past Before Us: Contemporary Historical Writing in the United States,* edited by Michael Kammen. Ithaca, NY: Cornell University Press, 1980, 408–432.

Maier, Charles S. "Marking Time: The Historiography of International Relations." In *The Past Before Us: Contemporary Historical Writing in the United States,* edited by Michael Kammen. Ithaca, NY: Cornell University Press, 1980, 355–387.

McCormick, Thomas J. "Drift or Mastery? A Corporatist Synthesis for American Diplomatic History." *Reviews in American History* 10(December 1982): 318–329.

Nichols, Roy F. "History Teaching in this Intellectual Crisis." *Historical Outlook* 24(November 1933): 357.

Nichols, Roy F. "The Dynamic Interpretation of History." *New England Quarterly* 8(June 1935): 163–178.

Ravitch, Diane. *The Troubled Crusade: American Education 1945–1980.* New York: Basic Books, 1983.

Reilly, Kevin, ed. *The Introductory History Course.* (Proceedings of the AHA Annapolis Conference on the Introductory History Course.) Washington, DC: American Historical Association, 1984.

Robinson, James Harvey. *The New History.* New York: Macmillan, 1912.

Schlesinger, Arthur M., Jr. *The Age of Jackson.* Boston: Little, Brown, 1945.

Sellers, Charles G. "Andrew Jackson versus the Historians." *Mississippi Valley Historical Review* 44(March 1958): 615–634.

Singal, Daniel Joseph. "Beyond Consensus: Richard Hofstadter and American Historiography." *American Historical Review* 89(October 1984): 999.

Smith, Hilda. "Women's History and the Humanities." Organization of American Historians. *OAH Newsletter* (May 1983): 12–14.

Social Sciences Research Council, Committee on Historiography. *Theory and Practice in Historical Study.* Bulletin 54. New York: Social Science Research Council, 1946.

Susman, Warren I. *Culture as History: The Transportation of American Society in the Twentieth Century.* New York: Knopf, 1985.

Toynbee, Arnold J. *A Study of History,* 12 vols. London: Oxford University Press, 1934–1961.

White, Morton G. *Social Thought in America: The Revolt Against Formalism,* revised ed. Boston: Beacon Press, 1957.

Winkler, Karen J. "The Greening of American Social History: Scholars Rediscover the Countryside." *Chronicle of Higher Education* 30(March 20, 1985): 5–6.

CHAPTER 2

FROM MONOPOLY TO DOMINANCE

Paul Robinson
and
Joseph M. Kirman

The overriding impression one gains from thoughtful observers is of little change in the mainstream pattern of history instruction over the past half-century. Despite the passage of decades and the absence of a national system of education, the topics students study in history courses, the sequence in which they occur, and the teaching practices by which they are conveyed are remarkably similar to what they were throughout the country 50 years ago. The reason for this stability does not seem simple. Explanations for this persistent model have been summarized as resulting from a set of unique historical events:

- Recommendations from influential professional organizations
- The politics and economics of textbook publishing
- The effects of teaching students massed in large groups within bureaucratic structures
- The absence of debate on fundamental issues of political-economic ideology in the society at large (Newmann 1985, 2)

Existence of this durable pattern should not imply, however, satisfaction on the part of educators or citizens. It should not even imply an awareness of such a pattern, for statements can be found frequently in educational literature that history instruction is in a more or less continuous state of change, ferment or reform. This chapter offers a description of the development of history instruction over the course of the past half-century, with some attention being paid to the Canadian experience.

Several caveats should be raised at the outset. First, the literature of school history is an extensive one, too broad in scope and diversified in sources for any one person to digest. So this chapter, while based on the literature, is also a personal statement, centered on the secondary level, that can hardly do justice to such an ambitious topic. Someone else, given the same task, could well outline a different set of issues.

Further, it might be noted that there is nothing especially significant about the half-century limits of this volume, other than marking the 50th anniversary of the National Council for the Social Studies' independently held meetings. The year 1935 was not a noteworthy watershed in the teaching of history, as were 1899, 1916 or the early 1970s. Nevertheless, we possess a benchmark of sorts, or a set of benchmarks, in the publication during the 1930s of the volumes in the American Historical Association's investigation of the social studies in the schools. In particular Rolla Tryon's 1935 contribution to the Report of the Commission on the Social Studies, *The Social Sciences as School Subjects,* provides a careful compilation of data on the status of history as a subject of study against which to consider today's circumstances.

Finally, it is difficult to distinguish the teaching of history from the teaching of the social studies. It is common, for instance, when speaking of history instruction to imply all instruction in the social sciences, and, conversely, one will frequently refer to the social sciences and have solely history in mind. Indeed, one of the persistent, salient issues in the teaching of history is the nature of the relationship between history and the social studies more broadly conceived.

In troubled times we ask ourselves existential questions about who we are and why we exist. In this troubled century we have asked periodically these same questions of history in the schools, for trends in thinking about history instruction cannot help reflecting societal developments. The next section considers the answers offered to questions of definition and purpose in history instruction. Following that discussion the chapter considers issues of methods, materials, students and other matters yet to be resolved.

ISSUES OF MEANING

The relationship between history and the social sciences has long remained an unsettled one. When the secondary school curriculum was clearly delineated for the first time, in 1892, there was no such field as the social studies. The Committee of Ten's Conference on History, Civil Government, and Political Economy had outlined a curriculum drawn almost exclusively from the discipline of history. For the next quarter of a century, as historians continued to dominate the national social studies curriculum committees, history continued to monopolize the recommended curricula. Social scientists claimed that their disciplines were too complex and intellectually demanding to become a part of the precollege curriculum. Historians, holding the initiative, allowed the social sciences to play, at best, a distinctly auxiliary role. By World War I, history had become "comfortably settled at the center" of United States social studies education (Hertzberg 1980).

The publication of the report of the NEA Committee on the Social Studies in 1916, a committee dominated by public school people rather than historians, signaled the end of history's monopoly. The term "social studies" became commonplace as a broad designation for history and social science related courses. Since that time supporters of the discipline of history on the one hand and advocates of either social science or citizenship-based courses on the other hand have contended for intellectual, if not programmatic, control of the curriculum. No clear winner has emerged; the debate—taking new forms—will undoubtedly continue.

Henry Johnson, professor of history of Teachers College, Columbia University, stands as a pivotal figure in the uneasy relationship between history and the social sciences. Prior to his retirement in 1933, he was perhaps the best known teacher of history in the country. He exerted a powerful influence on thousands of teachers through his methods textbook and his 27 years of teaching. Although considered the "foremost leader in the development of the teaching of history and social studies as a field of specialization," he "never accepted the field of the social studies," according to Edgar Wesley (Robinson 1982, 15). He viewed the development of the social studies movement in the first half of this century as being captured by "militant educational reformers." These reformers, more attuned to issues of method than of content, seemed to Johnson to exemplify the doctrine that "scholarship had no rights which pedagogy is bound to respect" (Johnson 1940, 77). Johnson's lifelong balancing of the sometimes competing demands of scholarship and pedagogy in the field of history teaching is a process that others are still very much concerned with today.

Canadian Perspectives

In Canada other forces have been at play, leading to a distinctive situation. It is clear that Canada has many similarities to the United States and also important differences. Similar to the situation in the 50 states, Canada's 10 provinces retain control over education. The provinces jealously guard this legacy of the British North America Act. Thus curriculum development is a provincial responsibility. Coupled with this legal right is a noticeable element of regionalism expressed in provincial history studies that stress each province's history.

Another expression of regionalism is found in the way the curriculum can call for an examination of other areas of the world in comparison with the province. While examining the history of the nation, the provincial historical element is emphasized. For example, in the current Alberta social studies curriculum children in grade 4 study "Alberta's history: Early settlement, the Depression, the War Years, and Modern Times." There is a noticeable difference to be found, however, in how Quebec deals with its history compared to English-speaking regions. In Quebec there appears to be a measure of "divine heroic" emphasis regarding French-Canadian settlement, which may be related to cultural survival in a majority-English-speaking nation (Hodgetts 1968).

As Canada matured from a British colony to full nationhood, the emphasis in English-speaking areas on the history of England decreased and was supplanted with Canadian history. This trend became most obvious in the late 1960s and early 1970s. It probably reflected growing Canadian nationalism cast within a framework of regionalism. Ontario was singled out in 1974 for not providing a compulsory secondary level course on Canadian history (Herbert and Milburn 1974). The nationalist element also found expression in a new emphasis on Canadian publication of social studies textbooks rather than relying on United States or British publications. Although Canadian studies remains a popular subject, another more recent popular development is a course in modern world history concentrating on "revolution, industrialisation, impe-rialism, ideologies and war" (Tomkins 1983).

This rise of nationalism in the 1960s and 1970s was expressed in Quebec as French cultural nationalism rather than as Canadian nationalism. As a result the Quebec separatist party was swept into power in that province. At the same time vehement antimonarchist sentiments were also being expressed in some English-speaking areas. Further, Canadians began to be sensitive to the dis-tinction between themselves and Americans. One outcome was the Canadian Studies Foundation, created in 1969 to foster teacher-developed Canadian cur-riculum material including the preparation of local histories. This sensitivity to Canadian-American distinctions stands in contrast to the claim of the Cana-dian humorist Stephen Leacock earlier in the century that Canadian writers could use the word "American" for "the literature and education of all the English-speaking people between the Rio Grande and the North Pole" (Leacock 1916). It is axiomatic that how people view themselves will be reflected in how they teach about themselves.

Many in the United States have not been aware of this new Canadian nationalist sensitivity. For example, at a National Council for the Social Studies annual convention banquet in the early 1970s, Canada was not mentioned when participants from other countries were introduced. This omission was pur-poseful to avoid "offending" the Canadians who were thought not to consider themselves foreigners in the United States.

One trend in the teaching of history in Canada that parallels the experience in the United States is an increased sensitivity to minority cultures. The sen-sitivity in Canada has been a spin-off from that nation's location as a haven of refuge for the dispossessed following World War II, and of the immigration policy earlier in the century that encouraged the settlement of Europeans in the west. The multicultural growth in both countries has found expression in the development of a Canadian or U.S. cultural mosaic metaphor to replace the melting pot metaphor. Some of the earlier history texts in both countries contained material either offensive to minorities or else made little mention of their contribution to the nation, state or province. A measure of sensitivity has been introduced when teaching about the history of foreign areas or internal minorities along with a general trend to avoid what might be considered ethnocentric (Werner, Conners, Aoki, and Dahlie 1977; Banks 1979).

Similarly in the United States, events of the 1960s, the civil rights movement, the women's movement and the antiwar movement precipitated major chal-lenges to traditional curricula and materials. The content of much of the history curriculum was identified as being racist, sexist, and class biased. Organizations representing specific constituencies, such as the American Indian Historical Society, became active in a campaign to revise history textbooks and course materials. Although content analyses of history textbooks tell us that changes in textbooks have been mainly cosmetic rather than substantive, the legacy of the 1960s has been significant. Our ideas about the ideal history course and materials were permanently changed. These changes are reflected in curriculum guidelines, textbook evaluation instruments, publishers guidelines and state education codes that promote diversity in the history curriculum.

Search for Coherence

After nearly three-quarters of a century of "social studies" in the United States, informal evidence suggests that the actual courses to be found, at least at the secondary level, rarely are entitled social studies or social science. Rather, they remain overwhelmingly U.S. history, world history and government. Whether or not such traditional disciplinary-based course titles cover courses that are actually taught in an integrated manner is subject to controversy. Disciplinary purists claim that the virtues of their field have been watered down and washed out by what they view as the shallow, sloppy amalgams of the social studies. In many teachers' minds, however, it may be suspected that history looms as a distinct subject not to be confused with broader approaches to content.

The pattern of high school social studies curriculum, which was established via the 1916 NEA Committee on the Social Studies, has withstood a steady stream of reform efforts. Neither the AHA Commission on the Social Studies in the 1930s, nor the controversy over the strength of U.S. history instruction, played out in the pages of the *New York Times* during the early 1940s, nor the New Social Studies movement of the late 1960s and early 1970s could dissolve that curricular pattern, anchored as it was in the discipline of history. Sufficient reformist attacks had been mounted, however, so that by the early 1980s those who had a stake in the future of the field had little confidence in the fragmented pieces that remained. As Hertzberg concluded in her excellent survey of social studies reform over the past century, a "search for coherence" is the one "definite, identifiable trend" in the social studies today (Hertzberg 1981, 183).

Recent indications suggest that a curricular compromise is being fashioned. On the one hand, there is not room in the school curriculum for all the academic disciplines to be taught separately; yet, on the other hand, courses in "social studies" can connote a "shallow presentism." The emerging compromise is to combine disciplines, but in an explicit manner, retaining their disciplinary titles. Thus, for example, California's new *Model Curriculum Standards* call for three years of "history-social science": one year entitled "United States History and Geography," a second year of "World History, Culture, and Geography," and a third year of "American Government, Civics, and Economics." Although the model curriculum standards for these three courses are only guidelines, they reflect "growing public and professional support for a core curriculum" (*Education Week* January 16, 1985, 9). "People really understand and sympathize with the notion that all kids need to be connected to their culture, to the past, and to their responsibilities as citizens," claimed a state education official involved in the creation of the standards. California's efforts are an indication of renewed sentiment in favor of a common core and coherent design for school curriculum in general and history in particular.

Canada too has had to wrestle with the relationship of history to the rest of the social studies. Over the past half-century there appeared to be a specific curriculum for history, rather than history as part of a comprehensive social studies program. Geography was also isolated as a specific curriculum. The major exception occurred in Alberta where an integrated social studies program was introduced in the mid-1930s. This was the *Enterprise,* an elementary level program that used a project approach to teach social studies. It lasted until the 1960s when it appeared unable to deal with the then current values challenge.

In 1971 Alberta introduced a radically different curriculum—one of the most advanced in North America for both elementary and secondary levels. It set off a flurry of curriculum revision across Canada. Shortly after, the first revised Saskatchewan curriculum was modeled on it. In 1972 Quebec prepared a prototype curriculum that appeared to be an integrated social studies program instead of only history and geography courses. British Columbia was also piloting a new curriculum. Later Ontario brought out a highly integrated program in which social studies itself was not a distinct course of study but seemed to be subsumed in the overall curriculum. Paradoxically, Alberta is returning to history as a distinct rather than integrated social studies subject on the secondary level.

The century-long tension between history and the social sciences should not be interpreted simply as pitting historians as a professional body against other educators. The position of professional historians vis-à-vis school history has always been problematic. Viewing historians as a unified block, supporting history in the schools against all curricular challengers, would be a mistake. Many historians have demonstrated little interest in the problems of school curriculum and instruction; moreover, they frequently argue among themselves. As Edwin Fenton pointed out nearly 20 years ago, historians disagree markedly, not merely on matters of historical interpretation, but on how to define their discipline and how to describe its structure. Fenton opted for Collingswood's definition of history as "a kind of research or inquiry." He described its structure as most appropriately characterized—the "heart" of history—by the use of analytical questions, rather than the development of generalizations of the construction of basic concepts. His emphasis on disciplinary structure and his revitalization of inquiry as the basic mode of thinking in history provided intellectual leadership for the wave of New Social Studies curriculum projects that commanded attention among educators in the late 1960s and early 1970s, even though many of them were not historically based.

Fenton cared about history in the schools; many historians have not. One way to view the past half-century is to see it as a recurring struggle by historians to recapture control, interspersed with periods of neglect and disregard, if not outright disdain. Frequently left to their own devices, social studies educators tried to fashion a history curriculum responsive not only to the "spirit and letter of scholarship," but to the "realities and ideas of the society in which it is carried on" and to the "nature and limiations of the teaching and learning process at the various grade levels across which it is distributed" (Beard 1932, 2). Periodically historians would rediscover that the curriculum had become presentist in orientation. Young people were said to lack both knowledge and the long perspective cultivated by thinking in historical terms. Historians decided that either history in the schools needed to be beefed up and teachers more thoroughly grounded in the discipline or, more rarely, that they needed to devote greater attention and energies to the school's history curriculum.

The National Council for the Social Studies has embodied the tensions between history and the social studies in the ups and downs of its relationship with the American Historical Association. Although 1985 marks the 50th anniversary of the Council's independently held annual meetings—prior to 1935 the Council met as a part of the American Historical Association's meetings—it should be remembered that the AHA in time transferred full ownership of the social studies journal, *Social Education,* to NCSS and continued to provide a subsidy for it. As Hazel Hertzberg points out:

> the AHA's generous arrangement helped the NCSS to become a more independent, stable, and self-assured organization and again underlined the historian's continuing commitment to social studies education . . . (Hertzberg 1981, 54–55)

Yet the presidential address given at the 1984 meeting of the AHA referred to the fact that by the 1960s AHA committees no longer addressed themselves "in any extensive way to the role history should play in the education of students in secondary schools," and claimed that historians had "unthinkingly abandoned" the promotion of history in secondary schools (*Education Week,* January 9, 1985, 5). The president, Arthur S. Link, urged "the recovery of a crucial role for the AHA in the determination of the curricula of our secondary schools."

The front page headline in the November 28, 1984, issue of *Education Week* proclaimed, "Social Studies: Amid Criticism, Still in Search of a Clear Rationale." The article that followed reported the ongoing debate over the diffuse nature of the social studies field. Under discussion was a preliminary position statement on the social studies curriculum issued by the National Council for the Social Studies. According to the newspaper account, those considering the position statement—"In Search of a Scope and Sequence for Social Studies"—could not agree on whether the report focused too much on history or whether it gave history short shrift in the curriculum.

The search for meaning, for a firm rationale for history in the schools, continues. School governing boards need to be reminded of the historical importance of historical instruction, and students need to be continually persuaded of its long-range value. A recent and cogent expression of a rationale for history reads:

> The subject of history . . . should be restored as an integral part of the school curriculum because it is central to all fields of humanities. . . . The study of history is important . . . precisely because it helps students simultaneously understand their intellectual inheritance and their civic responsibilities. (Downey 1984, 10)

METHODS, MATERIALS AND STUDENTS

Almost any social studies methods text one might consult recommends that teachers have at their command and employ a broad repertoire of strategies in teaching history. Part of this common injunction relates to the simple need for variety in one's teaching and part relates to the need for the appropriate matching of method with instructional goals and type of materials being used. The fact of the matter is, however, that teaching methods have remained remarkably narrow in range and standardized in application. Teaching methods in the social studies, especially in history, came under fire in the 1960s. In Canada, too, following a national survey, it was claimed that almost everywhere history was being taught in a very boring, dry and factual manner (Hodgetts 1968). Despite the rhetoric of the New Social Studies, lecture and recitation dominate now as they did a half-century ago. This domination is not for lack of alternative models. Henry Johnson stressed and exemplified in numerous ways the importance of getting the subject matter into the direct experience of young people 45 years ago (Johnson 1940). The persistence in the use of lecture and recitation can be—and certainly has been—attributed to the presence of dull and uninnovative teachers in the classroom. More recent and more thoughtful assessments suggest that history teachers rely on lecture and recitation methods for well-founded reasons relating to the structure and philosophy of the schools themselves (Shaver, Davis and Helburn 1979; Cuban 1982).

Looking beyond classroom pedagogy, we find that calls for the inclusion of multiple perspectives and social justice in history curriculum precipitated an appreciable stream of materials and inservice workshops for teachers. The content of this body of supplementary history materials reflected the quiet revolution that took place in historical scholarship in the 1960s and '70s. Curricula and courses in U.S. history were enriched by the particular histories of immigrants, women, Afro-Americans, native Americans, Asian-Americans, Hispanics and other groups who constitute the "mosaic of American history." Books—such as *My Backyard History; What Was It Like When Your Grandparents Were Your Age; We, The American Women, A Documentary History;* and *Teaching Ethnic Studies*—are typical of the flood of supplementary materials that emerged from the period and found its way into workshops, classrooms and curricula guides.

Assisting in efforts to reform curricula were the Department of Education, the National Endowment for the Humanities, the Organization of American Historians, the American Historical Association and the National Council for the Social Studies. These groups and many others sponsored and encouraged the development and dissemination of curriculum materials. They also supported inservice programs, such as summer institutes, and included information for teachers in their publications and annual programs.

Conceptual frameworks and theories on the restructuring of history and history teaching emerged along with new materials. Gerda Lerner (1976) worked out a framework that is very useful for understanding the progression of the history of women and other groups who have been excluded from history textbooks. The first level, "women worthies" or "compensatory history," documents the achievements of great women. The second level, contributory history, identifies and explains the contributions of women to various dimensions of our national life. The contributions of women to abolition, to the labor movement and to the reform movement are typical issues considered at this level of history development. A third level of history is feminine-centered history. Female-centered history requires a new periodization of history based on women's collective experiences. It calls for an alternative methodology, focusing on the actual experiences of all women and utilizing letters, diaries, autobiographies, oral histories and oral traditions.

Mary Kay Tetreault has expanded Gerda Lerner's categories of history in a five-stage conceptual framework for the adoption of women's history by teachers. Her work represents the level of sophistication we have achieved in thinking about how to reform traditional history curricula.

A striking feature of the literature on the history of history teaching is the long-standing disapproval of history textbooks. Acknowledged since the early 19th century to be the basic material for the history curriculum—if not in many cases *the* curriculum itself—they have been widely criticized on every conceivable ground (FitzGerald 1979). Although the era of the New Social Studies seemed to usher in a receptiveness to a greatly expanded range of materials in addition to the textbook, or in some cases in lieu of the textbook, the last decade appears to suggest a retreat from the use of artifacts, original documents, case studies and various media. The trend is toward renewed reliance on textbooks and accompanying worksheets.

Most of the literature on the history of history teaching focuses primarily on the curriculum. Comparatively little has been written on the interaction of the curriculum with students or on students' response to the curriculum. This neglect can be attributed in large part to the difficulty and expense of obtaining such information. What little we know about the relation of students to the history curriculum might be summarized in three generalizations:

- Over the past 50 years students' tendency to dislike instruction in history has remained rather constant.
- The overall history curriculum has been rather steadily simplified to respond to a perceived decline in students' abilities.
- Not a great deal of attention has been paid to adaptations of the history curriculum to suit different subgroups of students.

RECENT DEVELOPMENTS

Dennis Gunning has made a helpful analysis of recent developments in general educational theory that have had an impact on history teaching. Three prime examples may be found in the work of Jerome Bruner, Jean Piaget and Benjamin Bloom. Bruner has been instrumental in promoting the "structures of subjects" as the main concern of a learner. The concepts, skills and mode of inquiry characteristics of history, for instance, were to replace history considered as a body of information to be passed on by the teacher. As mentioned previously, Fenton developed this structural perspective and applied it directly to the development of the history curriculum.

Piaget has been responsible for a greatly increased awareness of the importance of concepts in the teaching and learning of any subject, including history. To the extent that teachers and curriculum guides have come to emphasize the centrality of concepts, they have called into question the importance of history for its own sake and its dependence on chronology as the major organizing principle. Historical occurrences become settings or illustrative topics within which to explicate key concepts rather than episodes embedded in a historical narrative.

The third source of educational theory that has had an impact on history teaching has been Benjamin Bloom's work. He and his associates developed the powerful idea of a hierarchy of cognitive skills. (The development of a parallel hierarchy of affective skills has had considerably less influence.) Gunning contends that the idea of "skills" is of great importance to teachers of history because it enables them to move from vague expressions of desired outcomes (e.g., students should think for themselves, or should understand history) to much more precisely targeted and sequenced goals. He concludes that the work of Bruner, Piaget and Bloom has combined to produce "a marked development in creative thinking about history and connected fields of study" (Gunning 1978, 13).

Gunning has also raised the issue of whether the academic discipline called history has to be the same as the school subject called history. From his utilitarian perspective, the true test of whether a fact, concept or a skill should be taught to particular students is the question: "Of what use, or potential use, is this knowledge to them?" Thus he plays down the notion of the "key concepts of the subject" in favor of the "large number of specific social, political, economic concepts involved in the understanding of any historical topics," and plays down the idea of the "skills of the historian" in favor of concentration on a wider range of skills. Expressed in another way, to the extent that a concept or skill is particular to history as a subject, it is less valuable for teaching than a concept (e.g., revolution) or a skill (e.g., extrapolation), which has broader application or utility.

A reaction to the pragmatic skills orientation has recently been set in motion. Although the notion of learning concepts and techniques, which can be transferred to an infinite number of future tasks, is an attractive one to the pragmatic U.S. mind—an argument for efficiency in education—it tends to downplay or ignore entirely the content of the subject matter. People concerned with the connections between the school subject of history and culture-making argue that a focus on skill development misses these connections and thus leads toward cultural fragmentation. Expressions of this concern may be found in the calls for cultural literacy, a common core of curriculum, and a coherent design in the social studies.

The struggle between those who favor making history a useful source of skills and concepts development on the one hand, and those who wish to restore the subject to its former role as a prime conveyor of humanistic values and national tradition on the other, is likely to become a painful and persistent issue in history teaching into the 1990s.

Another issue that merits further thought and investigation revolves around what might be called the psychology of school subjects. Are there particular features of history as a source of curriculum and an object of instruction that require attention because they impinge heavily on how young people understand, relate to, or employ history? Two examples have been discussed recently. One is the concept of time and how students react to its central role in history differently according to their stages of psychological development or to cultural norms (Hertzberg 1984).

A second example is the question of whether the "expanding horizons" conception used as the most common structure for history development in the elementary school curriculum is in actuality suitable for the ways in which young people's minds develop (Egan 1980).

Unlike the issues of the nature or functions of history, or of the proper relationship between history and the social sciences—for which there are no empirical solutions—questions about psychological development are amenable to empirical investigation. They deserve further attention and exploration.

In summary, then, history instruction over the past half-century has been characterized by a persistence in method and materials. The claims of academic history and the pull toward a broader-based social studies orientation have maintained an uneasy tension. New efforts at balancing these positions are being attempted as educators struggle with the appropriate place of history instruction in modern society. A movement from history as a separate subject to one of the social studies appears to have gained more ground in Canada than in the United States. Leading educational theorists have influenced how we think about history in the schools, if not how we practice it. In Canada the growth of nationalism and the maintenance of regionalism have been societal developments influencing history teaching. Sensitivity to minorities and cultural pluralism have become major factors in both the United States and Canada. Issues of cultural continuity versus presentism and diversity, and of how the study of history actually affects young people remain to be resolved.

NOTE

The author acknowledges valuable suggestions for this chapter by Jane Bernard-Powers.

REFERENCES

Anyon, Jean. "Ideology and United States History Textbooks." *Harvard Educational Review* 49(August 1979): 361–385.

Banks, James A. *Teaching Strategies for Ethnic Studies,* 2nd ed. Boston: Allyn and Bacon, 1979.

Beard, Charles A. *A Charter for the Social Sciences in the Schools,* Report of the Commission on the Social Studies, Part I. New York: Charles Scribner's Sons, 1932.

California State Department of Education. *Model Curriculum Standards: Grades Nine Through Twelve.* Sacramento: California State Department of Education, 1985.

Cook, Ann, Marilyn Gittell and Herb Mack. *What Was It Like When Your Grandparents Were Your Age?* New York: Pantheon Books, 1976.

Council of Ministers of Education. *A Survey of Provincial Curricula at the Elementary and Secondary Levels.* Ottawa: Council of Ministers of Education, Canada, 1982.

Cuban, Larry. "Persistent Instruction: The High School Classroom, 1900–1980." *Phi Delta Kappan* 64(October 1982): 113–118.

Downey, Matthew T. "The Status of History in the Schools." In *History in the Schools,* edited by Matthew T. Downey. Washington, DC: National Council for the Social Studies, 1984.

Education Week, November 28, 1984, p. 1.

Education Week, January 9, 1985, p. 5.

Education Week, January 16, 1985, p. 9.

Egan, Kieran. "John Dewey and the Social Studies Curriculum." *Theory and Research in Social Education* 8(Summer 1980); 37–55.

Fenton, Edwin. "A Structure of History." In *Concepts and Structure in the New Social Science Curricula,* edited by Irving Morrissett. New York: Holt, Rinehart and Winston, 1967.

FitzGerald, Frances. *American Revised: History Textbooks in the Twentieth Century.* Boston: Little, Brown, 1979.

Gunning, Dennis. *The Teaching of History.* London: Croom Helm, 1978.

Hahn, Carole L., Jane Bernard-Powers, et al. "Sex Equity in Social Studies." In *Handbook for Achieving Sex Equity Through Education,* edited by Susan S. Klien. Baltimore, MD: Johns Hopkins University Press, 1985.

Hertzberg, Hazel Whitman. "The Teaching of History." In *The Past Before Us: Contemporary Historical Writing in the United States,* edited by Michael Kammen. Ithaca, NY: Cornell University Press, 1980.

Hertzberg, Hazel Whitman. *Social Studies Reform, 1880–1980.* Boulder: Social Science Education Consortium, 1981.

Hertzberg, Hazel W. "Students, Methods and Materials of Instruction." In *History in the Schools,* edited by Matthew T. Downey. Washington, DC: National Council for the Social Studies, 1984.

Hodgetts, A. B. *What Culture? What Heritage?* Toronto: Ontario Institute for Studies in Education, 1968.

Johnson, Henry. *Teaching of History in Elementary and Secondary Schools with Applications to Allied Subjects.* New York: Macmillan, 1940.

Leacock, Stephen. *Essays and Literary Studies.* Toronto: S. B. Gundy, 1916.

Lerner, Gerda. "Placing Women in History." In Berenice A. Carroll, *Liberating Women's History.* Urbana: University of Illinois Press, 1976.

Milburn, G., and J. Herbert. "Is Canadian Nationalism Out of Step?" In *National Consciousness and the Curriculum: the Canadian Case,* edited by G. Milburn and J. Herbert. Toronto: Ontario Institute for Studies in Education, 1974.

Millstein, Beth, and Jeanne Bodin. *We, the American Women: A Documentary History.* Palo Alto, CA: Science Research Associates, 1977.

Newmann, Fred M. "The Radical Perspective on Social Studies: A Synthesis and Critique." *Theory and Research in Social Education* 13(Spring 1985): 1–18.

Robinson, Paul. "The Earliest Master: Henry Johnson (1867–1953)." *Journal of Thought* 17(Fall 1982): 12–26.

Shaver, James P., O. L. Davis, Jr., and Suzanne W. Helburn. "The Status of Social Studies Education: Impressions from Three NSF Studies." *Social Education* 43(February 1979): 150–153.

Taxel, Joel. "Justice and Cultural Conflict: Racism, Sexism and Instructional Materials." *Interchange* 9(1978–1979): 56–84.

Tetreault, Mary Kay. "Stages of Thinking About Women in History." Paper delivered at the College and University Faculty Association Annual Meeting, 1984. Washington, DC.

Tomkins, G. "The Social Studies in Canada." In *A Canadian Social Studies,* edited by J. Parsons, G. Milburn and M. van Manen. Edmonton: Faculty of Education, University of Alberta, 1983.

Tryon, Rolla M. *The Social Sciences as School Subjects.* Report of the Commission on the Social Studies, Part XI. New York: Charles Scribner's Sons, 1935.

Werner, W., B. Conners, T. Aoki, and J. Dahlie. *Whose Culture? Whose Heritage?* Vancouver: Centre for the Study of Curriculum and Instruction, Faculty of Education, University of British Columbia, 1977.

Weitzman, David. *My Backyard History.* Boston: Little, Brown and Co., 1975.

CHAPTER 3

THE EVOLVING NATURE OF GEOGRAPHY

Salvatore J. Natoli

Mark Muro wrote, "only in crisis do Americans decide to learn geography" (*Boston Globe,* November 13, 1984). His words remind us that in times of peace and economic well-being many of us are content to ignore the geographic surroundings that continually affect our lives. Muro's observation might explain, too, why so many Americans are abysmally ignorant not only of the rest of the world's geography, but of their own as well.

If any nation was blessed by its geography in its formative years, it was the United States. Not only did its territory possess a variety of climates and landforms, but it also had an abundant endowment of high quality land, minerals, vegetation and physical resources essential for industrial and commercial enterprises. Unlike the geographic setting of its Canadian neighbor, severe climatic conditions did not confine cities, towns and farmlands only to a small portion of the national territory. Unlike the land of its Mexican neighbor, rugged topography did not present insurmountable barriers to internal communication and transportation systems.

Perhaps the ignorance of people in the United States concerning geography, then, was derived from geography's beneficence throughout much of the history of the United States, and the fact that geography was so obviously an asset to national development. Thus, Jeffersonian democracy established its basis on a hospitable land, and our patriotic songs affirmed nature's abundance and expansiveness. Nevertheless, as the United States advances into the third century of its nationhood, we may be forced to rewrite our anthems to abundance and to relearn our geography. For example, World War II and the succeeding conflicts in Korea and Vietnam required an intimate knowledge of other nations, not only for potential bombing targets, battlefields, staging areas and bases for deploying troops, but as a means of helping to reconstruct troubled nations and societies in a period of transition.

What is more, in the 40 years following the end of World War II, a number of significant events severely tested the natural resources, self-sufficiency, self-confidence and national security of the United States. Other nations have challenged the technological and military superiority of the United States, and their challenges can no longer be ignored.

Meanwhile, in the United States, burgeoning suburbs have created ambiguous patterns of urban morphology and spatial interaction. Highways and their complex interchanges have overrun prime agricultural land. Waste products of industrial productivity have strained and overwhelmed the capacity to neutralize or dispose of them safely. Many charge that large populations have been placed at risk, that there has been dangerous contamination of water and air by industrial wastes, and that wasteful and injudicious foreign adventures have exposed our fuzzy international knowledge to the rest of the world.

Recent energy shortages have revealed the overdependence of the United States on foreign suppliers of petroleum. The nation's once-awesome industrial productivity has shown signs of becoming an aging and increasingly inefficient industrial complex, and one that is growing less competitive among formerly almost unassailable foreign markets. It is clearly time, then, for U.S. citizens to take seriously the geographic aspects of their situation and to strengthen their understanding of the scholarly findings in the discipline of geography.

In this task, concerned and involved geographers can be of invaluable assistance; for the discipline of geography has evolved, changed, and enlarged its capabilities impressively. No longer is there justification for the statement: "Now that all parts of the world have been discovered, there is nothing left for geographers to do."

Geographers today focus on a variety of vital topics: urban blight; the change, decline, and expansion of farmland; new disease vectors; frontier outposts in the inner city; emerging suburban morphologies; changing laborsheds and market areas; contoured risk surfaces; risk mosaics; natural and technological hazard zones; landscapes of fear; life-spaces; place-utility fields and equilibrium market areas, to name a few. As a result, geographers—both theoretical and practical—can provide a deeper knowledge and appreciation of the meaning of the planet Earth, and furnish insights and methods for its survival as a fitting home for humankind.

NEW DEAL TO END OF WORLD WAR II

Fifty years and one month ago I came to Washington to save the nation. . . . It was the New Deal; we were there to get the country going again, to right the inequities of the Great Depression, and . . . to remedy the onslaught of erosion, drought, and flood. (White 1985)

Gilbert F. White spoke these words at the opening session of the 1984 meeting of the Association of American Geographers and recalled the crisis he perceived as a fledgling civil servant during the Great Depression.

Every geographer was not so altruistic, but many "saw the New Deal programs as ways to broaden their professional opportunities, particularly outside the teaching field. . . . [Such] opportunities in government [were] quite limited in periods other than national emergencies" (Kollmorgen 1979). Geographers in the Federal Service contributed mainly to developing land classification schemes with a view toward improving natural and human resource use. They were part of a planning effort resulting from the Ogburn Report on Recent Social Trends (President's Research Committee 1933), which expressed the belief that improved national policy might be fashioned on the basis of careful social science analysis.

During this period, academic geography constituted only a small segment of higher education. Between 1935 and 1945, only 134 Ph.D.s were awarded from 18 institutions, with 6 of these accounting for almost three-fourths of the degrees granted. Although the academic training of geographers included important and required field courses (essential for much of the applied geography in the Federal Service), only a small proportion of Ph.D. recipients sought nonacademic employment during this period. World War II, however, created a huge demand for foreign area specialists and field-trained geographers.

Programs for precollege teachers were geared largely to the existing curriculums in the schools, rather than reflecting the disciplinary content of geography in the graduate schools. Not all geographers acquiesced to what was being taught. Richard Hartshorne (1937), for example, gave his outspoken reaction to what school teachers had told him was expected in geography instruction in the Minneapolis elementary schools, which was said to be the absence of map work and the focus on complex and dubious environmental determinism.

A few years after Gilbert White's entrance into the Federal Service, with some successes and failures the New Deal seemed to have become institutionalized (White 1985). The entrance of the United States into World War II set off another wave of intense activity in geography and provided many professional positions for geographers. Ironically, the statement was made that "World War II was the best thing that happened to geography since the birth of Strabo. Before the war the discipline was academic, afterwards it was oriented to nonacademic interests" (Stone 1979). Preston James noted in a similar vein: "I suppose really there are two professional fields that do in fact benefit from a war: one is medicine and the other is geography" (quoted in Buttimer 1983, 71).

These wartime experiences influenced profoundly the growth and development of the discipline in the postwar years. Cartography was one of the major beneficiaries of the wartime activities. Prior to World War II, cartographic studies played minimal roles in training U.S. geographers. Engineers and draftspersons drew most of the government's maps. But World War II demonstrated the need to obtain, digest and report information of value about foreign areas to operational agencies of the government. Despite inadequacies in their technical training in cartography, geographers were well-equipped to analyze, interpret and demonstrate how this information could be best presented in mappable form.

According to Arthur Robinson, who joined the Research and Analysis Branch of the Office of the Strategic Services in the Geography Division, "the greatest cause for concern . . . was that we were never really confident that we were doing the right thing, both technically and conceptually . . . the present student of cartography . . . would find it difficult to appreciate our ignorance." By the end of the war it became clear that academic programs in geography had to enlarge their instructional offerings in geographical cartography. It was stated that

The wartime experience of geographer-cartographers in Washington was duplicated in other countries, and one of the great lessons of the war was that thematic maps of all varieties were going to be much in demand. Increased planning and controls called for maps: restoring devastated cities and areas required maps; rebuilding the economies of nations demanded maps: expansion of transportation facilities delayed by the war needed maps; analyses of the consequences of development called for maps; integrated water use in drainage basin organization necessitated maps; and so on almost without end. (Robinson 1979)

The work of geographers in the war drew praise, and their foreign area experiences gave them perspectives for research. The war also opened up opportunities for postwar government service. In business, as a result of geographers' personal contacts, the value of geographical training became apparent. During the war, the Army Air Force Training Program, the ASTP-Area-Language Programs, the Navy V-5 and V-12 (for deck officers and aviators), and the Civil Affairs Programs all demanded geographical courses. The number of geographers left on campuses was insufficient to fill the instructional needs, and geographers were pressed into training individuals from allied fields to teach some of the courses.

Because many university administrators saw the field's significance in these training programs, they were willing to support geography programs after the war. Returning veterans wished to know more about where they had been, and "the overall effect of a global war—which most people knew we were hardly prepared for—led to the formation of areal institutes and the rapid expansion of departmental offerings" (Stone 1979).

Practicing geographers became aware of the deficiencies of geographic training in equipping them for a variety of tasks they were expected to do. An introspective period after the war led to some significant changes in the nature of geographical training and research. Surprisingly, a seminal work, Richard Hartshorne's *The Nature of Geography* (1939), became overlooked somewhat in the war-mobilization efforts. The course of history since that time has cast a range of perspectives on the significance of this work. For the first time in the history of the emerging discipline, a work provided a reflection upon the antecedents of geography and a discourse on its organization and scholarly objectives. The book had its origins in a suggestion to Hartshorne by Derwent Whittlesey, then editor of the *Annals of the Association of American Geographers*.

The volume presents the historical background of American geography, the deviations from the course of historical development, the justification for the historical concept of geography as a chorographic science, "landschaft" and "landscape," and the relation of history to geography. It further outlines the limitation of the phenomena of geography to things perceived by the senses, the logical basis for the selection of data in geography, the concept of the region as a concrete unit object, the methods of organizing the world into regions, and the relation of geography to science. The *Nature of Geography* did not resolve the philosophical questions about the nature of the discipline. It did, however, raise the consciousness of geographers about their discipline's scientific methodology and position among the sciences, especially vis-à-vis the physical and social sciences. The book also stimulated many critical rejoinders and, most notably, an alternative view, expressed in Schaefer's (1953) "Exceptionalism in Geography: A Methodological Examination." Hartshorne himself in 1959 provided a retrospective monograph on his original work.

GROWTH, TRANSITION AND CHANGE AFTER WORLD WAR II

The interest in geography generated by wartime contacts with foreign cultures and the energies and monies pumped into the postwar reconstruction of devastated countries encouraged geographers to conduct foreign field research, a largely neglected field prior to World War II. The benefits of the GI Bill swelled college enrollments and made higher education available to larger segments of the population than in any period of the nation's history. The composition of that population would, in less than a generation, drastically alter the sociology of U.S. higher education during some of its most turbulent years. The GI housing benefits also helped to change the landscape.

Suburbs grew at an unprecedented rate, and, in a short period, compelled urban students to re-examine the city-suburb dichotomies and their symbiotic relationships. The increasing use of automobiles transformed the morphology of the suburban landscape from bedroom communities to exurban minicities. Nonfarm populations occupied increasingly larger acreages of land within and adjacent to the large metropolitan areas.

It is, of course, somewhat misleading to relate direct causal attributes of the changes in our landscape to the problems receiving increasing attention in U.S. geographical research; but we cannot ignore that possibility. Research in urban, industrial, and transportation geography expanded in the postwar period. Geographers developed useful models and raised serious questions about the complex spatial interactions of city systems, industrial reorganization and transportation planning.

To many, the "quantitative revolution" of the late 1950s and early 1960s marked a watershed in U.S. geographical research and, in Kuhnian terms, expressed a paradigm for scientific geography (Kuhn 1970). The geography departments at the Universities of Washington and Iowa loomed large in this period as centers for the diffusion of innovations in quantitative methodology. William Garrison, who introduced and expounded the new methodologies at the University of Washington, shed some light on this period by going beyond a concern with statistics and quantification. His "central concern" was the logic of method (Garrison 1979).

Other writers of this period also identified the principal source of this movement to be the individuals who were present in the Department of Geography at Washington—particularly, G. Donald Hudson, who championed questioning and who encouraged his students to be concerned about the status of geography and its relatively low esteem. In addition, Torsten Hägerstrand spent an academic year in the department carrying his innovative ideas of human geography from Sweden; the Hartshorne-Schaefer debate was on; and the new geographers were dissatisfied with their own work. In general, regional and systematic geographers clashed, and paradigms for studying urban areas, transportation, and regional science emerged. It was said: ". . . (W)e played with methodological ideas and produced a generation of students who liked to play with ideas about the logic of method" (Garrison 1979).

The happy coincidence of the adoption of quantitative methodologies and the growth of urban, economic (industrial), and transportation geography provided a more practical value to the "revolution" than merely as a scientific paradigm for the discipline. It introduced students to theoretical modeling of regions and to sophisticated mathematical and statistical tools useful for practical applications in solving real world problems. With the growth and accessibility of computer technology, geographers became valued consultants and practitioners for large-scale regional planning programs in both the developed and developing worlds. The new methodologies spread slowly to other geographical subfields and, in particular, to cartography via the pioneering work of Waldo Tobler, who introduced the concept of the "warping of geographical space under various mental or physical influences" (Gould 1979).

The new methodologies also transformed the geographer's view of the world by providing new tools for analyzing and synthesizing how people perceive their environments. These geographers shifted from relying entirely upon their trained observers' eyes to seeing the world through the eyes of those who experienced their environments most directly. Studies of people under environmental stress, of the natural and technological hazards that influence and affect human activities, of the varieties of culturally biased attachments to land and landscapes, and even of landscapes of the past all became objects of careful scrutiny. These resulted in developing behavioral models to help scholars enlarge their knowledge of the world by observing differently than in the past why people chose to live where they lived and behave the way they did. Research in perception demonstrated that many of these ideas were indeed not really new but required a fertile atmosphere for their further development and use (Wright 1925, 1966).

In 1954 the Association of American Geographers (AAG) sponsored the publication of *American Geography: Inventory and Prospect,* a stock-taking to mark the 50th birthday of the Association. The authors said that "if the project stimulates the *doing* of geography instead of merely talking about it, much will have been accomplished" (James and Jones 1954). For a brief period this volume became required reading for every graduate student in geography. It also provided evidence of the diminished role that physical geography had played in the recent history of the discipline. The intellectual ferment that grasped the discipline in the 1950s soon turned this landmark document into.a useful historical record.

In 1956 an equally significant volume, *Man's Role in Changing the Face of the Earth,* provided a showcase for the persistent human-environment theme as envisioned for a more livable world, not only by geographers but by anthropologists, sociologists, and other students of the human landscape. In its preface, Paul Fejos wrote that the present undertaking would "further the recombination and synthesis of available and new knowledge, looking toward the development of a more comprehensive science of man" (Thomas 1956). Marvin Mikesell in 1984 wrote that "the publication was out of phase to the larger public interest [at that time], and had it appeared a dozen years later, on the eve of Earth Day, geographers might have enjoyed a public recognition that they have often yearned for but seldom achieved."

Meanwhile Gilbert White and his students contributed widely to the literature and method of perceptual and behavioral models in their work on natural hazards and their mitigation for the populations at risk (White and Haas 1975).

The geographer's continuing concern for methodology and for defining and articulating the discipline's position among the sciences led to periodic statements on the methodological aspects of the discipline. Following the *Nature of Geography* in 1939 and Schaefer's rejoinder in 1953, there appeared Ackerman's 1958 monograph on *Geography as a Fundamental Research Discipline,* Hartshorne's *Perspective on the Nature of Geography* (1959), and two major disciplinary statements. *The Science of Geography* (Ad Hoc Committee on Geography 1965) surveyed research directions in physical geography, cultural geography, location theory and political geography. In 1970, Taaffe presented a report entitled *Geography,* which examined the social scientific aspects of the discipline. The number of such statements continued to expand as the number of subfields and viewpoints within geography matured (James and Martin 1981).

From Geographic Discipline to Inquiring Student

No chronicle of the 1960s can be complete without mentioning the High School Geography Project (HSGP). At the time, elementary and secondary school geography bore only a faint resemblance to professional and academic geography. The federally funded curriculum improvement projects of this period provided the means to bring school geography into line with the rest of the discipline. The successes and failures of the High School Geography Project have received ample coverage elsewhere in this volume, and it suffices to say that the HSGP was designed to provide opportunities for students to "do" geography; that is, the activities developed attempted to replicate how geographers solve problems. The intensive participation of academic geographers in this project introduced these scholars to the problems and prospects for improving geographic education in the schools. For many, it established life-long commitments to educational efforts and developed sensitivities to the relationship between school geography and college geography (Patton 1980).

Similarly, the work of the NSF-funded Commission on College Geography (CCG) in the 1960s and early 1970s focused on the content and quality of teaching of geography in the colleges and universities. In many respects its objectives were to achieve a greater parity between the "strong" and "weak" departments. The CCG also brought many university professors in touch with the mainstream of college-level instruction and raised their consciousness about the significance of the quality of teaching and the role of geography in liberal education (Geography in Liberal Education Project 1965).

In 1984 a joint National Council for Geographic Education/Association of American Geographers (NCGE/AAG) committee published the *Guidelines for Geographic Education—Elementary and Secondary Schools,* designed to inform educational decision makers about the need to institute, update, and enrich geography programs in our schools. The guidelines address the growing problem of geographical illiteracy and provide a blueprint for developing a sequence of programs that will improve the teaching and learning of geography in the elementary and secondary schools. Acting upon the favorable public response to the guidelines, the NCGE and AAG agreed to combine their efforts to implement the recommendations of the guidelines nationwide. The American Geographical Society and National Geographic Society joined with them to form the Geographic Education National Implementation Project (GENIP). GENIP is a national project to improve the status and quality of geographic education in grades K–12 in the United States. GENIP is in the process of seeking funding to implement the guidelines' goals and provide detailed curriculum and course outlines, initiate plans for a nationwide testing and evaluation program for geographic education, and support other activities that will improve geographical literacy.

ENVIRONMENTAL CRISIS

The logical progression from work on natural hazards to concerns for environmental quality increasingly occupied the attention of many geographers. Although geography had a rich tradition in environmental studies extending from the 1920s through the 1930s, it required a philosophic move away from the work of the environmental determinists, notably Huntington and Semple. A careful rereading of their work today reveals them to be less open to scholarly criticism. It was the translation of their work into oversimplified studies of cause–effect relationships and blind acceptance of spurious concepts in school textbooks that overlooked some of their elegant and original thinking and research. The thread of environmental studies remained intact in the Depression era, when conservationist–geographers worked on the dust bowl problems of the prairies, and the deterioration and erosion of agricultural land in the post-cotton belt economy of the traditional south.

Rachel Carson's *Silent Spring* (1962) raised the nation's conciousness about environmental degradation. Environmental studies were revived, then proliferated by the end of the 1960s. Suddenly the public began to notice the many obvious wounds on the landscape wrought by air, water and noise pollution. Native animal and plant populations were jeopardized or destroyed by extensive use of pesticides on farmlands and forests. Health problems from drinking water supplies that were contaminated by carelessly chosen toxic waste-disposal sites increased exponentially. Bills were coming due from our disregard for basic geographical and ecological principles to achieve the agricultural, mining and industrial maturation of the American dream Hammond et al. 1978.

The quality of life in cities deteriorated, creating hostile environments and "landscapes of fear" (Tuan 1979). Crises again aroused the population to demand that these problems be corrected, but action was hindered by the collective ignorance on the part of the public and the government of basic geographical and ecological processes, environmental degradation, and the cultural aspects of environmental quality. Most of all, geographers brought a global perspective to the study of environment, a departure from the American ethnocentrism so characteristic of much of the environmental crusade (Zelinsky 1970).

The AAG's Task Force on Environmental Quality called attention to aspects of geographers' professional backgrounds that equipped them for effective environmental teaching and research. These professional backgrounds included abilities to synthesize information from complex sources, to provide complex explanations, to use a range of information sources and methodologies, to focus attention on location and spatial relationships, and to employ the human-environmental equation (Lowenthal et al. 1973). The environmental movement placed geographers squarely in their element and to some extent unified the discipline by re-emphasizing the physical science aspects of geography and the need for an integrative, holistic view of the human–land perspective (Marcus 1979; Orme 1980).

Federal environmental legislation in the clean air and water acts, environmental impact statements, and a myriad of other federal, state and local laws necessitated a spatial portrayal of practically every environmental problem. Fortunately, the vastly improved abilities of cartographers to give expression to these spatial relationships created an enormous demand for their services. Increasingly sophisticated computers assisted the compilation and analysis of massive data outputs from sensitive monitoring instruments, remotely sensed imagery, and field observations. These data could be mapped accurately and quickly. The maps could convey graphically all manner of problem areas, scenarios of short-term and long-term effects, and alternative solutions. Cost-benefit analysis, used so successfully in ordering alternative decision-making processes for assessing mitigation of natural hazards, could be applied to many environmental problems, especially those attributed to unrestrained or unchallenged technological advances (White and Haas 1975).

SOCIETY IN CRISIS

The Vietnam War and the civil rights movement spurred a period of geographical research and teaching often overlooked or underrepresented in the professional literature. The traditional scholarly approach of analyzing social or physical phenomena but shying away from making recommendations no longer seemed justified, as the content of scientists' work now demanded accountability.

Geographers, long silent on many issues within their purview and reticent behind a façade of scientific objectivity, belatedly proclaimed—at first only to each other—a "Resolution on National Priorities," now referred to as the Kates' Resolution. Robert W. Kates brought it before the 1969 business meeting of the AAG, and, in eloquent terms, it catalogued the wasteful and environmentally destructive war in Vietnam while the rest of the world and domestic social ills and inequities went unnoticed or were given scant attention. The resolution called upon geographers and

> all Americans to join in reversing our national priorities, to commit our wealth, our intelligence and our skills to the vast challenges of inner space; the health, happiness and hope of the individual, the survival and embellishment of our collective places, the preservation for all of the wonder of nature, and the mutual sharing of the riches of the earth. ("Resolution on National Priorities" 1969)

Geographers were also painfully aware that minorities and women played minimal roles in the discipline. More significantly, the record of human geography research and teaching about these groups left much to be desired. Black geographers constituted less than 3% of the academic practitioners. In 1969 Donald Deskins wrote;

> Before geographers can address themselves to the question: What research contributions can the geographical profession make that will contribute to a solution of the racial dilemma presently facing America? they have to answer the question: What have geographers done in the past to contribute to the resolution of American racial problems?

Deskins later headed the AAG's Commission on Geography and Afro-America, a federally funded program to help institutionalize the discipline's efforts in recognizing blacks. This multipronged effort provided funds to support talented black students in geography graduate departments, faculty exchanges between leading geographic research centers and predominantly black colleges, faculty leadership conferences and workshops, and summer institutes for geography teachers from predominantly black schools which also provided faculty teaching internships for graduate students.

The commission helped to increase greatly the number of black Ph.D.s in the profession. A large proportion of these black geographers returned to predominantly black campuses, and many have achieved national reputations in research and teaching. However, the abatement of social consciousness in recent years and the current state of federal "benign neglect" of the problems of minorities have blocked the full entry of the black population into the mainstream of our economic prosperity and into a major role in U.S. higher education.

Harold Rose, the first (and only) black to be elected to the presidency of the AAG, recalled in the preface to his 1978 presidential address the attentiveness accorded Professor Parsons' presidential address as he delved into a characterization of his 30 years of field work in Latin America.

> I have chosen to call [Parsons' address] the geography of happiness. . . . [I]t reflected the personal rewards . . . of one's experience as a practicing geographer. I made a note to myself . . . that my geography was the geography of despair and that my presidential address would reflect that. . . . Thus, I have chosen to emphasize the rising incidence of acts of lethal violence as they are becoming increasingly important as killers of selected populations. (Rose 1978)

The geographical literature of the 1960s began to indicate rising concern about the plight and conditions of minority groups and their geographical expression (Deskins 1969). Minority group coalitions and caucuses such as blacks, women, gays, Native Americans and others have pressed for increased recognition in textbooks and research, as well as in participation in the governance of the Association. Women geographers, in particular, who today represent only about 20 percent of U.S. geographers, have increased in numbers steadily but slowly over the past decade and constitute an active advocacy group. Women, however, are significantly underrepresented in tenured or in full professorial positions in college and university departments of geography.

In a 1982 paper, Monk and Hanson suggested two alternative paths to producing a gender-balanced approach to the study of geography. One path is "to develop a strong feminist strand of research that would become one thread among many in the thick braid of geographic tradition." But this was considered insufficient.

> The second approach, which we favor, is to encourage a feminist perspective within all streams of human geography. In this way issues concerning women would become incorporated in all geographic endeavors.

The feminist perspective compelled many human geographers to examine carefully, in both their teaching and research, the male-weighted gender imbalance in treating geographical research questions, particularly in the shadow economies, economic productivity measures, migration patterns, population studies, and cultural ecology (Mazey and Lee 1983; Rengert and Monk 1982).

PLURALISM IN GEOGRAPHY

The information presented in this chapter highlights the developing pluralism within the discipline. This pluralism occurred despite some commonly shared goals, and it is a hallmark of modern geography. There is pluralism in methodologies, even within subfields—such as in regional development approaches that use both regional science and more traditional regionalization methodologies—and in the proliferation, consolidation and recombination of several subfields. It exists, too, in examinations of a variety of epistemological approaches, such as humanistic or phenomenological geographies. Meanwhile, historical studies have been revived and flourish, especially in local studies on historic preservation (Mikesell 1984).

The call for research accountability on social problems has generated a whole spectrum of applied studies and projects and widespread attention to public policy questions. Pluralism and applied studies seem to have formed an unusual marriage.

> Geography attracts people with an aversion to intellectual boundaries, with an instinct that physical artifacts on the landscape are important in understanding processes—people with curiosity, eclecticism, and practicality. These attributes make geographers *useful* [emphasis added]. But the main explanation is that public policymaking in the United States is exquisitely geographic, at least at the material level . . . [where] spatial patterns, relationships and structures are at the heart of policymaking. (Wilbanks 1985)

Even the map, the major tool of geographic expression, becomes demonstrable evidence of public policy in a spatial setting. Adopting a policy orientation requires fundamental modifications in cartographic education by de-emphasizing traditional methods of map production and integrating "instruction in graphic representation, remote sensing, digital cartography and spatial analysis, and [making] a formal attempt to deal with policy issues affecting geographic information" (Monmonier 1982.)

Geographic information systems development has been a response to the enormousness of the data now available about the earth, and a necessary organizational method for defining and implementing public policies. Such integrated systems attempt to develop and manage a variety of significant data bases organized within a variety of spatial units. Pluralism is evident nearly everywhere.

In a little more than a generation, geographers have been forced to relinquish the luxury of maintaining an objective distance from environmental and social problems. Academic geography today keeps in close contact with the world we call our home and with our stewardship of its resources. It is no longer conscionable for us to ignore the significance of the geographical space in which we play out our lives. We cannot forget that this space must support increasing numbers of people who will place demands upon it and each other. *Where* will we produce the food to sustain the world's increasing population? *Where* will we find and harness the energy and marshal the technological resources to fuel the world's burgeoning industries? *Where* will we house the billions who will populate the earth and procure the materials to house them? *Where* will we locate the social institutions and health-care facilities to serve optimally and equitably an increasingly mobile and aging population? *Where* will we site the infrastructures to guarantee the well-being of all people with food, services, recreation and employment? Political, social and economic perturbations add alarming complexities to these difficult questions. The world today is

> basically unlike those earlier worlds [of detachment and profligacy]. The differences are in kind, not in quantity. In considering them, geographers are not dealing with trends; they are dealing with discontinuities at long last perceived. The globe is finally seen as an intricate set of systems of tectonic movement, atmospheric circulation, and biogeochemical flows supporting dynamic communities of plants and animals, all subject in greater or lesser degree to human perturbations. The human family is seen as mutually dependent for its livelihood and as standing to survive or not according to its wisdom—or luck—in social management of the basic systems. Now it is tortured and driven by its newfound capacity to throw the whole set of processes out of kilter by one violent action. . . . All of us are members of a world community that is coming to see itself whole. (White 1985)

So we have come full circle from focusing on the nation to focusing on the world. Geographers see clearly that the constructive and creative development of other lands and other peoples—indeed, *all* lands and *all* peoples—is a major part of their responsibility.

> Why might geographers think we can help in [this enterprise]? The answer is plain and modest: because we have shown in limited but practical and tested ways that we can do so in teaching, in research, and in policy analysis. (White 1985)

REFERENCES

Ackerman, Edward A. *Geography as a Fundamental Research Discipline.* Chicago: Department of Geography Research Paper 53, 1958.

Ad Hoc Committee on Geography of the Earth Sciences Division, National Research Council. *The Science of Geography.* Washington, DC: National Academy of Sciences/National Research Council, Publication 1277, 1965.

Adams, John S. "The Geography of Riots and Civil Disorders in the 1960s," *Economic Geography,* 48 (January 1982): 24–42.

Berry, Brian J. L. "Monitoring Trends, Forecasting Change and Evaluating Goal Achievements: The Ghetto vs. Desegregation Issue in Chicago as a Case Study." In *Urban Social Segregation,* edited by Ceri Peach. London: Longman, 1975, 196–221.

Brown, W. "Access to Housing: The Role of the Real Estate Industry," *Economic Geography,* 48 (January 1982): 66–78.

Bunge, William. *Theoretical Geography.* Lund, Sweden: University of Lund (Lund Series in Geography), 1966.

Buttimer, Anne. *The Practice of Geography.* London: Longman, 1983.

Buttimer, Anne, and David Seamon, eds. *The Human Experience of Space.* London: Croom Helm, 1980.

Carson, Rachel. *Silent Spring.* Boston: Houghton Mifflin, 1962.

Chorley, Richard J., and Peter Haggett. *Models in Geography.* London: Methuen, 1967.

Chorley, Richard J., ed. *Directions in Geography.* London: Methuen, 1973.

Committee on Geographic Education, Association of American Geographers/National Council for Geographic Education. *Guidelines for Geographic Education—Elementary and Secondary Schools.* Washington, DC, and Macomb, IL: AAG/NCGE, 1984.

Committee on Geography and International Studies, Association of American Geographers. *Geography and International Knowledge.* Washington, DC: Association of American Geographers, 1982.

Davies, C. Shane, and David L. Huff. "Impact of Ghettoization on Black Employment." *Economic Geography* 48(October 1972): 421–427.

Deskins, Donald R., Jr. "Geographical Literature on the American Negro, 1949–1969: A Bibliography." *Professional Geographer* 21(May 1969): 145–149.

Dresch, Jean. "Reflections on the Teaching of Geography." *Prospects* 9(March 1979): 287.

Garrison, William L. "Playing with Ideas." *Annals of the Association of American Geographers* 69(March 1979): 118–120.

Geography in Liberal Education Project. *Geography in Undergraduate Liberal Education.* Washington, DC: Association of American Geographers, 1965.

Gould, Peter, "Geography 1957–1977: The Augean Period," *Annals of the Association of American Geographers,* 69 (March 1979): 139–150.

Gross, Richard E. "The Status of Social Studies in the Public Schools of the United States: Facts and Impressions of a National Survey." *Social Education* 41(March 1977): 194–200, 205.

Hägerstrand, Torsten. *Innovation Diffusion as a Spatial Process.* Translated by A. Pred. Chicago: University of Chicago Press, 1967.

Hammond, Kenneth A., George Macinko and Wilma Fairchild, eds. *Sourcebook on the Environment: A Guide to the Literature:* Chicago: University of Chicago Press, 1978.

Hartshorne, Richard. "Geography for What?" *Social Education* 1(March 1937): 166–172.

Hartshorne, Richard. *The Nature of Geography.* Lancaster, PA: Association of American Geographers, 1939. (Reprinted, with corrections by the author, 1961.)

Hartshorne, Richard. *Perspective on the Nature of Geography.* Chicago: Rand McNally, 1959.

Helgren, David M. "Place Name Ignorance is National News." *Journal of Geography* 82(July–August 1983): 176–178.

James, Preston E. "The Significance of Geography in American Education." In *The Social Sciences and Geographic Education,* edited by John M. Ball et al. New York, John Wiley and Sons, 1971.

James, Preston E., and Clarence F. Jones, eds. *American Geography: Inventory and Prospect.* Syracuse, NY: Syracuse University Press for the Association of American Geographers, 1954.

James, Preston E., and Geoffrey Martin. *All Possible Worlds: A History of Geographical Ideas,* 2nd ed. New York: John Wiley and Sons, 1981.

Kenworthy, Leonard S. *Social Studies for the Eighties.* New York: John Wiley and Sons, 1981, 28.

Kollmorgen, Walter M. "Kollmorgen as a Bureaucrat." *Annals of the Association of American Geographers* 69(March 1979): 77–88.

Kuhn, Thomas S. *The Structure of Scientific Revolutions.* Chicago: University of Chicago Press, 1970.

Ley, David F. *The Black Inner City as Frontier Outpost: Images and Behavior of a Philadelphia Neighborhood.* Washington, DC: Association of American Geographers. Monograph Series 7, 1974.

Ley, David F. "The Street Gang Milieu." In *The Social Economy of Cities,* edited by Harold Rose and G. Gappert. Beverly Hills, CA: Sage, 1975, 247–273.

Lowenthal, David, et al., "Report of the AAG Task Force on Environmental Quality," *Professional Geographer* 25 (February 1973): 39–47.

Manners, Ian R., and Marvin W. Mikesell. *Perspectives on Environment.* Washington, DC: Association of American Geographers. Commission on College Geography. Publication 13, 1974.

Manson, Gary. "An Analysis of the Status of Geography in American Schools." (Paper Presented at the Annual Meeting of the Association of American Geographers.) Louisville, KY, April 1980.

Marcus, Melvin G. "Coming Full Circle: Physical Geography in the Twentieth Century." *Annals of the Association of American Geographers* 69(December 1979): 521–532.

Mazey, Mary Ellen, and David R. Lee. *Her Space, Her Place: A Geography of Women.* Washington, DC: Association of American Geographers. Resource Publications in Geography, 1983.

Mikesell, Marvin W. "Developments in North American Geography." In *Geography Since the Second World War: An International Survey.* Edited by R. J. Johnston and Paul Claval. Totowa, NJ: Barnes & Noble Books, 1984.

Monk, Janice, and Susan Hanson. "On Not Excluding Half of the Human in Human Geography." *Professional Geographer* 34(February 1982): 11–23.

Monmonier, Mark. "Cartography, Geographic Information and Public Policy." *Journal of Geography in Higher Education* 6(April 1982): 103–104.

Morrill, Richard L. "The Negro Ghetto: Problems and Alternatives," *Geographical Review,* 55 (July 1965): 339–361.

Orme, Antony R. "The Need for Physical Geography." *Professional Geographer* 32(May 1980): 141–148.

Pattison, William D. "The Four Traditions of Geography." *Journal of Geography* 63(May 1964): 211–216.

Patton, Donald J., ed. *From Geographic Discipline to Inquiring Student* (Final Report on the High School Geography Project). Washington, DC: Association of American Geographers, 1970.

President's Research Committee on Social Trends. *Recent Social Trends,* 2 vols. New York: McGraw-Hill, 1933.

Rengert, Arlene, and Janice Monk, eds. *Women and Spatial Change: Learning Resources for Social Sciences Courses.* Dubuque, IA: Kendall/Hunt, 1982.

"Resolution on National Priorities," *AAG Newsletter.* (December 1969).

Robinson, Arthur H. "Geography and Cartography: Then and Now." *Annals of the Association of American Geographers* 69(March 1979): 97–102.

Rose, Harold M. "The Geography of Despair." *Annals of the Association of American Geographers* 68(December 1978): 453–464.

Schaefer, Fred K. "Exceptionalism in Geography: A Methodological Examination." *Annals of the Association of American Geographers* 43(September 1953): 226–249.

Stone, Kirk H. "Geography's Wartime Service." *Annals of the Association of American Geographers* 69(March 1979): 89–96.

Taaffe, Edward J., ed. *Geography* (The Behavioral and Social Sciences Survey). Englewood Cliffs, NJ: Prentice-Hall, 1970.

Thomas, William L., Jr., ed. *Man's Role in Changing the Face of the Earth.* Chicago: University of Chicago Press, 1956.

Tuan, Yi-Fu. *Landscapes of Fear.* New York: Pantheon Books, 1979.

White, Gilbert F. "Geographers in a Perilously Changing World." *Annals of the Association of American Geographers* 75(March 1985): 11–16.

White, Gilbert F., and J. Eugene Haas. *Assessment of Research on Natural Hazards.* Cambridge, MA: The MIT Press, 1975.

Wilbanks, Thomas J. "Geography and Public Policy at the National Scale." *Annals of the Association of American Geographers* 75(March 1985): 4–10.

Wise, John H., "Geographic Education and the Anticipation of World Events," *Journal of Geography* 79 (April/May 1980), 154–155.

Wright, John K. *The Geographical Lore of the Time of the Crusades.* New York: American Geographical Society, 1925. Reprint. New York: Dover, 1965.

Wright, John K. *Human Nature in Geography: Fourteen Papers, 1925–1965.* Cambridge, MA: Harvard University Press, 1966.

Zelinsky, Wilbur. "Beyond the Exponentials: The Role of Geography in the Great Transition." *Economic Geography* 46(July 1970): 498–535.

CHAPTER 4

TEACHING AND LEARNING IN GEOGRAPHY

Barbara J. Winston

Education for citizenship is an enduring instructional goal in K–12 social studies, and geography helps to augment that goal. Geographic knowledge and skills are perhaps more important now than at any other time in human history, for we are faced daily with concerns about the state of the planet and world affairs.

Many of these concerns deal with factors of location, patterns of distribution and movement, human/environmental relationships and other factors pertinent in geography. Thus, with every effort to set disciplinary chauvinism aside, it seems reasonable to argue that geographic knowledge and skills help citizens to:

- Formulate enlightened opinions on complex global issues related to peace, hunger, trade, environment, refugees, development, or overpopulation, to name a few;
- Cast informed votes for government leaders with stands on the above issues, and evaluate whether records of leaders' actions reflect that they know and take account of geographic realities surrounding the issues;
- Make informed decisions about personal foreign policies, and evaluate related individual and group behaviors;
- Gain perspectives about similarities and differences in ways people in other societies live and interact with each other and their environments—a preliminary step to reduce ethnocentric and stereotypic thinking;
- Understand, and find creative solutions to, problems such as those in community or urban planning;
- Deal with regional issues such as open space or transportation problems;
- See ways in which apparently local, regional or national issues are linked inextricably to global issues;
- Gain skills to select and use maps with understanding because comprehension of so many issues depends on one's ability to use media that answer questions about "where?" "how far?" or "in what direction?"

The points above and others that could be made suggest that United States citizens should be knowledgeable about geography, and the subject should be important in social studies programs in our schools. The evidence, however, makes it clear that this is not the case. Instead, the current realities are: (1) U.S. children and many adults are deficient in geographic knowledge, skills and affective learning; and (2) geography is less significant than it might be as a component in social studies. These two points are primarily responsible for producing the overarching issues that are discussed in this chapter, which is designed to explore perspectives on persistent concerns related to teaching and learning in geography over the last 50 years.

THE OVERARCHING ISSUES

1. U.S. children and many adults are deficient in geographic knowledge, skills and affective learning.

In January 1983, a university professor in Florida quizzed his class in introductory geography on the locations of several important places (Helgren 1983). More than one-half of the students (N-128) could not locate Cairo, Algeria, Sahel, Chicago and Moscow, among other places. Anyone who has given a similar quiz might not be surprised at these results.

Recently, the Committee on Geographic Education of the Association of American Geographers and the National Council for Geographic Education reported that among 12-year-old students in eighty highly industrialized nations, U.S. students ranked a weak fourth among those taking a geography examination.

The National Assessment of Educational Progress measured students' knowledge of worldwide spatial distributions, as well as knowledge about interrelationships within and among physical and cultural environments. The results of that study were also dismal.

A report published in the 1970s on overall results of state assessments and nationwide tests by the National Assessment of Educational Progress concluded tentatively that among the social sciences, students had the most serious deficiencies in knowledge of geography and economics. Students were also most deficient in skills that required the use of maps, tables and graphs (Wiley 1977, 249).

In a study done to measure global understanding by college students, results revealed that less than one-third of the freshmen surveyed knew that cultivation of crops over time contributed most directly and extensively to environmental alteration on earth. (Most attributed this to urbanization.) In the same study, less than one-half of the freshmen had accurate information about current population trends, and about the same proportion felt that overpopulation was a world issue in which they had very little interest. The study also revealed that only slightly more than 10 percent of the freshmen surveyed believed geography courses contributed to their awareness of world problems (Barrows 1981).

The above examples offer current evidence of deficiencies in geography, but the problems are not new. Further, many readers could probably supply several of their own stories illustrative of geographic illiteracy, but perhaps these are sufficient to make the point here.

2. Geography is less significant than it might be as a component in social studies.

The most comprehensive data on the status of school geography appeared as part of a larger study in the 1970s (Wiley 1977). In that study, the Social Science Education Consortium assessed practices and needs in precollege social science education during the period 1955–1975. Results described in that study are the sources of most information described here.

One indicator of a subject's perceived importance is whether it is a separate requirement for secondary school graduation. Using this criterion, U.S. history was the most important social studies subject in the period 1955–1975. In addition, while U.S. government and world history courses were important requirements in many states, geography was not mentioned at all, either as a required course or as a content requirement within another social studies course.

A second indicator of perceived importance is inferred from advisement practices in schools. A common practice in secondary schools is to counsel college-bound students into world history as a social studies elective, rather than into world geography. Since geography is rarely required at the university level, it is possible that students are never exposed to a geography course. This point is corroborated with results of a study that revealed that about two-thirds of a large sample of college seniors had never taken any university courses in geography (Barrows 1981, 150). In the vocational programs of the past, commercial geography was considered a suitable course for noncollege-bound students. It is possible that present counseling practices are an outmoded carry-over from that period of time.

Another indicator is whether schools have separate geography course offerings. Gross found, in 1973, that the subject was offered to about one-half the more than 20,000 junior high and secondary schools surveyed, a result that did not differ dramatically from the cases in world history and U.S. government. It is likely that geography and many other traditional social studies subjects experienced a decline during the period of 1973 to 1980. This period coincided with a time when new social science courses were added to the curriculum (e.g., sociology and psychology) along with new interdisciplinary courses.

Comparative enrollment patterns for school subjects can also be examined to weigh the importance of geography. Gross showed that while total enrollment in middle and secondary schools increased 59 percent between 1961 and 1973, enrollment in secondary world geography increased only 24 percent. This figure was compared to larger increases in U.S. government courses (+67 percent), U.S. history (+74 percent), economics (+120 percent), sociology (+175 percent), psychology (+323 percent). The only increase more modest than that attributed to geography was in world history (+5 percent)—a finding that is also disturbing.

In a 1982 editorial comment, the Association of American Geographers' newsletter cited more current information on this point. "The U.S. Department of Education estimates that less than 9 percent of all secondary students in the U.S. are enrolled in geography courses and this percentage is about 60 percent of what the enrollment figures showed for 1960–1961."

Teachers' academic preparation is another area to scrutinize. It was concluded that geography represented a subject in the 1950s and 1960s in which secondary social studies teachers "were least well-prepared academically" (Wiley 1977, 143). Many who taught high school social studies had earned no academic credit in geography; in addition, those who taught geography as a separate subject did not always fully meet state or university requirements. More recently, based on state certification requirements published in 1982, it appeared that one state allowed teachers to offer secondary geography with only six credits of study in the discipline (Woellner 1982).

For elementary teachers, Roeder's study on geography requirements was reported for 860 teacher training institutions (Wiley 1977, 132). Results revealed that more than one-third (39.9 percent) of the institutions surveyed required no credits in geography for elementary social studies teachers, and about one-third (32.2 percent) required only three semester hours in the discipline.

In summary, no evidence was found that geography was important enough to be a required secondary school subject, the number of geography offerings was relatively low prior to 1980, geography did not expand at a pace proportional to increases in the total student population, and educational programs for social studies and geography teachers were inadequate in terms of a geography component.

It is possible now that some of these trends are reversing. A growing number of commercially published, middle school and secondary geography texts are emerging, and several recent newspaper articles imply growing public interest in a strengthened and improved geography component in social studies. For example, four secondary schools in the Chicago metropolitan area are expanding their geography offerings.

Meanwhile, it seems reasonable to wonder what went wrong in the case of geography, and to undertake a serious review of past practices. These practices indicate basic confusion about the nature and purpose of geography in the schools. Geography has been widely viewed as a fact-centered, overloaded collection of trivia to be memorized. It has also frequently consisted of content that has reinforced ethnocentric and stereotypic thinking in students. These points represent observations to be treated in the following pages.

CONFUSION ABOUT THE NATURE OF GEOGRAPHY

People like to have a clear definition of things they use and take seriously, and they expect such a definition of geography. Geographers over the years have agreed on the unifying characteristics of the discipline. They have not, however, agreed on a simple definition, nor have they clearly articulated geography's complexities or value to educators, students and the general public. Manson referred to "the failure of geographers to explain their discipline to nongeographers and to school people in particular" in a discussion of the status of geography in U.S. schools.

A detailed discussion of geographers' struggle to define the nature and purpose of the discipline appears elsewhere in this publication, but a few points that bear directly on issues related to geography as a social studies subject should be highlighted here.

While most people probably could tell you that in history, students study changes over time, many could not tell you that in geography, students study similarities and differences in phenomena over space—earth's space. Geographic study might be organized by regions (e.g., the geography of Anglo-America, climatic regions, the Chicago metropolitan area); by time periods (land use in Orange County, 1950–1980); by topics (geography of transportation or soils, urban geography); or by a combination arrangement (geography of United States working women since 1975). In all instances, the organizing perspective will focus on spatial patterns—patterns revealed from arrangements of things that occur in earth's space. Further, like historical data, geographic information is subject to complex thought processes needed to understand and utilize the information effectively. In geography, however, reflection will generally focus on the importance of location and on interrelationships, as well as on similarities and differences in spatial patterns.

In a classic paper, Pattison wrote on the spatial tradition in geography.

> [It] allows one to see a bond of fellowship uniting the elementary school teacher, who attempts the most rudimentary instruction in directions and mapping, with the contemporary research geographer . . . [It can] open the eyes of many teachers to the potentialities of their own instruction. . . . . Looking outside geography, one may anticipate benefits from the readiness of countless persons to associate the name "geography" with maps. Latent within this readiness is a willingness to recognize as geography, too, what maps are about—and that is the geometry of and the movement of what is mapped.

It is worth noting that geographers seem to avoid use of the term spatial when they are speaking or writing about geography for the public, teachers and K–12 students. There are important exceptions, of course, but generally the word is not used as often as it might be. Perhaps wiser thinkers feel the term adds to nongeographers' confusion about the nature of the subject. Yet, the public, teachers and students understand and use terms such as legal, vital, special, regal, frugal, and even historical. Perhaps the term spatial should be added to the list of frequently used descriptors in order to increase understanding of the term and the important characteristics of the perspective.

Communicating the nature of a geographic perspective is one of at least two confusing factors necessary to understand the nature of the discipline. A second problem relates to the question of whether geography is indeed a social science.

GEOGRAPHY IN THE CURRICULUM

Geographers specialize. Over the years, they have divided themselves based on a practical need to focus on smaller parts of the larger field. Accordingly, they developed methodologies, as well as specialized research and teaching interests such as urban geography, physical geography, political geography, or biogeography. The divisions among geographers seem to foster confusion among the public and among educators about whether geography is a physical or social science, both, or neither. Fifty years ago, A. C. Krey, serving as Chair of the Commission on the Social Studies of the American Historical Association, referred to the issue when he wrote, "Whether geography is a physical or a social science is a question for the geographers, perhaps, for each geographer to decide" (Quoted in Bowman 1934).

More recently Dresch commented that the issue was responsible for "bewilderment within the general public trained in [elementary] and secondary education as well as among schoolchildren themselves, their teachers and education authorities who did not quite know what to do with geography in . . . education." It may be worthwhile to look for sources of this confusion.

Physical geography is concerned with spatial interrelationships within and among natural systems, and its scholars use natural science methodology in related research efforts. Thus, physical geography in its purest sense is cast as a natural rather than a social science.

Human geography, on the other hand, focuses on interrelated spatial patterns and processes associated with human beings and social phenomena. Concerns here relate to demography, behaviors and culture traits in human groups, as well as to the landscapes human beings create. Typically, school treatment of this dimension of geography draws on topics such as population, migrations, languages, governments, religions, settlements patterns, technologies and economic activities of human groups. Since human geography deals with the wheres and whys of people and the things they do and create, and related research reflects social scientific methods, this aspect of the discipline is cast as a social science.

A quick glance at content and method in these two strands in geography makes it seem easy, proper and even useful to separate them. This is true when it comes to organizing specialized geographic research or curriculum for geography majors in higher education. It is also useful to highlight whether natural or human factors are the organizers for geography courses in universities. Separation of the two strands, however, is not useful in at least one respect— it does not hold up under scrutiny.

First, in physical geography, it would be irresponsible, if not impossible, to study natural systems without considering the effects of human beings on these systems. This becomes more apparent as pressures on natural systems increase from population growth, resource consumption and waste production. Further, since natural resources are culturally defined, they could not be studied without attention to the social context for the term itself, as well as effects of human consumption on such resources. Thus, while natural systems might be used to provide a central focus and organize content in a physical geography course, such a course, if taught responsibly, would also incorporate social considerations.

Turning to human geography, one could not understand the location and nature of problems in cities or other human settlements without attention to the natural environment. Dependence and effects on the natural environment are also important to the study of economic activities or migrations of human groups. Even the spread and practices attributed to particular religions, languages or political thought can be affected by or affect natural phenomena.

Thus, instruction in human geography incorporates significant attention to factors in nature.

It appears that as long as we must live with persistent and awkward classifications of knowledge, geography must be recognized as both a natural and social science. The overriding purpose in the discipline augments understanding of interrelationships within and among spatial patterns in both the natural and human-made environments.

QUALITY OF GEOGRAPHY IN THE SCHOOLS

Any effort to explore major problems in geography should include evaluations of geographic content and teaching over the years. Before turning to this complicated task though, it will be useful to summarize some past and present characteristics of geography in the schools. A detailed discussion of these characteristics appears elsewhere and provides some of the material highlighted here (Vuicich and Stoltman 1974; James 1971).

Geography as a social study in the 1930s was geared to expanding the knowledge students had about people and places in their own country and others, knowledge about human dependence on the natural environment (called "man-land" relationships then), and knowledge about United States and worldwide economic interdependence. The latter, via commercial geography courses in high schools, focused on study of patterns associated with resources, production, movement and consumption of goods.

Eventually, especially after two world wars, U.S. citizens became more interested in people and places around world, and regional geography courses increased in popularity in secondary schools. The regional emphasis absorbed some of the products and trade information formerly important in commercial geography, but focused largely on description and comparison of the natural and social environment in regions of the world.

In the 1960s, post-Sputnik reforms led the social studies to a more discipline-centered curriculum, and geography's response was the High School Geography Project (HSGP) of the Association of American Geographers. The project was designed specifically to improve geography in the secondary schools, largely through narrowing the gap between the discipline as it was taught in high school classrooms and the frontiers of current research and professional thinking in geography. Instructional strategies in the project were aimed at teaching "selected ways the discipline looks at the world, . . . questions geographers ask about the world, and . . . methods geographers employ. . ." (Patton 1970).

HSGP content and activities centered on topics in geography (as opposed to regions). Students used theories, concepts and methods of inquiry used by professional geographers. Inquiry-learning strategies replaced the description associated with study of world regions, and students were expected to participate actively in the learning process. The HSGP provided strong emphasis on skills to acquire, process and report information, with repeated opportunities for practice. This emphasis paralleled a commitment generally in social studies toward skills development along with other kinds of transferable learning.

49

Weiss reported that by 1977 less than five percent of a sample of high school districts was using the HSGP. In 1980, using newly published secondary geography textbooks as an indicator, Manson reported few alternatives to the world regional approach in high school geography. Thus, over the years, a regional approach has dominated geography in secondary school social studies.

The picture in elementary school geography is less complex. Since the 1930s, geographic learning experiences were incorporated in social studies, and sequenced on an expanding environment principle. Very young students focused on topics and places that were familiar and in close proximity, and expanded to topics more distant in space, time and familiarity. A recent NCSS Task Force report recommended against relying "solely" on this sequencing practice, because even the small child's life space is affected today by global events and interconnections.

There are imperfect means to assess the quality of past and present geography instruction. Scientific evidence on which to base conclusions is scarce, and notions about criteria or indicators of "good" geography differ among groups. There are additional complications because of the confusion among nongeographers regarding definitions of the subject and its place in the social studies. With these problems in mind—and there are more that confound the task of evaluating geography in the school—we can turn to the following observations. These are organized around traditional categories in social studies instruction: knowledge, skills, and affective learning.

Knowledge

In the period 1930–1980, the following geographic themes were employed persistently in social studies programs:

- Knowledge about people and places
- Knowledge about human dependence and effect on the natural environment
- Knowledge about economic interdependence and world trade
- Knowledge about natural and social environments.

The themes were organized spatially—beginning with the home community for young children, later expanding to the state and country, and finally to the world—with information treated globally sometimes, or, more often, in a region-by-region analysis.

The themes and spatial organization seem reasonable enough for geography as a social study. Treatment of these, however, was often inadequate and probably caused considerable damage to the credibility of school geography over the years. The following is a discussion of some of the more serious problems.

- Geographic ideas often taught in the schools were judged as out of date.

The NCSS curriculum guidelines of 1979 called for social studies programs to draw from "currently valid knowledge representative of human experience, culture and beliefs," and declared that ideas from geography "are often badly out of date and culturally biased." This appears to be both a fair and a serious criticism that should be examined closely.

When interest in human geography emerged in the 20th century, with emphasis on human/environmental relationships, there were no established treatments of this strand. Most geographers had been trained primarily in physical geography, and most school teachers and books focused on the physical aspect of the subject. It was not surprising, therefore, that newer treatments of human geography were closely tied to the better known physical geography. Geography for a social education once again studied spatial patterns, but emphasis was on factors in the natural environment as causal explanations for human activities.

This type of explanation, called environmental determinism, suggested that "everything, or nearly everything about [humankind] is traceable to some aspect of the physical environment" (Murphey 1973). Though environmental determinism had short-lived credibility among geographers, the concept had long and wide exposure in U.S. textbooks and teaching philosophies. Even today, one runs into the perspective occasionally.

• Geographic knowledge, as it is often taught in the schools, is a collection of unrelated facts to be memorized.

From time to time, the public cries out about geographic illiteracy. Usually this implies specifically that students and adults do not know locations of currently newsworthy places. One hopes we will not return to memorization of place names as a dominant activity in geography. It is a dull task, and retention is low without a context for learning. One critic of such teaching looked forward to a revival of geography in the schools, but raised the following concern.

> There is a danger that the return of geography to the curriculum will mean a return to the horrible teaching which caused it to be removed or minimized a few years ago. The criticism then was that geography concentrated on the memorization of the name of the capitals, the states, the leading products of the places, the major rivers and their lengths, and similar minutiae, without regard to the more important topic of relationships of people and places. (Kenworthy 1981)

An earlier comment noted, "A preoccupation with factual detail—as opposed to a search for concepts, models, and principles—has traditionally been the lot of the young victims of an outmoded geography" (Bacon 1967, 611).

The HSGP, as discussed earlier, was designed in part to address weaknesses described above. The project is an example of good geography for students at the secondary level. There are complex reasons for its limited acceptance, but among these, one emerges—the lack of teacher preparedness to use a program that departs dramatically from prevailing treatments of geography. Thus, as in cases to be discussed later, priorities related to teacher preparation must be addressed before dramatic, constructive changes will occur in K–12 geography.

The essence of what geographers are doing today bears little resemblance to the geography taught in most schools. While some lag time is expected before school treatment of a subject catches up with contemporary thinking in the discipline, evidence pertaining to geography suggests that this is happening much too slowly. Better teacher preparation can help close the gap. This does not merely mean more geography courses at the university level, but rather specific learning experiences designed for teachers to help them grasp and translate for youngsters the essential geographic concepts, principles, skills and methods of inquiry—experiences to help their students do geography in order to discover the valuable insights that accompany spatial analyses in problem solving.

- Current emphasis on global education requires a revision of traditional regional geography.

Global education is defined by Anderson and Anderson as "education for responsible citizen involvement and effective participation in global society." The NCSS position statement on global education urges teachers to "cultivate in young people a perspective of the world which emphasizes the interconnections among many cultures, species and the planet." Further, the 1984 NCSS position statement on a scope and sequence for the social studies recommends that subject matter at all grade levels reflect a global perspective.

Anderson argued that curriculum aimed toward citizenship education in a global age must shift from a region-centered perspective.

> Curriculum based on a region-centric perspective portrays the world's nations and geographic regions as if they were isolated and self-contained units with no relations with one another. In contrast, curriculum embodying a global perspective treats individual nations and regions as part of a larger whole. (Anderson 1979)

Region as a concept, and regional study as a method have been widely used in geographic research; regions are manageable and coherent units of analysis as geographers attempt to study complex natural and social phenomena on earth. To be sure, both the concept and method have enduring value. World regional geography, however, as it is persistently taught in U.S. schools, often divides the world, and treats natural and social phenomena within each region as if these were discrete units. Such treatment tends to obscure the global nature of natural systems and the global character of human experiences in the world today.

Educators in the United States attest again and again to the importance of students' knowledge of the world's people and places as well as knowledge about the state of the planet and human interdependence. Efforts to achieve these goals, however, may be counterproductive in a business-as-usual, region-centered curriculum in which teachers teach as they have been taught and publishers publish what is traditionally taught.

There are some signs of improvement. Recently, the Committee on Geography and International Studies of the Association of American Geographers highlighted several ways that geographic curriculum can contribute to global education. A secondary school textbook by Backler and Lazarus is an excellent example of ways to promote a global perspective.

Undoubtedly, other examples of curriculum materials exist that align geography with the goals of global education, but breaking the patterns as they exist today will require creative, cooperative and sustained efforts by geographers and social studies educators.

Skills

Skills development is a well-established instructional goal in social studies. An NCSS Yearbook devoted an entire volume to "skills for democratic citizenship, . . . skills to locate, collect, organize, evaluate, and test data; skills to absorb and express information and skills to define and solve problems" (Carpenter 1953). Winston and Anderson wrote about skills as "tools for self-renewal and lifelong learning."

Map skills, of course, have received the most attention in geography, as students learn operations to use maps and globes for work with spatial data, make inferences, formulate and test hypotheses, and exercise other higher order thinking. A recent publication by the National Council for Geographic Education offers many ideas to develop thinking and information-reporting skills in concert with use of skills to obtain spatial information (Winston 1984). The HSGP provides notable attention to skills development. The project fosters students' active participation, and emphasizes students' use of aerial photos and maps, along with diagrams, graphs, tables and other media.

More examples could illustrate the fine attention to skills development in selected geography classrooms over the years. Most often these are provided by teachers who have been trained and understand the intellectual processes involved in human thought as well as child development considerations. Such training is provided in geography courses designed especially for teacher education programs, and there are far too many teachers without this training in our schools.

Affective Learning

Efforts to decrease ethnocentrism and stereotypic thinking are well-recognized social studies objectives. Many teacher education programs and curriculum materials are aimed at promoting cultural pluralism and world-mindedness among our students, and reducing biases related to gender, race and ethnicity.

Geographers, for a long time, have been deeply concerned about these considerations. As mentioned earlier, they quickly dismissed environmental determinism. In the 1960s, popular fascination in geography was focused on "strange lands and exotic people" (Bacon 1961, 610). Bunge discussed racism in geography, by highlighting ways the subject is taught in western societies: "to enhance the ethnocentrism of the white race." These and other writers raised consciousness about how such biased treatments in geography unintentionally reinforce ethnocentric and stereotypic thinking, some more obvious than others. Examples include the following:

- Portraying the author's home country and people therein as most fortunate, most honest, capable, industrious; most advanced; and having other positive attributes; negative characterizations (primitive, barbaric, lazy, stupid), on the other hand, are attributed to people with cultural traits least like those of the people of the author's home country or region;
- Suggesting that discovery of a place does not occur until Westerners arrive, regardless of how long the place was inhabited before their arrival; ignoring

the notion that discovery of people is a mutual experience—one people discovers another;

- Referring to unexplored or newly explored places without attention to the question of whose explorations count and whose do not;
- Using terms on maps and in texts such as the "dark continent" or the "Far East." Many today would ask "dark" or "far" to whom?
- Treating human groups unevenly on maps and texts (e.g., more attention to English settlers in the United States than to African settlers); extensively treating western trade systems with little or no attention to non-western systems;
- Implying that the world centers on North America or Europe by using maps that exclusively reflect this perspective;
- Using maps that exaggerate the size of northern hemisphere continents;
- Selecting the most startling and exotic portrayals of non-western people, perhaps to heighten interest in geography; implying that attributes of one group could be generalized to people on an entire continent. (One teacher devoted so much time and detail to pygmies smeared with elephant dung, who scrambled up to elephants for a kill with blow darts, that there was little time to learn about other groups in Africa. One wonders about students' images of Africa, Africans and geography from this kind of teaching.)
- Discussing in texts and classrooms non-American people and places that implies a we-they world view;
- Using imperfect categorizations on maps and in texts, such as developed and underdeveloped; neglecting analysis of the criteria for these categories; neglecting evaluations of the judgments that such categories imply;
- Implying notions of importance to certain regions of the world by spending more time on them, and skipping one or two regions because of limited time or teacher preferences.

There are other bias-related issues where attention and remediation are just emerging. Efforts to reduce language bias and gender-role stereotypes have progressed somewhat in geography, probably about as fast as in the other social sciences. Other related issues, however, are deeply rooted and complex, and these are more resistant to change.

One of these issues focuses on questions about ways of knowing and the validity of geographic knowledge itself. As Monk and Hanson point out, "Knowledge is a social creation, and its treatment is shaped by the people engaged in acquiring and producing that knowledge." In geography (as well as most other disciplines), knowledge over the past fifty years was acquired and produced largely by white, western males.

Indeed, their particular vantage points influenced selection and definition of research problems and findings, as well as knowledge transmitted to teachers through university programs and textbooks used in our schools. Accordingly, limited perspectives were at the center of geography, and the knowledge that was generated ignored or trivialized some things and inflated others.

Thus, there are gaps in geographic information, and seemingly invisible topics, such as women's experiences in migration, women's location decisions or travel patterns, the effect on women of development in traditional societies, women's central roles in agriculture and trade in many parts of the world, and geographies of black women's work.

First steps are being taken to focus research that will fill the gaps and produce resources for teachers at all levels. An entire issue of the *Journal of Geography* was devoted to women in geographic curriculum. Learning modules focusing on women and spatial change were produced in another excellent set of learning materials (Rengert and Monk 1982). A resource publication on a geography of women was recently produced (Mazey and Lee 1983). Several sessions on women are appearing at professional conferences; university courses and bibliographies, as well as journal articles, are emerging with a focus on women's spatial experiences and perspectives.

It is encouraging to see the nature and quantity of these activities. A great deal of work must be done, however, before U.S. school children will benefit from geography curriculum that incorporates perspectives on women generally, as well as on women and men of color. Perhaps one of the most exciting challenges in geography today arises as one wonders if our mental maps and images of landscapes—people, as well as geographic issues—might be different with the missing perspectives at the center of the geographic discussion.

CONSTRUCTIVE CHANGE

There is no scarcity of issues surrounding teaching and learning of geography in U.S. schools over the last several decades. Many social studies educators and geographers, as well as members of the general public, deplore the status of the subject in the schools, the lack of attention to geography in teacher preparation, and prevailing geographic illiteracy among students and many adults. These involve the larger issues that are possibly connected to causes, such as confusion about the nature and purpose of geography, confusion about the place of geography in social studies, and problems with geographic content and teaching in schools for the last 50 years. The previous pages highlighted some examples of efforts aimed at constructive change, and others can be cited.

In October 1984, the Committee on Geographic Education of the Association of American Geographers and the National Council for Geographic Education published, for the first time, a position statement on guidelines for geographic education in the elementary and secondary schools. The guidelines are aimed at improving and strengthening geography in the schools and in teacher education and providing a scope and sequence for K-12 geography. The position statement reflects several of the problems mentioned here and sets several goals, including the following.

- Influencing standards in geographic curriculum and certification;
- Improving teacher expertise with provision of consultants, course work and workshops;
- Setting up networks of individuals at all levels who can serve as consultants in geography education; identifying geography departments that can develop teacher education programs for preservice and inservice teachers, and identifying elementary and secondary teachers who can organize workshops;

- Increasing visibility of geography;
- Improving materials for the teaching of geography by critically reviewing existing materials, producing new materials and establishing materials exchange programs to access geographic education materials published outside the United States.

The guidelines reflect the importance of a spatial perspective (although the term spatial is not used—perhaps an unfortunate decision). In addition, the unique contributions of geography to public policy decisions are emphasized. Finally, the guidelines identify fundamental themes in geography and suggest how these, with specific knowledge, skills and perspectives, can be used systematically in an organized program of study.

The guidelines are recommendations will be widely circulated, fleshed-out and subject to revision. They are a giant step toward focusing attention on the need to improve geography in the schools, and several implementation steps have been taken to date.

Another dimension of constructive change relates to the fact that, for too long, professional geographers in universities and applied fields took little interest in school geography. Some professional geographers even disparaged their colleagues who actively worked in research or in the production of curriculum materials for school geography and social studies.

Perspectives may be changing on this score as geographers begin to see relationships between the health and credibility of the discipline as a whole, the public images of geography, and the status of the subject in elementary and secondary schools. Perhaps changing perspectives will lead to a growing number of geographers working on curriculum design for elementary and secondary schools, on textbook preparation, on new or improved courses and entire programs for teachers, on teachers' workshops, and on improved certification standards. These efforts, if they are to be useful, must be mounted in cooperation with classroom teachers and other social studies professionals who share an interest in improved geography as a vital part of a student's social education.

REFERENCES

Anderson, Charlotte C., and Lee F. Anderson. "Global Education in Elementary Schools: An Overview." *Social Education* 41(January 1977): 34–37.

Anderson, Lee. *Schooling and Citizenship in a Global Age: An Exploration of the Meaning and Significance of a Global Education.* Bloomington, IN: Mid-America Program for Global Perspectives in Education, 1979.

Anderson, Lee, and Charlotte Anderson, eds. *Windows on Our World.* Boston: Houghton Mifflin, 1980.

Association of American Geographers. *AAG Newsletter* 17(January 1, 1982): 24.

Association of American Geographers. High School Geography Project. *Geography in an Urban Age.* Toronto: Macmillan, 1970.

Backler, Alan, and Stuart Lazarus. *World Geography.* Chicago: Science Research Associates, 1980.

Bacon, Phillip. "Changing Aspects of Geography and the Elementary Curriculum." *Social Education* 31(November 1967): 609–611.

Barrows, Thomas S. *College Students' Knowledge and Beliefs: A Survey of Global Understanding.* New Rochelle, NY: Change Magazine Press, 1981.

Bowman, Isaiah. *Geography in Relation to the Social Sciences.* New York: Charles Scribner's Sons, 1934.

Bunge, William. "Racism in Geography." *The Crisis* 72(October 1965): 494–497, 538.

Carpenter, Helen McCracken, ed. *Skills in Social Studies.* 24th Yearbook of the National Council for the Social Studies. Menasha, WI: George Banta Publishing, 1953.

Committee on Geographic Education, Association of American Geographers/National Council for Geographic Education. *Guidelines for Geographic Education in the Elementary and Secondary Schools.* Washington, DC, and Macomb, IL: AAG/NCGE, 1984.

Committee on Geography and International Studies, Association of American Geographers. *Geography and International Knowledge.* Washington, DC: Association of American Geographers, 1982.

Dresch, Jean. "Reflections on the Teaching of Geography." *Prospects* 9(Fall 1979): 287.

Gross, Richard E. "The Status of Social Studies in the Public Schools of the United States: Facts and Impressions of a National Survey." *Social Education* 41(March 1977): 194–200, 205.

Helgren, David M. "Place Name Ignorance Is National News." *Journal of Geography* 82(July–August 1983): 176–178.

James, Preston E. "The Significance of Geography in American Education." In *The Social Sciences and Geographic Education,* edited by John M. Ball et al. New York: John Wiley and Sons, 1971.

Kenworthy, Leonard S. *Social Studies for the Eighties in Elementary and Middle Schools.* New York: John Wiley and Sons, 1981.

Manson, Gary. "An Analysis of the Status of Geography in American Schools." Paper presented at the annual meeting of the Association of American Geographers, Louisville, KY, April 1980.

Mazey, Mary Ellen, and David R. Lee. *Her Space, Her Place: A Geography of Women.* Washington, DC: Association of American Geographers, 1983.

Monk, Janice, and Susan Hanson. "On Not Excluding Half of the Human in Human Geography." *Professional Geographer* 34(February 1982): 12.

Murphey, Rhodes. *The Scope of Geography.* Chicago: Rand McNally, 1973.

National Assessment of Educational Progress. *The First Social Studies Assessment: An Overview.* Princeton, NJ: Educational Testing Service, 1974.

"National Council for the Social Studies Position Statement on Global Education." *Social Education* 41(January 1977): 36–37.

National Council for the Social Studies Task Force on Curriculum Guidelines. "Revision of the NCSS Social Studies Curriculum Guidelines." *Social Education* 43(April 1979): 268.

National Council for the Social Studies Task Force on Scope and Sequence. "In Search of a Scope and Sequence for Social Studies." *Social Education* 48(April 1984): 252–253.

Pattison, William D. "The Four Traditions of Geography." *Journal of Geography* 63(May 1964): 212.

Patton, Donald J., ed. *From Geographic Discipline to Inquiring Student.* (Final Report on the High School Geography Project.) Washington, DC: Association of American Geographers, 1970.

Rengert, Arlene C., and Janice Monk, eds. *Women and Spatial Change: Learning Resources for Social Sciences Courses.* Dubuque, IA: Kendall/Hunt, 1982.

Vuicich, George, and Joseph Stoltman. *Geography in Elementary and Secondary Education.* Boulder, CO: ERIC Clearinghouse for Social Studies/Social Science Education Consortium, 1974.

Weiss, Iris R. *Report of the 1977 National Survey of Science, Mathematics, and Social Studies Education.* Research Triangle Park, NC: Center for Educational Research and Evaluation, 1978, B-25.

Wiley, Karen B. *The Status of Pre-college Science, Mathematics, and Social Science Education: 1955–1975.* Boulder, CO: Social Science Education Consortium, 1977.

Winston, Barbara J. *Map and Globe Skills: K–8 Teaching Guide.* Macomb, IL: National Council for Geographic Education, 1984.

Winston, Barbara J., and Charlotte C. Anderson. *Skill Development in Elementary Social Sciences: A New Perspective.* Boulder, CO: Social Science Education Consortium, ERIC Clearinghouse for Social Studies/Social Science Education. 1977.

Woellner, Elizabeth H., ed. *Requirements for Certification of Teachers, Counselors, Libarians, Administrators for Secondary Schools, Junior Colleges.* Chicago: University of Chicago Press, 1982.

"Women in Geographic Curricula." *Journal of Geography* 77(September/October 1978).

CHAPTER 5

POLITICAL SCIENCE: PROMISE AND PRACTICE

John G. Gunnell

Political science in the mid–1980s can be personified as understanding itself primarily as a policy science concerned with the various stages of public policy, including agenda–setting, formulation, implementation, and impact. This self–image has formed the identity of the discipline from its inception, and one might well ask how else a social science devoted to the study of politics and government would conceive of itself.

Yet, while political science must, almost by definition, be construed as devoted to the analysis of public policy, there has been, characteristically, a certain tension between its methods and its goals—between its commitment to science and its commitment to social relevance. These have seldom been understood as incompatible, but they have given rise to questions of priority and to a certain dialectic within the field that has informed its development during the past 50 years.

What has been called the behavioral revolution in political science began in the 1950s and evolved into a movement that, by the 1960s, came to constitute mainstream political science. Behavioralism was defined by its devotion to the development of a scientific study of politics that would emulate the methodology of the natural sciences. Although this goal was never jettisoned, there has been, during the past 15 years, a definite shift in emphasis marked by a renewed concern about the relationship of political science to political practice. This "policy turn" is in part attributable to changes in the historical and social context of field, but it is also a consequence of the dynamics of the discipline's internal intellectual structure. Both elements and the relationship between them must be taken into account.

While one might point to waves of European influence on the discipline of political science and, particularly, to the impact of German thought at various points (including its formative years in the latter part of the 18th century, the early 1900s, and the late 1930s), political science, of all the social sciences, has been most distinctly an American invention, or, as Bernard Crick put it, an American science of politics. While we imported many fields of study, we have exported political science. From the beginning, political science has been intricately tied up with an American vision of liberal democracy.

ORIGINS AND EARLY DEVELOPMENT

The origin of political science in the United States could be reasonably located in the idea of a science of politics or constitution–making referred to in the

Federalist Papers. From its earliest appearance in the university curricula, political science was conceived as a practical science concerned with the study and improvement of our nation's institutions and with the political education of citizens and public servants. Francis Lieber at Columbia is usually credited with founding the systematic study of politics in the late 1850s. Following the Civil War and the expansion of our university system, political science developed as a standard part of the university curriculum. Departments appeared throughout the country; and by the late 1800s, through the work of individuals such as John Burgess at Columbia, political science had been established as a general field of study devoted to the historical and comparative study of the state.

Departments of political science continued to proliferate in U.S. universities during succeeding years. The American Political Science Association was created in 1903 for the purpose of "advancing the scientific study of politics in the United States." The drive for autonomy was in many respects more a result of a desire to break off from the field of history and establish a definite professional identity with a practical orientation than a product of a clear sense of the domain of political science. From the beginning, political science with its subfields (such as political theory, American government, comparative government, international relations and constitutional law) was in some ways more a "holding company" for some quite diverse pursuits; but the quest for professionalism created a growing demand for the integration of the field and for the development of its scientific character.

Although there was an increased emphasis in the early 1900s on an eschewal of speculative and metaphysical thought in favor of scientific methods, empirical research, and realistic analyses of facts, the pursuit of science still implied basically practical concerns and social utility. Political science, like many of the social sciences, had originally wished to be "scientific" and professional in order to gain authority for claims about political and social reform. Eventually, the call to science and the concerns of professionalism would come close to overshadowing social purpose; but in the formative years of the discipline the goal of political knowledge was to produce good government and enlightened citizens, to effect political change and overcome corrupt politics, and to ameliorate some of the effects of modern capitalism.

The end of the Progressive era and the advent and aftermath of World War I were not occasions for optimism for political scientists. Neither citizens nor governments, international or domestic, had seemed to indicate much capacity for democratic enlightenment, and the question of the character and role of a science of politics was re-evaluated. The dominating figure in the discipline during the 1920s was Charles Merriam. His influence shaped the future of the profession and, particularly, its idea of science and its relationship to politics.

Merriam had been active in the movement for Progressive reform; but, like many academics of the period, he increasingly believed that the principal path to change would be less through direct practical involvement than through more scholarly effort toward the development of a professional, interdisciplinary, and methodologically rigorous political science that would compare favorably with the achievements of modern natural science and command social authority. Merriam claimed that, historically, political inquiry had evolved through three basic stages: *a priori* and deductive up through 1850; historical and comparative between 1850 and 1900; a tendency toward observation and measurement from 1900 to the present.

The future of political science, in his view, pointed toward a more psychologically and theoretically based study of political behavior. Such a science, located in the university, would continue to educate citizens, but it would also turn away from historical and institutional studies and seek causal scientific explanations. It would also be the vehicle for the full realization of democratic values and institutions by contributing to responsible government and to social control.

Merriam's vision of scientism had a significant impact on the self-image of the discipline and was perpetuated, and accentuated, during the 1930s in Harold Lasswell's arguments about a therapeutic behavioral science. However, changes in disciplinary practice were not pronounced. The use of quantitative methods and other tools of systematic political analysis increased, but legal, historical and institutional modes of study still dominated literature of the field. On the whole, the 1930s was a period of political crisis both internationally and domestically, and these crises occupied the attention of political scientists whose liberal democratic faith was being challenged in both theory and practice and who found no easy answers in science. The resurgence of scientism that would mark the behavioral movement and fundamentally shape contemporary political science in the 1950s did not appear suddenly. The continuities as well as the innovations deserve attention.

Merriam had stressed the need for theoretical advances if the scientific promise of political science was to be realized. Individuals such as George Catlin kept the scientific message alive while at the same time recognizing the need to shore up democratic ideology. By the early 1940s, before the end of World War II, political scientists were already thinking once more about how to advance political science as a more scientific discipline. Individuals such as Benjamin Lippincott criticized the field for equating empiricism with fact collection and called for a more theoretical approach. Others such as William Foote Whyte argued for more attention to the description and analysis of political behavior and less concern with ethical and evaluative issues.

Such emphasis on value-free scientific theory was in part the legacy of the discipline's characteristic commitment to science and its sense that it had not realized its scientific promise, but it was also increasingly part of a response to a challenge to the traditional U.S. faith in the triad of science, liberal democracy and social progress. This challenge entered political science mainly through the work of émigré scholars such as Leo Strauss, Hannah Arendt, Eric Voegelin and Herbert Marcuse, as well as certain U.S. political theorists such as John Hallowell.

For these individuals, the formative political experience was totalitarianism, which they equated with a fundamental crisis in Western thought and politics that signaled a decline. Furthermore, whether their ideological stance was to the left or right, they viewed this crisis as partly a consequence of the intellectual tendencies associated with modern science, positivistic social science, and historicism or value-relativism, as well as certain related weaknesses of liberal democracy. Their basic answer was to seek the source of error and recover truth from the great tradition of political thought, from Plato to the present, that they believed informed modernity.

Although American political scientists during the 1930s and 1940s had found it necessary to search for a more self-conscious defense of democratic ideology in the face of European authoritarianism, the abiding faith was in the historical and symbiotic progress of democracy and science. This was the history of politics and political ideas as told by historians of political theory such as George Sabine. It was a story of progress, despite the aberrations of Nazism and Communism, and not of decline. Value-relativism and the inability of science to underwrite political values was not the dilemma that it was for émigrés such as Arnold Brecht. Liberal values and their historical confirmation had been the assumed framework of U.S. political science.

THE EMERGING BEHAVIORAL REVOLUTION

The impending conflict between "traditional" and "scientific" theory, between mainstream political science and the history of political theory, that would mark the behavioral era in U.S. political science was, thus, at least in part, a conflict growing out of this intellectually exogenous threat to the values of science, liberalism and progress. The behavioral revolution was in a sense a conservative revolution in defense of assumptions and principles that had informed the discipline from its beginnings. However, while the basic goals regarding the science of politics had remained quite consistent and while the tenets of behavioralism were almost identical to the program articulated by Merriam, the practice and accomplishments of the discipline had lagged far behind the vision. This in part accounts for the one area in which there was a distinct shift in position.

While the characteristic idea of political science had been that of a practical science devoted to the reform of politics and government, the behavioral image of science placed priority on the development of a purely descriptive and explanatory, rather than an applied, form of inquiry. This retreat from relevance would be a constant source of the criticism of behavioralism.

Although the behavioral revolution can be interpreted as an instance of the discipline's perennial affirmation of its commitment to science, there were important circumstances that informed its particular restatement of that commitment. The post-World War II era was one of both political quiescence and constraint. Many social scientists, such as Daniel Bell, Seymour Martin Lipset and Robert Lane, subscribed to the "end of ideology" thesis, which suggested that Western democratic society embodied the ultimate values and that what remained was basically only to eliminate certain deficiencies in material prosperity and transform politics into administration. This was not an unusual or untraditional position in U.S. social science with its assumptions about a liberal consensus, except for the fact that the applied tasks were now not understood as great or as pressing as in the Progressive era or in time of Merriam and the New Deal.

Under these conditions, a science of politics might concentrate on perfecting its scientific principles and methods. As Lasswell noted, it was not that application should be neglected but that science and theoretical knowledge should precede practice. The "Cold War" also had its effect. In the age of McCarthy, political scientists were less than willing to talk about political reform, and they were wary about involvement in political affairs. But maybe even more important was the general emphasis on scientific development that characterized the postwar years and the types of funding that were involved. Political science was pressured to legitimize itself as a true or "hard" science, and there was a definite sense that it had not achieved the scientific status of such social sciences as economics.

The behavioral revolution laid the basic foundations of the discipline and profession of political science as it stands today. During the critical period of the rise of the behavioral movement, from the end of World War II to the early 1970s, membership in the American Political Science Association increased five-fold, and the behavioral persuasion became the orthodoxy of an increasingly professionalized field. This did not take place without a struggle, but by the early 1960s leaders of the behavioral approach, such as Robert Dahl, counted the revolution a success.

It is difficult to say exactly what constituted the behavioral revolution, especially since the basic credo, as set forth by individuals such as David Easton, echoed long-standing values and aspirations in the field regarding its status as a science.

It cannot be said that the most basic goals, such as creating a general science of political behavior comparable to physics, were ever achieved—or could have been achieved. But the practice of the discipline did change in many ways, and political science matured as a profession. Quantitative methods such as those involved in survey research and the statistical analysis of data finally began to replace more traditional kinds of research, and one could reasonably speak of being "trained" to be a political scientist in a way that would not have been possible in an earlier period. Comparative politics, or the study of foreign political cultures and institutions, received more emphasis. In many respects, then, one must seek the evidence of the revolution in the transformation of research programs and the accoutrements of increased professionalism. But there is also an important sense in which the behavioral revolution was a theoretical revolution.

First of all, the revolution was initiated in the name of theoretical change. David Easton's famous critique of the field fastened on what he called the "decline of political theory" (Easton 1953). This involved what he claimed was the degeneration of theory into the writing of the history of political ideas rather than the creation of relevant value theory and, most important, empirical theory that would transcend mere fact-gathering and technique and form the core of a truly scientific study of politics based on the methodology of the natural sciences. Although political theory had become identified with the history of political thought, the individuals that Easton singled out for attack, such as Sabine, had not been hostile to the scientific goals of political science.

The split between "scientific" and "traditional" or historical theory was a new development. It was in part a result of the need of behavioralism to find something to revolt against in a field that had always been, at least in principle, committed to the basic goal of a scientific study of politics. It was also in part a consequence of the growing influence of the antiscientific/liberal spirit of the émigré scholarship that was influencing the study of the history of political theory.

In the succeeding years, the controversy about behavioralism was in large measure a controversy in and about political theory. Easton and other behavioralists located the decline of political theory in the work of those who emphasized historical ideas and normative concerns. But the critics of the "new political science" such as Leo Strauss claimed that although there was in fact a decline, it was a function of the positivist approach of the discipline and its rejection of classical political philosophy in favor of a commitment to the idea of a scientific value-free political science that was blind to the crisis of our time. By the early 1970s, traditional political theory and mainstream political science would largely go their separate ways.

The behavioral agenda included these characteristics: an interdisciplinary focus that would take advantage of what was understood to be the methodological advances in other fields such as sociology; increased use of statistics and other quantitative techniques for gathering and organizing data; the separation of propositions involving "is" and "ought"; and the priority of pure science. Although behavioralism was changing the practice of political research in many ways, its basic identity was found in its image of theory as the search for explanatory and predictive generalizations about the uniformities and regularities of political behavior.

In part, this search for universal theory was a response to the "universalization" of political science in the postwar years and the increasing task of making sense of the vast amount of data that were being generated both at home and abroad. Political science was becoming more than a science of United States politics in terms of both its subject matter and employment. The 1960s was the age of the "conceptual framework" in political science, and the work of David Easton, Karl Deutsch and Gabriel Almond was oriented toward constructing models and schema of analysis, often around the concept of the "political system," for the conduct of political inquiry.

These quite abstract analytical constructs, which were offered as prototypes of a general theory of politics and political behavior, were complemented by attempts to build theory more inductively from generalizations derived from empirical research. But it was widely agreed that the basic goal of political science was a general theory ultimately based on, and verifiable in terms of, experientially grounded facts.

COUNTERREVOLUTION

Despite the continuity between behavioralism and certain basic and early goals of political science, the movement occasioned considerable opposition on its path to hegemony within the discipline. Some of this criticism eventually contributed, by the early 1970s, to significant changes. For example, both political scientists whose basic concern was political philosophy or the more humanistic study of politics and those whose emphasis was on practical affairs were alientated by the behavioral "mood."

The subfield of political theory remained split between those who remained committed to the traditional study of the history of political theory and those committed to the scientific study of politics modeled after the natural sciences. Although it would be fair to say that by the mid-1960s behavioralism governed political science, the revolution had by no means gained universal support.

Critics of behavioralism tended also to be critics of liberalism and pluralism. Many of them argued that this liberal bias of behavioral political science was reflected in its research models, the selection of data, and its less than reflective attitude toward the processes and institutions of U.S. politics. Despite its claim to scientific objectivity, behavioralism, it was charged, constituted an apology for the status quo and neglected political issues and problems of democracy in the United States and in other countries. What had begun as a science dedicated to political reform and economic change had, many claimed, withdrawn, in the name of scientific objectivity, from an engagement of relevant social issues. At the time, society was faced with problems such as Vietnam, civil rights tensions, the possibility of nuclear war, student unrest on college campuses, and poverty and urban decay. But such topics were, by the late 1960s, scarcely noted in the literature of political science, which emphasized voting studies and other aspects of normal politics.

This professional dissatisfaction was manifest in the creation, in 1967, of the Caucus for a New Political Science, which represented a variety of complaints about the political science establishment. One complainant spoke for a generation of critics of behavioralism, and particularly for political theorists, when he charged that the "vocation of political theory," represented in both the classics of the history of political thought and in the transmission of political wisdom through the study of that literature, had been undermined by the "methodism" that dominated political science (Wolin 1969). This narrow image of empirical inquiry embraced by the discipline, it was said, destroyed scientific creativity and contributed to political complacency in the face of modern political crises. By the end of the 1960s, then, behavioralism was the dominant persuasion in political science, but it was also being subjected to pointed criticism. And this criticism involved more than the problem of the relationship between political science and politics.

The vision of science adopted by behavioralism was based on mediated images of scientific explanation ultimately derived from the literature of logical positivism. Despite the emphasis on emulating natural science, there was little indication that behavioralists had any very direct acquaintance with the actual practice of these fields. By the mid-1960s, the work of philosophers such as Thomas Kuhn had severely called into question the picture of natural science that had for so long dominated the literature of philosophy. This critique began to spill over into the social sciences, which had long attached themselves to these ideas.

Claims about scientific explanation, theory and method that had characterized behavioralism could no longer be taken as an adequate account of scientific practice.

In addition, a significant body of literature had by this time developed in the philosophy of social science, around the work of individuals such as Peter Winch and Alfred Schutz, which challenged many of the behavioralist claims about the nature of social phenomena and the character of social scientific inquiry. Behavioralism was now being criticized internally in terms of its very notion of science and scientific method, rather than in terms of the limitations inherent in its commitment to scientific as opposed to other ways of studying politics. This critique was fully developed during the 1970s, but by that point mainstream political science was actively involved in changing its self-image.

David Easton, who continued to be a principal spokesman for the behavioral movement, had, as late as 1968, defended behavioralism in terms of its success in separating fact and value and moving political science away from prescriptive, problem-oriented studies. But in his presidential address to the American Political Science Association in the following year, he called for "a new revolution in political science." This "postbehavioral revolution" was, he claimed, the product of a deep dissatisfaction with the lack of politically and socially relevant research in the discipline, and the goal was to give more attention to the public responsibilities of the field and to pressing public problems and issues. Advances in behavioral science were to be applied to substantive studies that were responsive to the problems of the time, and attention was to be given to the implementation of solutions. This was to take precedence, at least in the immediate future, over the further development of techniques of scientific inquiry (Easton 1969).

This statement set, or represented, a new mood in the discipline, and it could well be construed as the official birth of the contemporary policy turn in political science and the self-image that has characterized mainstream political science during the past 15 years. There is little indication that the basic assumptions about the nature and demands of scientific methods have been fundamentally transformed, but the idea of political science as first and foremost a "pure" science has clearly been re-evaluated.

POSTBEHAVIORALISM

It is difficult to generalize about what has commonly been understood as the postbehavioral era in political science, from the early 1970s to the present. The new revolution, if it can reasonably be understood as such, was, in part, much like the behavioral revolution, a response to both internal demands and external pressures. The promulgation of the idea of political science as primarily a policy science served, among other things, to defuse internal criticism by highlighting social relevance and de-emphasizing scientism. Externally, a significant shift occurred in scholarly funding that pushed research toward domestic political issues and problem-solving approaches as well as a considerable inducement to attempt to approach the consultative status that economics had enjoyed. One question that might be asked is whether postbehavioralism has signaled a return to the original commitment of political science to political relevance through science.

This is in part difficult to answer, because, like many of the social sciences today, political science is in a state of dispersion. Despite the perennial quest for unity and identity during the past decade or more, any such solidarity of practice and concerns has not been forthcoming. For all its difficulties, behavioralism was a significant attempt to achieve disciplinary unity in terms of a scientific creed; but in that respect, it must ultimately be counted a failure. That unity was to have been based on the achievement of a core of scientific theory, but such a core does not exist. With few exceptions, there is no attempt to devise a core of scientific theory—particularly on a disciplinary-wide basis. The search, during the 1960s, for a general theory of the political system has largely been abandoned.

Although the public policy image is pervasive and textbooks have been reformulated to reflect this definition and emphasis, the issue of what the general relationship between political science and politics is, and should be, has not been a topic of focused attention among current mainstream political scientists. The literature of political science research clearly reflects the policy emphasis, but, just as clearly, there is no particular substantive policy goal or set of goals that informs research in the discipline.

Some political scientists identify policy analysis with political science as a whole, while others see it as a particular approach or type of approach in the discipline. Whatever its scope, there is a variety of perspectives regarding what kind of research is involved. These include acquiring knowledge about policy processes; making recommendations for the improvement of such processes; studying issues of general social concern and importance; providing information for policy makers; problem solving or providing consultative support to decision makers; formulating and rationalizing social and political goals; and prescribing means for the achievement of policy goals. But despite all this, the aspirations of contemporary political scientists are, in general, far removed from those that characterized the Progressive era and the activities of individuals such as Merriam.

To some extent public policy studies have amounted to little more than new bottles for old wine, but there has been a return in many quarters to an emphasis on the state and institutions of governance as instruments of policy and on the outputs of government and their impact on society. Such fields as political economy have enjoyed a renaissance. But it is difficult to find a great deal of intellectual and ideological coherence in the diverse world of public policy analysis and even more difficult to isolate areas of pointed controversy.

The postbehavioral era can be characterized and evaluated in a number of ways. For some, it indicates the failure of the behavioral program, while for others it signifies its success and its extension. Even some of the leaders of the behavioral movement today view its past goals regarding a science of politics as unrealistic, but few would deny that the discipline and its research programs were fundamentally transformed during the behavioral era. Postbehavioralism is probably too broad a concept to suggest an identity for the field. Nearly everyone would identify it in terms of a greater concern with political relevance.

While some view it as the rejection in some measure of the scientism of behavioralism, others view it as the adaption of science to policy-research. Although the behavioral movement generated a great deal of controversy, the debate did provide a central issue which is now lacking; and to some degree, that lack can be attributed to, or is at least symbolized by, the exodus of political theory.

By the early 1970s, behavioralism declared victory in terms of its attempt to make political science scientific. It also sought to mollify or disarm critics by its commitment to public policy and renewed concern with normative issues. Many of the political theorists who had opposed the behavioral notion of theory and emphasized historical and ethical concerns had, by this point, largely written off mainstream political science. They either, like the followers of Leo Strauss, turned inward to pursue their own concerns or identified themselves more closely with the emerging interdisciplinary (history, philosophy, sociology, economics, political science) field of political theory. For example, the work of individuals such as John Rawls and Jurgen Habermas began to have a great impact on the field by the early 1970s. With the exception of some individuals, such as William Riker, who continued to defend behavioralism, discussions about the nature of theory largely disappeared from the literature of political science by the late 1970s.

SCHOLARSHIP AND ADVOCACY: THE UNRESOLVED DILEMMA

There is little doubt that political science in the 1980s remains uneasy about its identity, its unity and its accomplishments. Much of the underlying uneasiness about the state of the discipline involves the question of whether it has, even in terms of its recent commitment to public policy, fulfilled its promise as a science devoted to democratic change or whether the drive toward scientism and professionalism has rendered it impotent, if not irrelevant. Charles Lindblom, in a recent presidential address, argued that the discipline had adopted a complacent view of politics and government and would do well to pay attention to a more radical model and the views of the dissenting academy.

Two recent comprehensive studies of the evolution of political science have suggested that the discipline has not lived up to its promise and that rather than seeking democratic reform it has tended to revise democratic theory to make it conform to U.S. politics. David Ricci has claimed that the tragedy of U.S. political science is that its search for scientific professionalism has ended in a debasement of its commitment to democratic politics. And Raymond Seidelman has traced what he claims is the failure of a tradition within political science that attempted to blend successfully scholarship and political advocacy.

Such complaints have been consistently voiced about the behavioral movement and postbehavioral era by political theorists, but they, too, have not been able completely to bridge the worlds of political theory and political action. Part of the problem is that although the social sciences in the U.S. grew out of an impetus toward social and political reform, the academization of these fields, in the context of the relationship between politics and the university in the

United States, made it impossible for them to reconcile, in any very easy way, the demands of science and democracy. It may not always be possible to make the goals of social action compatible with requirements of social scientific scholarship. The relationship between academic and public discourse and the proper and possible social function of social science scholarship and teaching is a matter fraught with paradox and ambiguity.

It may in part be the depth of political science's original commitment to democratic reform and the teaching of democratic citizenship that makes its inadequacies appear unduly stark. After all, one hardly expects sociology to perfect society, anthropology to save humanity, or economics to ensure prosperity. For political science to charge itself with the role of saving democracy may be more than can be expected from an academic discipline caught in the bureaucratic structures of differentiated modern society. Political science may warrant criticism and suffer a continual crisis of identity from its failure to live up to its promise, but an authentic commitment to social change may require social scientists to step outside the world of scholarship. It may not always be possible to effect the former in the course of pursuing the latter.

REFERENCES

Catlin, George. *The Story of the Political Philosophers.* New York, McGraw-Hill, 1939.

Crick, Bernard. *The American Science of Politics: Its Origins and Conditions.* Berkeley: University of California Press, 1959.

Dahl, Robert A. *Who Governs? Democracy and Power in an American City.* New Haven: Yale University Press, 1961.

Deutsch, Karl, et al. *Nerves of Government.* New York: The Free Press, 1963.

Easton, David. *The Political System: An Inquiry into the State of Political Science.* New York: Knopf, 1953.

Easton, David. "The New Revolution in Political Science." *American Political Science Review* 63(December 1969): 1051–1061.

Eulau, Heinz. "Skill Revolution and the Consultative Commonwealth." *American Political Science Review* 67(March 1973): 169–191.

Gunnell, John G. *Between Philosophy and Politics: The Alienation of Political Theory.* Amherst, MA: University of Massachusetts Press, 1985.

Habermas, Jurgen. *Knowledge and Human Interests.* Boston: Beacon Press, 1971.

Hallowell, John. *Main Currents in Modern Political Thought.* New York: Holt, Rinehart & Winston, 1950.

Kuhn, Thomas. *The Structure of Scientific Revolutions.* Chicago: University of Chicago Press, 1962.

Lane, Robert E. "The Politics of Consensus in an Age of Affluence." *American Political Science Review* 59(December 1965): 874–895.

Lindblom, Charles. "Another State of Mind." *American Political Science Review* 76(March 1982).

Lippincott, Benjamin. "The Bias of American Political Science." *Journal of Politics* 2(May 1940): 125–139.

Lipset, Seymour Martin. *Political Man: The Social Bases of Politics.* Garden City, NY: Doubleday, 1960.

Rawls, John. *A Theory of Justice.* Cambridge, MA: Harvard University Press, 1971.

Ricci, David. *The Tragedy of Political Science: Politics, Scholarship, and Democracy.* New Haven: Yale University Press, 1984.

Sabine, George. *A History of Political Theory.* New York: Holt, Rinehart and Winston, 1937.

Schutz, Alfred. *The Phenomenology of the Social World.* Evanston, IL: Northwestern University Press, 1967.

Seidelman, Raymond, and Edward J. Harpham. *Disenchanted Realists: Political Science and the American Crisis, 1884–1984.* Albany, NY: State University of New York Press, 1985.

Strauss, Leo. *What Is Political Philosophy?* Glencoe, IL: The Free Press, 1959.

Truman, David B. "Disillusion and Regeneration." *American Political Science Review* 59(December 1965): 865–873.

Voegelin, Eric. *The New Science of Politics.* Chicago: University of Chicago Press, 1952.

Whyte, William Foote. "A Challenge to Political Scientists." *American Political Science Review* 37(August 1943): 692–697.

Winch, Peter. *The Idea of a Social Science.* London: Routledge and Kegan Paul, 1958.

CHAPTER 6

CIVICS AND GOVERNMENT IN CITIZENSHIP EDUCATION

James P. Shaver and Richard S. Knight

The most persistent issue in the teaching of civics and government, as well as in the teaching of social studies generally, is exemplified by the organization of this book. That is, chapters by prominent social scientists about the issues in their respective content areas are followed by chapters by social studies educators focused on issues in regard to teaching the social science content areas. This division symbolizes well the perennial dilemma over the role of the social sciences in social studies education.

Regarding government and civics specifically, the issue can be posed in terms of whether the curriculum for elementary and secondary school students is to reflect essentially the scholarly interests of those in the field of political science and government or whether there is some broader, more encompassing civic purpose for K–12 social studies education that should provide an orientation for the teaching of government and civics (see Quillen 1966). From the latter perspective, a social studies course with a government label might look quite different from courses in government taught in a department of political science or government, and it might go rather far beyond those courses in attempting to specifically prepare students to reflect on and participate in the civic life of the society.

Of course, this broad issue as to whether courses in a social studies curriculum should reflect the interests and conceptualizations of social scientists or be based on a broader conception of citizenship education is a complex one. It would be a major oversimplification to say that social scientists are not interested in citizenship, or to imply that courses organized around the content of a social science "discipline," such as political science or government, have no contribution to make to citizenship education. Similarly, it would be erroneous to suggest that those who propose that social studies should be citizenship-based are not interested in the social sciences or believe that social science concepts have no contribution to make to citizenship education. The matter is much more complicated than that, as we shall attempt to make clear by raising several subissues in this chapter.

HISTORICAL CONTEXT

The report of the Committee on Social Studies of the NEA's Commission on the Reorganization of Secondary Education in 1916 has been very influential in social studies education. Not only has the consistency in the overall structure of the social studies curriculum since that report been remarked on frequently (e.g., Jarolimek 1981; Morrissett 1981), but the academic discipline-citizenship dilemma was implicit in it. Government and civics courses were very much a part of the proposed structure, with civics to be taught at the ninth grade and government at the 12th grade. Yet, while using those labels, the Committee urged that citizenship should be the aim of "social studies," which should be organized around the study of important societal problems of interest to students, rather than structured as formal courses in the social sciences (Butts 1980).

Tension between the citizenship-societal problems orientation and the formal-study-of-government orientation has continued to this day. It is, in its broadest sense, represented by two competing definitions of social studies: One, attributed to Edgar Wesley (usually with the incorrect connotation that he was opposed to problems or issues-oriented social studies—Wronski 1982), defines the social studies as the social sciences simplified and adapted for pedagogical purposes; the other defines social studies as that part of the elementary-secondary school curriculum for which citizenship education is the primary goal and for which content is drawn from the social sciences, including political science, along with other fields, as is deemed appropriate.

An ironic manifestation of this tension has been a curricular structure in which the problems of democracy or American problems course has been a separate entity from civics and government courses, suggesting rather clearly that social studies educators have not grappled directly nor very satisfactorily with integrating the study of societal problems into the total social studies curriculum. In that regard, the social studies curriculum is fragmented. Although there is considerable variability from classroom to classroom, students in courses with social science titles—such as government—tend to study the formal content of the discipline, while the study of problems tends to be reserved for courses with that term in their title. This pattern not only contributes to a disjointed curriculum, but, many would argue, to a fragmented conceptual structure for students, so that the relevance of social science concepts to decision making about societal problems is often not evident.

The general demise of the civics and the problems of democracy course noted by Gross (1977) suggests that the study of problems is becoming even less of a factor in the social studies curriculum. One might be tempted to think that these courses are disappearing because the study of societal problems is becoming an integral part of social studies courses with social science labels, but this does not appear to be the case. The content of the textbooks that dominate social studies instruction continues to be largely social science-based.

Civics textbooks over the years have usually been a rather amorphous mixture of material on the structure of government and a soft-handed, rather abstract, touching upon of societal problems, with the formal structure of governmental decision making the predominant topic. The textbooks for government courses have been even more strongly oriented toward the formal structure of government, although occasionally they have been focused on decision making—usually as a rather difficult-to-trace overall theme, represented primarily by brief exercises at the ends of the chapters.

An explicit, straightforward, and unembarrassed approach to values could be found in many textbooks of 50 years ago. For example, during the 1930s, Lippincott published citizenship readers at various levels. One, entitled *Makers of America* (Sewell 1930), was an anthology of articles about famous men and women. In a manner somewhat akin to that of the McGuffey readers of the 1800s, traditional values like honesty, thrift, ambition, freedom, virtue, and patriotism were advocated directly. Such an approach is likely to seem quaint, even slightly embarrassing, to the sophisticated civics and government teacher of the 1980s, at least as their views are exemplified by the textbooks they are likely to be using.

A typical current text, for example, *American Civics* (Hartley and Vincent 1983), has well-done and eye-catching print, graphics and pictures, with a very subtle approach to values designed to offend no one. The sense of realism is greater, with less mythical quality. Textbooks like *Makers of America* are difficult, if not impossible, to find among modern-day curriculum materials. Although such texts were clearly aimed at commitment to and preservation of a valued way of life, they were not imbued with the reconstructionist philosophy of the 1930s, from which the schools were viewed as major agents of social change.

The national trauma of the Great Depression brought considerable support from progressive educators for the Committee on Social Studies' proposal that the focus of social studies be on citizenship education and, in particular, on the study of social problems. The emphasis, Butts (1980) has pointed out, was on economic social reconstruction, with fairly clear ideas about what the reconstructed society should be like (Shermis and Barth 1985). With their fundamentally anticapitalist views, the progressives and social reconstructionists came to be viewed by power interests as radicals. In reaction to their proposals, there was movement back again to the more traditional emphasis on the structure of government and on patriotic values.

The New Social Studies movement of the late 1950s and the 1960s again heightened the delineation between social studies as social science based and social studies as citizenship based. The influence on the New Social Studies movement of Jerome Bruner's structure of the discipline cognitive psychology is well known. In terms of civics and government curricula, perhaps the most interesting observation about the New Social Studies movement is the comparative lack of involvement by political scientists. The involvement of anthropologists, economists, sociologists and historians is clearly evident in project titles (see *Social Education,* April 1965; April 1970; November 1972). Although political science was included in efforts to develop interdisciplinary social science curricula, the work of only one center, at Indiana University, was clearly political science based.

Ironically, of the first major New Social Studies projects, only one, the Harvard Project, was clearly citizenship focused. That project emphasized government because of a central concern with preparing students to participate in the political decision-making processes of the society, but teaching political science concepts was not a first-order priority. That project, and others that have grown from it, posed again the major issue in regard to the relative roles of government as an academic field and citizenship-based considerations in the teaching of civics and government. In addition, the Harvard Project approach makes evident specific subissues having to do with what should be taught about government, what role the process of decision making itself should play in civics and government courses, and how values should be handled.

WHAT TO LEARN ABOUT GOVERNMENT?

A perennial question has been whether the emphasis in government and civics courses should be on local, state, federal, or, recently, international government. A more fundamental question, however, is whether studying the formal structure of government is sufficient or whether students should learn about the inner workings of political decision making, a topic sometimes reflected in the work of political scientists themselves. Is it enough for students to learn about the three branches of government and the myth of separation of powers; or should they be made aware of the extent to which both the executive branch and the judicial branch have become involved in lawmaking, aware of the tremendous centralization of power in the office of the presidency, and perhaps even concerned about the dependence of Congress on the president for legislative leadership?

Is it enough that students understand the steps in the passage of a bill; or should they understand factors such as the dealing and tradeoffs, the power wielded by committee chairs, the role of lobbyists and the influence of political contributions on legislators' votes? Or, at a more fundamental level, should students understand that the legislative process only scratches at the surface of decision making in our society? Should they come away from their civics and government courses with a clear conception of how minority groups have shaped the law of our society through both protests and the judicial system, of how pressure groups are organized at the local, state and even national levels to influence policy, and, even more fundamentally, of how political contributions and other favors influence legislative and executive decisions?

Such issues, of course, raise questions about the context within which the study of government and civics should take place. In that sense, the materials available to students are of the first order of importance. That is, do their textbooks provide a realistic sense of the ways in which policy decisions are influenced and made? Can textbooks give that sense and still be acceptable to the conservative elements that influence textbook selection and, therefore, textbook writing? Is it possible to publish materials that would help students become adept at the social criticism, which some individuals, such as Harold Berlak and Shirley Engle, have argued should be a major aim of social studies education?

A more fundamental contextual question is whether learning about the processes of governmental decision making can take place in the isolated environment of the classroom. Should—as Gillespie and Mehlinger proposed—the school itself as a political institution be subject to study by students as a basis for understanding political decision making? Further, ought students, as part of their supervised learning experiences, be involved in their community as a basis for learning not only how community decision making proceeds but how they can be involved in those processes?

Proposals for involving students in community participation as a basis for education for citizen action raise issues particularly pertinent to the teaching of civics and government. For one thing, at least implicitly they focus attention on what is meant by "citizen action." Traditionally, the good citizen has been defined as one who votes. That is a very limited conception of participation or action. Moreover, abstaining from voting when none of the choices is acceptable can be a rational form of political expression. So, paradoxically, nonaction might be the desirable state of action when only voting is included in citizen participation.

Most social studies educators would, however, agree that voting behavior is not sufficient for a definition of citizen action in a democracy. Therefore, an important question is what types of social action should be treated in civics and government courses, if action, rather than only an understanding of formal government, is to be dealt with at all. Should students learn how to affect government decisions through the pressures of large political contributions or massive protest movements? In an already highly litigious society, should they be helped to learn how to use the court system more adroitly in advancing political causes?

Such queries raise fundamental questions. Should social studies educators involve students in the consideration of political action versus nonaction as a serious civic issue? If so, what types of prospective action should be included? The 1960s illustrated vividly the importance of the latter question. Political action ranged from quiet discussion and voting (or nonvoting) to protests through peaceful demonstrations, to violent demonstrations and riots, to underground revolutionary activities. Each raises different issues if justification is to be based rationally on the values of a democratic society.

The question about the types of citizen action to which students should be exposed raises an interesting pedagogical issue. That is, to what extent is the type of realistic social action in which students can be involved limited by the structure of the school? Can students be meaningfully involved in national or even state movements? Must they inevitably—except for letter writing and passive participation in national organizations—be limited to local community participation? It is ironic that, as Newmann (1981) has pointed out, the major focus in social studies is on societal decision making, while the most reasonable entrée for involvement of students in social action is at the local community level. How can we deal, in civics and government courses that include social action, with this paradox?

Of course, one might note that the paradox validly reflects reality. For reasons of personal investment and geographic-economic limitations, most people, if they participate at all beyond voting, do so passively at the state and national levels (e.g., through political contributions) and/or through local action. Direct participation in state and national decision making is infrequent.

As society has become more abstract due to the growth of centers of population and world awareness, with the effects exacerbated by immediate reporting of worldwide details through media technology and by the threat of international destruction, it may also be well to ask whether, despite the importance of commitments to basic societal values, the manifestation of those values locally will not provide the sense of shared community that is an essential centripetal force for any society.

From that perspective, participation in local government and in local voluntary organizations—as Hartley and Vincent noted, George Washington, Benjamin Franklin and Paul Revere were all volunteer firemen—may be more essential than participation at the larger societal level, although concern with the latter is essential to a democratic nation. Involvement at the wider societal levels also is more inherently divisive because the presentation and discussion of issues often heighten differences, in contrast to the effects of working together on local projects with people who are not likely to be associated only with some special interest or issue.

Students engaged in local participation may gain not only a greater sense of efficacy and self-determination, but increased identity with and knowledge of how to participate in a comprehensible community. The result could be a greater sense of realistic existence within a complicated technical-industrial nation and volatile world. How to strike an appropriate balance between local community participation and the study of societal and global issues is a major unresolved issue in political education. So is the issue of the extent to which efforts to involve students in local participation should extend to voluntary organizations such as charities, church groups, boy scout and girl scout groups, and neighborhood organizations.

DECISION MAKING IN CIVICS AND GOVERNMENT

Another underlying issue has to do with whether the making of decisions about policy issues should itself be an explicit part of civics and government instruction. It is one thing to study the social and political structure and processes through which decisions are made, but quite another to consider conceptual frameworks through which such decisions might be formulated and justified.

The Harvard Project (Oliver and Shaver 1966) was the only early New Social Studies project that had as its central focus helping students to become more conscious of and adept at societal political-ethical decision making. In other words, it was assumed that students should not only understand the social-political processes through which policy is made, but be aware of the relevant concepts and thinking skills for coming to warranted conclusions in regard to various questions, including what issues are important, what are the best resolutions for those issues, and whether one should become involved in the political process in order to attempt to affect the outcomes as different interest groups compete to influence policy.

If one admits that decision making is a legitimate part of courses in government and civics, what model of decision making should provide the basis for instruction? For example, there has been until recent years a tendency in social studies to accept a Deweyean pragmatic model of decision making. Thinking is assumed to proceed from "perplexity, confusion, or doubt," to the definition of a problem, to the formulation of an hypothesis in regard to a plausible solution, to the gathering and analysis of factual evidence in the context of the problem to be solved, and, finally, to testing of the hypothesis in action (Dewey 1933).

The pragmatic emphasis is on the formulation of hypotheses and the gathering of relevant data. It is not entirely foreign to another frequently taken approach to decision making in social studies education—a focus on the empirical orientation of the social scientist. Students are urged to formulate the types of problems in which political scientists are interested, to develop hypotheses, and to gather data relevant to those hypotheses.

A much different model is suggested by an approach that focuses on public issues as basically involving questions of political-ethical import. Here the emphasis is on the formulation of problems, which, when defined, involve much more than the gathering of data. The model calls for the consideration of conflicting values, the examination of one's own frame of reference, and the careful analysis of language as it might affect one's decision, as well as the collection and analysis of empirical evidence related to the decision.

In social studies, the Deweyean pragmatic approach has been largely superseded by the social science approach to inquiry; the political-ethical approach has made few significant inroads into the textbooks that provide the basic source of instruction in civics and government, although some include sections on values and value judgments (e.g., Mehlinger and Patrick 1974; Gillespie and Lazarus 1979). Which of these models should be the focus of instruction in civics and government, when decision making is admitted as a legitimate concern, is a major unresolved issue.

An even more perplexing issue, raised by recent work in psychology, is whether any of the decision-making models used in civics and government instruction, as well as in social studies generally, is realistic in terms of the complexity of the elements in the decisions to be made and the contexts which ought to be taken into account in making them. Some researchers have found that decision making by school-age teenagers does not reflect comprehension of basic concepts of law and government, and teenagers seem unable to form coherent political philosophies (Adelson 1972; Gallatin 1980). It has been suggested that what appear to be shortcomings in political decision making may be a function of the difficulty of comprehending and keeping in mind the various bits of information, points of view, and intellectual moves that are relevant in the discussion of complex public issues (Keating 1980). The demands may be overwhelming for the human brain.

The limited capacity of human intellect has been addressed by Simon in his "bounded rationality" model of thinking. He maintains that classical models of rationality assume an imaginary, oversimplified world in which it is possible to make "perfectly justified" decisions that take into account all relevant factors; but societal decision making is actually incredibly complex, and in reality we must simplify in the face of that complexity and muddle through to imperfect, but workable, decisions.

In short, it may be not only that the scientific view of decision making, with its neglect of ethics and values, is too restricted a model of citizen decision making, but that models of decision making which attempt to take into account the great contextual as well as conceptual intricacy of decision making may not be practicable. They may not be applicable by people faced with a multitude of decisions on various levels of their lives, and with inadequate time and resources to address most of them. How a civics or government teacher interested in decision making might approach such instruction from a "bounded rationality" point of view is a question of a different order from the one that has usually been addressed by those interested in citizenship decision making.

VALUES IN CIVICS AND GOVERNMENT

Consideration of citizen decision making as a matter of ethical reasoning raises the question of the role of values in the teaching of civics and government; for ethical decisions are rooted, implicitly if not explicitly, in our moral standards or principles—that is, in our moral values. What to do about values has been a perennial, although often subdued, issue over the years. As Butts (1978) has pointed out, the movement from private to public schooling in the early years of our nation was based in part on the belief that the survival of the society depended upon the promotion of fundamental values upon which the republic was founded. Civics instruction has persistently been concerned with the promotion of values; an enduring question has been what kinds of values ought to be involved. Efforts to inculcate the basic values of the republic to which Butts alluded have often been replaced by more superficial concern with "patriotism"—especially during the two World Wars—with patriotism defined as affection for and commitment to the American society and government as presently constituted.

The emphasis on democratic values, or on patriotism, has not been as obvious in government as in civics courses. The study of comparative government was even rather extensively advocated—although probably rarely carried out in the schools—by specialists in government during the late 1960s, but has since ebbed in popularity. So while one issue in the teaching of civics and governments is how much emphasis there should be on comparative government to acquaint students with alternative solutions to the conundrum of how to govern societies, the more basic issue is what role should values play in the study of government? And, if values are to play a role, which values?

The issue in regard to values is a particularly difficult one, in part because a basic value of our democratic society is freedom of thought. The difficulty is also a reflection of the domination of the social studies by the social sciences, which are primarily concerned with empirical, factual decision making. In the social science model, the emphasis is on the testing of hypotheses, and decisions are not to be influenced by values other than fundamental scientific commitments to truth, honesty, independence, freedom of expression, originality, and respect for ideas (Bronowski 1977). Indeed, there is a naïveté among some social studies educators, stemming at least in part from a misapprehension of the role of values in science, that social studies should be value-free so that instruction will not fetter the students' minds with value commitments (e.g., Shermis and Barth 1985).

At the rather superficial level that "patriotism" is often defined, it is difficult to deny the legitimacy of that concern. But at a more basic level, it may well be dysfunctional. It was, for example, a basic premise of the Harvard Social Studies Project, and of projects that have stemmed from it, that basic societal-constitutional values play a major role in societal cohesion as well as in decision making, and that civic education ought to take place within a context of commitment to those basic values, especially to the ultimate value of human worth and dignity.

From that point of view, building emotive commitment to the basic values of the society is an essential element of civic education. However, the democratic commitment to freedom of thought, to intelligence and dissension, means that specific definitions of the basic values or interpretations of the values in social policies must be matters of open debate. Also explicit in this approach to values is a recognition of conflict between the basic values, such as the continuing tension between freedom and order, which must be taken into account as part of a conceptual framework for decision making about societal issues. In short, then, from this position, developing emotive commitment to basic societal values should be a major concern of the social studies curriculum, but neither specific cognitive meanings and interpretations nor particular resolutions of value conflicts should be inculcated (although "outrageous" solutions, such as racism or genocide, should be opposed). Instead, value meanings and their applications to policy should be contemplated and discussed as an integral part of the curriculum.

An underlying issue here, too, is whether personal, life-style values should be dealt with in courses in which citizen decision making is a concern. Personal values have an impact on societal problems. Values in regard to sexual relations, for example, underlie problem areas such as teenage pregnancy, single-parent families, and the current epidemic of venereal diseases. How to deal with such values as relevant to societal decision making without infringing on personal-familial rights raises questions even more difficult than deciding when students' solutions are so atrocious as to be unacceptable.

A major issue, then, has to do with what role values should play in civics and government courses. Which values should be emphasized? Is value inculcation legitimate? How might the inculcation of values be related to cognitive civic education goals, such as helping students to be more aware, more insightful, and more capable of making sound decisions about the issues that confront the society? Can decisions by individuals about political–ethical issues be sound if such persons are not firmly committed to basic democratic principles and aware of how consciously to base positions on them?

The social science intellectual–empirical orientation toward decision making not only downplays the role of values but, in particular, the importance of commitment to values as a part of civic education. From that perspective, there is also a tendency to ignore other important aspects of decision making. Already alluded to has been the importance of examining one's own frame of reference (and, one might add, the rigidity of our frames of reference) as an important step in making decisions about public issues. Another area of equal importance, and equally ignored, has been the role of empathy—the ability to put oneself in the position of another—as a critical aspect of decision making in a democratic society. Whether the development of empathy as a basis for decision making should be an objective in civics and government courses has rarely been discussed by social studies educators. The failure to raise and grapple with the affective elements of citizen decision making is likely a result of the tendency to resolve the basic issue in the teaching of civics and governments mentioned at the beginning of this chapter, whether by intention or by default, in the direction of instruction that is social science based rather than citizenship oriented.

"HIDDEN CURRICULUM" AS AN ISSUE

Earlier, we questioned whether civics and government instruction can be done adequately within the confines of typical classrooms, without providing students with experiences in the community. Another dimension of the question has to do with the extent to which unplanned, unintended experiences (often referred to as the "hidden curriculum") affect, and even counteract, the teachings that occur in civics and government classrooms. The question here is: What do students learn about such matters as civic participation, the meaningfulness of basic democratic commitments, and respect for themselves as individuals and as intelligent decision makers, not only through what goes on in the classroom but also within the total context of the school?

If the frequent claims that the aims of civic education are subverted by the nondemocratic structure of classrooms and schools are accepted as valid, then there are more fundamental issues than whether the student should study the school as a social-political institution. They include whether teachers of civics and government, as well as teachers in general, have an obligation to structure their own teaching according to basic democratic values and attempt to affect the social-political structure of the school as a context for civic education that is broader, and perhaps more influential, than the individual classroom (Shaver and Strong 1982).

The role of civics and government, or social studies, teachers as schooling activists—and even the special obligation of such teachers to be activists in light of the central citizenship education concern in social studies—has not been widely considered by social studies educators. Yet, it is a latent major issue hinted at by those, such as Giroux (Giroux and Penna 1979), who write from a radical critique perspective.

Consideration of the school as an environment for civic education is often averted by asserting that schools cannot be defined and structured democratically. Such claims are frequently based on the rather simplistic view, reflected even in Kohlberg's "Just Community" schools, that to be democratic, institutions must operate on the principle of majority rule. This position leads some to conclude that schools cannot be "democratic," because majority rule encompassing students would not only expose the educational process to immature decision making, but would involve processes so complex and time consuming as to interfere with education. The limited applications of the Just Community concept to schools have not allayed these fears.

One must ask, however, whether majority rule must be a predominant characteristic of a "democratic" school. After all, even in the broader society, majority rule is not the paramount definitional criterion for a democracy. Otherwise, we would have no need for a judicial system to protect individual and minority rights.

Clearly, the society is constantly faced with consternation over how to balance its commitment to majority rule (in decision making generally the wishes of the many should have more weight than the wishes of a few), based on the fundamental value of human worth and dignity, against the need to preserve individual and minority rights, the other aspect of human worth and dignity. Just as denials of individuals and minorities by the majority must be carefully justified, so must denials of majority rule; but it can be argued reasonably that the educational rights of individual students and the needs of the society warrant greater restrictions on majority rule in schools than in the broader society.

Democratic values can permeate schooling through other avenues. As the Supreme Court has pointed out, failures to adhere reasonably to basic societal values—e.g., disrespect for the religious freedom of students (*West Va. State Board of Education vs. Barnette* 1943), disregard for due process in important decisions about students (*Goss vs. Lopez* 1975), and the denial of freedom of speech on important public issues (*Tinker vs. Des Moines* 1969)—are a major way in which school personnel fail to make schools "democratic" institutions and "teach youth to discount important principles of our government as mere platitudes" (*Barnette* 1943). Schools can be made more valid democratic institutions without going so far as to accept the potentially debilitating effects of full-scale student majority rule.

Cautioning against the overzealous application of majority rule does not, however, argue against increased involvement of students in more meaningful decision making. Such involvement would also be a proper step in the self-conscious application of societal ethical principles to the life of the school, which Dewey (1909) advocated as essential to fulfillment of the obligation to educate for membership in a democratic society. Unfortunately, the issue in regard to the role of civics and government teachers in affecting the school as an environment for civic education, and questions about the characteristics that classrooms and schools should take on in order that the "hidden curriculum" will be more conducive to appropriate civic education in a democratic society, are not only largely unresolved, but all too rarely recognized and debated in social studies circles (a recent exception is Hepburn 1983).

SOCIAL PROBLEMS IN GOVERNMENT AND CIVICS

As mentioned earlier, the report of the Committee on Social Studies in 1916 called for a focus on social problems, rather than for the study of formal social sciences, as the basis for the curriculum in order that students could be involved in issues that they viewed as vital, be prepared for effective participation in the various groups to which they belonged and would belong as citizens, and be able to gain the skills needed to be good citizens, rather than the more limited intellectual skills of evidence-gathering, criticism, and synthesis, which the social sciences emphasize. Although others over the years have advocated that the social studies curriculum in general, as well as courses in civics and government in particular, be focused on the analysis of social problems that are real to students—not problems as defined by social scientists (Barth and Shermis 1979)—the organization of the textbooks that underlie such courses is still largely shaped by other concerns.

How curricula can be developed and organized when they are to be based on problems of interest to students, or how problems that are identified by adults to be of vital interest to the society can be made meaningful and emotionally compelling for students, remain largely unresolved questions. In fact, the consideration of such questions is effectively circumvented by a curriculum structure based on textbooks that are not social problem-oriented and that provide little assistance in helping students to either generate problems or appreciate the vital issues facing the society. Because the texts tend to be based on a social science perspective, when problems are identified they tend to be of the empirical social science, rather than the ethical-citizenship, variety.

Certainly, a major challenge to those who teach civics and government courses, as well as those in the social studies generally, comes from research indicating that students do not find social studies interesting, do not see its relevance to their adult lives (Farman, Natriello and Dornbusch 1978), and do not behave as if differences in social studies programs had a discernible impact on their adult civic participation (Shaver in press). Can it be that such results, in a curriculum area that should have vital significance for the students' current and adult life, are largely due to our failure to find the means for making the teaching of civics and government, and social studies in general, not only problem focused, but focused on those problems in ways that make evident their significance to the society and to the students' individual lives? If so, that is a major indictment of a curricular area for which citizenship education is to be the highest priority.

CONCLUSION

The above question considered in relationship to the neglect of social problems in social studies is not independent of other issues discussed in this chapter. Each discussion implies reasons for students' lack of interest, inability to perceive relevance, and lack of differential citizenship behavior. Clearly, the extent to which civics and government instruction, as well as social studies instruction in general, can be meaningful citizenship education will depend in large part on how curriculum developers, textbook publishers, and teachers resolve a number of interrelated issues: Should citizenship education or the social sciences be the central focus of instruction? Should understanding the realities of government and influencing policy be emphasized? Ought civic education be preparation for active citizenship, and to what extent does such an orientation necessarily entail participation in the school and the community? Should there be an emphasis on decision making that goes beyond the empirical focus of the social sciences and calls for the involvement of students in the essential political-ethical dilemmas of a democratic society? Should decision-making models take into account the limits of human rationality? How should values be treated in civic education?

These issues have pervaded not only the teaching of civics and government but the social studies curriculum generally for the past 50 years. Consideration of them ebbs and flows, but the dominant feature of civics and government instruction, as of social studies education generally, is its stability—a stability that reflects a conservative commitment to the purveying of social science knowledge and the implicit and seemingly thoughtless inculcation of often superficial values, typically without explicit consideration of the implications for the view of civic participation which is promoted.

REFERENCES

Adelson, Joseph. "The Political Imagination of the Young Adolescent." In *Twelve to Sixteen: Early Adolescence,* edited by Jerome Kagan and Robert Coles. New York: Norton, 1972.

Barth, James L., and Samuel S. Shermis. "Defining Social Problems." *Theory and Research in Social Education* 7 (Spring 1979): 1–19.

Bronowski, Jacob. *A Sense of the Future.* Cambridge, MA: Institute of Technology, 1977.

Butts, R. Freeman. *Public Education in the United States.* New York: Holt, Rinehart & Winston, 1978.

Butts, R. Freeman. *The Revival of Civic Learning.* Bloomington, IN: Phi Delta Kappa Educational Foundation, 1980.

Dewey, John. *Moral Principles in Education.* Carbondale: Southern Illinois University Press, 1909.

Dewey, John. *How We Think.* Boston: D. C. Heath, 1933.

Farman, Grey, Gary Natriello and Sanford M. Dornbusch. "Social Studies and Motivation: High School Students' Perceptions of the Articulation of Social Studies to Work, Family, and Community." *Theory and Research in Social Education* 6 (September 1978): 27–39.

Gallatin, Judith. "Political Thinking in Adolescence." In *Handbook of Adolescent Psychology,* edited by Joseph Adelson. New York: Wiley, 1980, 382–384.

Gillespie, Judith A., and Howard D. Mehlinger. "Teach About Politics in the Real World—the School." *Social Education* 36 (October 1972): 598–604.

Gillespie, Judith A., and Stuart Lazarus. *American Government: Comparing Political Experiences.* Englewood Cliffs, NJ; Prentice-Hall, 1979.

Giroux, Henry A., and Anthony N. Penna. "Social Education in the Classroom: The Dynamics of the Hidden Curriculum." *Theory and Research in Social Education* 7 (Spring 1979): 21–42.

Gross, Richard E. "The Status of the Social Studies in the Public Schools of the United States: Facts and Impressions of a National Survey." *Social Education* 41 (March 1977): 194–200, 205.

Hartley, William H., and William S. Vincent. *American Civics.* New York: Harcourt Brace Jovanovich, 1983.

Hepburn, Mary A., ed. *Democratic Education in Schools and Classrooms.* Washington, DC: National Council for the Social Studies, 1983.

Jarolimek, John. "The Social Studies: An Overview." In *The Social Studies,* edited by Howard D. Mehlinger and O. L. Davis, Jr. Chicago: University of Chicago Press, 1981.

Keating, Daniel P. "Thinking Processes in Adolescence." In *Handbook of Adolescent Psychology,* edited by Joseph Adelson. New York: John Wiley, 1980.

Mehlinger, Howard D., and John J. Patrick. *American Political Behavior.* Lexington, MA: Ginn and Company, 1974.

Morrissett, Irving. "The Needs of the Future and the Constraints of the Past." In *The Social Studies,* edited by Howard D. Mehlinger and O. L. Davis, Jr., Chicago: University of Chicago Press.

Newmann, Fred M. "Political Participation: An Analytic Review and Proposal." In *Political Education in Flux,* edited by Derek Heater and Judith A. Gillespie. Beverly Hills, CA: Sage Publications.

Oliver, Donald W., and James P. Shaver. *Teaching Public Issues in the High School.* Boston: Houghton Mifflin, 1966. Reissued, Utah State University Press, 1974.

Quillen, I. James. "Government-oriented Courses in the Secondary School Curriculum." In *Political Science in the Social Studies,* edited by Donald H. Riddle and Robert S. Cleary. Washington, DC: National Council for the Social Studies, 1966.

Shaver, James P. "Implications from Research: What Should Be Taught in Social Studies?" In *The Educator's Handbook: Research Into Practice,* edited by Virginia Koehler. New York: Longman, in press.

Shaver, James P., and William Strong. *Facing Value Decisions: Rationale-building for Teachers.* 2nd ed. New York: Teachers College Press, 1982.

Sewell, James W. *Makers of America.* Chicago: Lippincott, 1930.

Shermis, S. Samuel, and James L. Barth. "Indoctrination and the Study of Social Problems: A re-examination of the 1930s debate in *The Social Frontier.*" *Social Education* 49 (March 1985): 190–193.

Simon, Herbert A. *Reason in Human Affairs.* Stanford, CA: Stanford University Press, 1983.

Wronski, Stanley P. "Edgar Bruce Wesley (1891–1980): His Contributions to the Past, Present and Future of the Social Studies." *Journal of Thought* 17 (Fall 1982): 55–67.

CHAPTER 7

IN SEARCH OF ECONOMIC IDEALS AND POLICIES

David D. VanHoose and William E. Becker, Jr.

Once known as the "dismal science," economics is the study of how individuals and society choose to make use of available resources for the production of final goods and services and of the manner in which these goods and services are allocated among individuals and groups in society. Although serious discourse on this subject dates back to Plato and Aristotle, the foundation for the modern study of economics was laid in 1776 by Adam Smith. Smith's great catalyst for economic growth was man's disposition to "truck, barter and exchange."

In the Smithian idea of capitalism, the forces of private consumer demand and producer supply interact via the "invisible hand" of the marketplace to produce wealth. Market prices allocate goods and services according to their costs of production and according to the preferences and wealth of consumers. Through increased wealth individuals are liberated and fulfilled.

Up to the 1860s, Smith's formulation was the major basis for discussion of economic issues. However, in 1867 Karl Marx described and analyzed what he considered to be the historically inevitable transition from a private property, market-oriented economy to one of full state ownership and allocation of resources, goods and services. Marx ignored Smith's other books in which Smith addressed the many sides of human motivation and admonished Smithian capitalism for causing people to lose their liberty in the pursuit of wealth. The Marxian system of socialism represents the antithesis to Smithian capitalism.

As this chapter will outline, the basic split between Smithian and Marxian ideas has persisted into the 20th century. The study of economics continues to be highlighted by debate over the importance of private property rights versus the need for government intervention.

SEARCH FOR ECONOMIC GROWTH: 1935–1940

Most Western European countries utilized a market system as the world entered the late 1920s, and the dominant Western European economists, such as A. C. Pigou at Cambridge (England), analyzed the functioning of the economy from the "classical" perspective of Smith. The 1917 revolution in

Russia and the formation of the Soviet Union as a socialist state were viewed as an experiment destined to fail. Economists argued that the growth of industrial capacity via private investment in capital goods, such as machines and factories, was the driving force behind economic growth. Given the significant expansion of industrial capabilities in the United States prior to and during the 1920s, leading United States economists, such as Irving Fisher at Yale University, predicted continued growth in labor employment and in living standards for market-oriented economies.

The prolonged economic contraction of the 1930s dealt a severe blow to these theories and predictions and dashed the hopes and dreams of a generation. The Great Depression of the 1930s also served as a watershed in the study of economics. Indeed, most developments in economic thought since the time of Smith and Marx have arisen from the disappointments and confusion of this period.

Relative to the five immediately preceding years, 1935 represented a year of recovery for the United States and for other nations as well. In fact, the period 1933–1937 witnessed a significant expansion of United States industrial production and a rekindling of confidence on the heels of the severe financial and industrial collapse of 1930–1933. Nevertheless, production and employment levels remained at abnormally low levels, and the prospects for a complete world economic rejuvenation appeared bleak. Classical economists were stymied.

In light of the failure of classical economists to foretell the economic collapse of the 1930s, the socialist viewpoint gained new adherents. The Depression seemed to be a proof positive of the breakdown of a market-oriented system. Oskar Lange of Poland and Abba Lerner of the United States were among the first to examine the practical issues involved in instituting socialist systems in fully industrialized nations. Although Lange, Lerner and other contemporaries uncovered numerous inherent pitfalls in socialist economics, they perceived a need for centralized planning and allocation to offset the large fluctuations in economic growth that can arise in private market systems.

A less radical departure from the status quo was recommended by the English economist John Maynard Keynes. Keynes' work became the most prominent of the attempts to provide a new approach to understanding the economic process. Keynes did not perceive a complete failure of the capitalist market system; however, he disagreed with the classical argument that technological change and growth in the supply of productive factors (land, labor and capital) are the key elements influencing the rate of economic growth. Instead, Keynes argued that the actual mainstay of growth and stability is the total level of demand for final goods and services. According to the basic Keynesian theory, excessive saving and the resulting underconsumption of final goods and services lay behind the severe downturn of the 1930s.

The sharp downturn in economic activity in 1937 and 1938 seemed to provide support for Keynes' contention that volatile levels of desired spending by individuals and businesses produced instability in aggregate production and employment. The renewed economic slump also appeared to reinforce Keynes' assertion that government action was necessary to alleviate the depressed conditions. He argued that the proper role of a national government is to make up for private underconsumption by undertaking its own spending on final goods and services and by reducing taxes to stimulate increased private spending.

Keynes' call for an enlarged governmental role was heralded by a growing body of young economists who looked upon classical economic theories and institutions as proven failures. In Western Europe and the United States, a consensus emerged that what was needed was a "mixed economy," which retained private ownership of resources and a role for price allocation via market forces overseen by a central government that would stand ready to intervene when necessary. Indeed, the governments in the democratic, industrialized nations began to intervene in the functioning of private markets on a large scale. For instance, the United States witnessed the passage of the Banking Acts of 1933 and 1935, which effectively made the federal government the supreme supervisor of all financial commerce, and the National Labor Relations Act of 1935, which gave the government authority to sanction union formation and to oversee wage-setting agreements in private labor markets. At an aggregate level, government spending began to increase, although at a small rate by more recent standards.

It will never be known whether, if left to their own peacetime devices, the governments of the democratic nations of this period would have voluntarily adopted the full recommendations of Keynes. The outbreak of war in Europe in 1939, followed by the worldwide military buildup and further escalation of war in 1941, produced an unprecedented rise in government demand for goods and services. This increase in spending played a key role in bringing an end to the Depression that the peaceful interplay of economic forces could not seem to overcome.

FORMULATION OF ECONOMIC GOALS: 1946–1950

At the conclusion of World War II, the search for economic growth began anew. For the victorious Allies, the primary concern was that the postwar period should not be allowed to degenerate into depression. The potential for a repetition of the 1930s clearly was present. In the Allied nations, much industrial capacity had been oriented toward production of military goods and services, and the sustaining component of aggregate demand during the war had been government spending. Economists held real fears that discharged servicemen and servicewomen would return to their home nations to find few prospects for employment in economies that were quickly winding down from their wartime production levels. Their apprehensions were magnified by the fact that the industrial economies of both the Axis nations and the battleground nations of central and eastern Europe had suffered major setbacks in their productive capacities as a result of their incredible human casualties and the wholesale destruction of business plants and equipment. Furthermore, political tensions were not fully extinguished by the Allied victory, so that the outlook for international trade appeared bleak.

By and large, most democratic nations chose at this point to adopt the type of policies that Keynes had advocated prior to the advent of war. The United

States took the lead in this regard when its Congress passed the Employment Act of 1946. This legislation formally established a role for the federal government as a key agent in the economy by directing the Office of the President to forecast annually the anticipated course of the domestic economy over near and intermediate time periods. To assist the President in this responsibility, a Council of Economic Advisers was established. In consultation with this Council, the President was charged with the responsibility of recommending government policies that would foster economic growth and stability. Much of Western Europe followed a similar course. The Soviet Union returned to its socialist economic plans, and several eastern European Soviet satellite nations followed that example.

As a result of its postwar economic and political dominance, the United States took the lead in the attempt to rebuild the industrial capabilities of Western Europe and Japan. Whereas the United States' domestic policies tended to be oriented toward governmental maintenance of spending levels, the Marshall Plan enacted in the years immediately following the war concentrated on the rebuilding of plants and equipment so as to expand the supply of goods and services. Furthermore, the Marshall Plan provided a basis for a renewal of trade between nations.

The period following the end of World War II marked a major turning point for economics as a social science. The passage of the Employment Act gave legitimacy to economics as an area of inquiry with real societal significance. Economists found themselves endowed with a legislated charge to make accurate predictions about the future course of economic activity and to propose solutions to the problems faced by modern economies.

SYNTHESIS OF ECONOMIC THEORY: 1951–1960

Simultaneous with the social recognition of economics as an applied science was a perceived need among economists to "operationalize" economic theories to yield hypotheses that could be tested scientifically. A natural response was that economists began to adopt the methods of mathematicians. In addition, the availability of the electronic computers in the 1950s made the estimation and testing of complex statistical structures possible.

Although mathematical and statistical methods had been used by some economists in the 19th century, many economists in the mainstream of the economics profession did not use sophisticated mathematical tools in their work prior to World War II. During and after the war, a virtual revolution swept through the economics profession as practitioners in the field became aware of the promises of mathematical and statistical modeling of real-world phenomena.

Indicative of the development of mathematical economics were books by John von Neumann and Oskar Morgenstern in 1944, and by Paul Samuelson in 1947. In each of these books, economic issues are analyzed via mathematical models of the behavior of individual units (e.g., households and business firms). These efforts began the task of formalizing theories of economic systems into mathematical variables and equations. Work on mathematical models by numerous economists continued throughout the 1950s, and a reflection of these efforts was Gerard Debreu's book, which effectively reduced the entire classical theory of markets of Adam Smith into a single mathematical formulation. The work by von Neumann and Morgenstern, Samuelson, Debreu and others helped form the basis for modern microeconomics, which is the sophisticated study of the interactions of consumers and firms in private markets. A major goal of much work in this area was the systematic investigation of the behavioral effects of government policy actions in a market system.

In addition, renewed attention was given to the Keynesian theory of aggregate growth and stability. Building on a mathematical interpretation of Keynes' ideas that was provided by John Hicks, macroeconomists interested in the functioning of the entire economy as a whole began to develop refined models of aggregate production and employment. Furthermore, they began to collect and utilize actual data on aggregate spending for use in projecting future economic growth. Early pioneers in these efforts were Wesley Mitchell and Simon Kuznets, whose exhaustive labors in collecting statistical data enabled economists to begin to make short-run predictions of the future pattern of overall economic activity.

The widespread adoption of mathematical and statistical methods truly represented a synthesis across the field of economics. Wassily Leontief, a promoter of socialist central planning, spearheaded "input-output analysis," which was designed to enable governments to predict accurately final outputs based on flows of resources utilized in production. Leontief's work has been used widely by socialist nations up to the present. However, Leontief's general approach of basing predictions on mathematical models paralleled work done by economists in market-oriented, mixed economies. By the end of the 1950s, economists around the world were virtually united in a common belief that economics had advanced to a level of sophistication that justified a claim that the field had become a social science in the most complete sense of that term.

EMERGENCE OF ECONOMIC ADVISERS: 1961–1969

By the beginning of the decade of the 1960s, mathematical and statistical economic models had advanced to the point at which economists felt comfortable that their predictions were highly dependable. The election of Kennedy to the presidency in 1960 gave United States economists a chance to prove this to the world. Kennedy had himself received some economic training, and he assembled a group of economists led by Walter Heller to staff the Council of Economic Advisers. This group made policy recommendations for governmental tax and spending policies that were based upon Keynes' basic theory of aggregate demand as the mainstay of growth and stability. Using their models of the economy, they felt able to make rather precise recommendations about the consequence of policy actions and the appropriate timing of such actions to ensure economic stability and expansion.

If one examines the performance of the economy during this period, it appears that these attempts to "fine-tune" the economy were successful. The variability of output and employment levels fell by a significant amount during this period, in which policies were designed to take advantage of a so-called

Phillips curve relationship. The Phillips curve shows an inverse empirical relationship between the rate of price inflation and the rate of labor unemployment (Figure 1). Named for A.W.H. Phillips, a British economist who discovered an inverse relation between money wage rates and unemployment rates in the United Kingdom between 1861 and 1957, the Phillips curve approach to policy held that high unemployment rates could be decreased, at the cost of only a little inflation, by Keynesian-type government-induced increases in aggregate demand.

Because these policies appeared so successful, the public stature of economics increased dramatically during the 1960s. Financial and nonfinancial businesses began to retain economists as full-time staff members or as consultants. Economists' advice was sought not only with respect to future performance of the economy as a whole but also as a guide to day-to-day decision making concerning financial affairs, tactics for competing with rival firms, and strategies for long-term corporate objectives. Government agencies hired economists to do studies and make policy recommendations on issues of social welfare, business antitrust enforcement, labor policy, agriculture, education, and national defense budgeting.

During the mid–1960s, economists were regarded with a new respect as true professionals, and they regained and surpassed the ground lost on the debacle of the Great Depression. In 1969, the first Nobel Prize in economics was awarded jointly to Ragnar Frisch of Norway and Jan Tinbergen of the Netherlands for their contributions to mathematical and statistical advances in the field.

In closing this discussion on the golden years of economics, it is worth noting that while economists were held in esteem in the 1960s, signs of discontent surfaced among a few British, Australian and U.S. economists regarding the assumptions on which much of mathematical economic theory was formulated. For example, the so-called "Cambridge Controversy" pitted Paul Samuelson and Robert Solow of Cambridge, Massachusetts, against Joan Robinson and Luigi Pasinetti of Cambridge, England. This controversy centered on the very definitions of capital, savings, and profit and their role in economic growth. In addition, the work of Herbert Simon during the 1950s and 1960s questioned the assumption underlying most economic models that individuals are completely rational in their decision making. He argued that uncertainty and human nature produce "bounded rationality" that constrains the abilities of individuals to make economic choices.

STRUCTURAL CHANGE AND DISILLUSIONMENT: 1970–1979

The high level of confidence held by the public about the role of economists was shattered during the 1970s. Beginning with the first two years of that decade, price inflation became a key problem. Since the late 1960s, economists had warned that funding the United States' war activities in Vietnam and maintaining our military involvement in Europe while also expanding social redistribution programs (such as Social Security and Aid to Families with

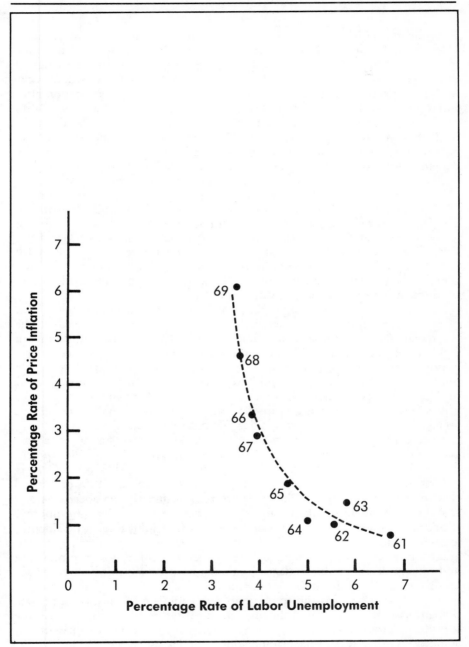

SOURCE: *Economic Report of the President,* 1985

FIGURE 1
Inflation and Unemployment Rates in the United States, 1961–1969

Dependent Children) were overstimulating the level of aggregate demand. Unfortunately, these warnings went unheeded. Throughout the democratic industrialized world, aggregate spending began to exceed the capacities of economies to produce goods and services. The resulting bottlenecks and backlogs in production placed upward pressure on prices. As higher inflation price expectations were formed, interest rates began their climb upward.

The wage-price controls of the first Nixon administration were advocated by few economists, and were criticized vehemently by many for attacking inflation's symptoms but not its cause—namely, the rise in total aggregate demand. When the controls were lifted in 1973, inflation resurged but this time with an unpredicted side effect—unemployment rates also rose.

In the 1967–73 period inflation was driven by aggregate demand. Starting in 1973 major supply shocks began to drive inflation. For example, dramatic oil price increases resulted first from the politically motivated Arab oil embargo in 1973 and later from the cartel pricing of the Organization of Petroleum Exporting Countries. Because oil is a key resource for producing energy for industrial production, the significant rises in oil prices caused immediate reductions in the industrial capacities of major nations. The resulting explosion in production costs added to the inflation problem.

The simultaneous stagnation in the production of output and rise in the level of prices, often referred to as stagflation, presented a problem for which the Keynesian demand approach could not offer a satisfactory solution. As shown in Figure 2, the simple Phillips curve trade-off between inflation and unemployment broke down in the 1970s and could no longer be relied upon as a guide for policy actions. As the Phillips curve relationship disintegrated, a rift in the economics profession emerged and widened as long-time, but ignored, critics of Keynesian-type aggregate-demand policies, such as Milton Friedman, attacked economic policy as misguided and mismanaged.

By the late 1970s, it had become clear that the consensus on aggregate economic policies had disappeared. Four types of responses to this development emerged.

First, the adherents to the activist Keynesian policies of the 1960s contended that the breakdown of the Phillips curve relationship was an aberration and that the government should not abandon its attempts to stabilize the economy.

Second, economists with a socialist bent, such as John Kenneth Galbraith, argued for an abandonment of "fine-tuning" policies in favor of permanent wage and price controls and government-business cooperation in production and pricing decisions. In England, economists with a socialist bent called for complete protection from foreign competition.

A third response was the recognition that complete reliance on aggregate demand policies had ignored the importance of technological change and the growth of productive capacity as crucial elements of economic growth and stability. A new group, called supply-siders and identified with Arthur Laffer, emerged. They argued for policies that would enhance business production, such as income tax cuts to spur work effort and tax incentives for capital investment that would enhance productivity (Canto, Joines and Laffer 1983).

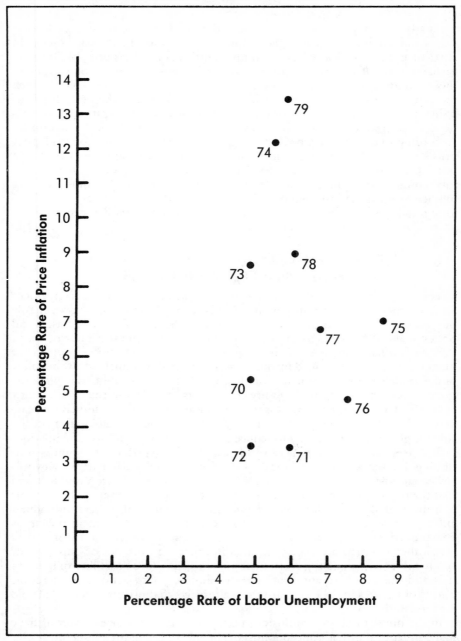

SOURCE: *Economic Report of the President, 1985*

FIGURE 2
Inflation and Unemployment Rates in the United States, 1970–1979

Finally, a group of economists under the intellectual leadership of Robert Lucas and Thomas Sargent began to question the basis of Keynesian theory in particular and statistically based economic predictions in general. Building on earlier efforts of Milton Friedman and other long-time critics of Keynesian theory, they argued that there is a natural rate of unemployment below which the actual rate of unemployment may not be lowered by the best efforts of policy makers. Initial theorists of this persuasion were called rational expectationists. More recently they have been dubbed the new classical economists. According to their theory, policies designed to stimulate production via higher prices will simply convince workers that the resulting inflation will erode the purchasing power of their incomes. Hence, no increase in employment will be forthcoming from the inflationary policies. Lucas argued that most existing mathematical and statistical models do not capture these types of private behavioral responses to government policy actions, so that such models provide poor predictions of policies' ultimate effects.

ECONOMIC THEORY AND POLICY IN TRANSITION: 1980–1985

The last five years have represented a period of continuing disagreement among economists and noneconomists alike concerning both the proper role of government in the economy and the position of economists as advisers and policy makers. With respect to the role of government, Lester Thurow (e.g., 1980, 1983) has echoed Galbraith's call for government-business cooperative planning and has been joined by others in advocating a national industrial policy under which the government would direct resources to industries with the greatest potential for growth. Many economists have denounced such a policy as one that would involve excessive government interference in private markets. Indeed, many supply-side economists have continued to advocate a smaller role for government as a way to reduce the burdens of taxation and regulation.

The debate between Keynesian and new classical schools of thought is continuing, but the distance between the two groups has tended to narrow. Keynesian economists generally have conceded that their models are imperfect and that the role of private anticipations of the effects of government policy actions is important. Nevertheless, they argue that the ability of private individuals and businesses to take actions that offset the effects of government policies is constrained by labor and business contracts. On the other hand, some new classical economists are beginning to admit that the existence of imperfect or costly information about government policies can reduce the ability of individuals and businesses to anticipate fully economic policy actions. As a result, effects of policies may be similar in some respects to those predicted by the old Keynesian theory.

In the midst of all this confusion, policy makers and ordinary citizens have lost a great deal of faith in economists. The most glaring manifestation of this fall in economists' reputations has been controversy about whether or not the Employment Act should be rescinded or at least amended to eliminate the Council of Economic Advisers. However, businesses and governments continue to employ microeconomists to study markets for specific goods or services, and macroeconomists remain in demand simply because even imperfect predictions are necessary if businesses or governments are to plan for the future.

Finally, while individual economists will continue to debate the pros and cons of a Smithian versus a Marxian type of social order, some agreement on several issues seems to exist at this time. In particular, a recent stratified survey of 2,072 economists in the United States, Austria, France, Germany and Switzerland (Frey, Pommerehne, Schneider and Gilbert 1984) suggests that there is a consensus among economists that the price system is an effective and desirable social choice mechanism and interventions by governments in its function generally are to be avoided. Wage-price controls, tariffs and import quotas, rent ceilings and employment guarantees are viewed by the consensus of economists responding to the survey as harming the economy. Furthermore, economists share common ground in their quest to achieve the broad goals of growth in living standards, high labor employment and low price inflation.

Even if the majority of economists respect the importance of the market system, a strong minority continues to advocate government interventionism and protectionism. Thus, it may be anticipated that division will continue to occur concerning specific policies to achieve the general goals of full employment, price stability, growth, and the liberation and fulfillment of humankind.

REFERENCES

Canto, Victor A., Douglas H. Joines and Arthur B. Laffer. *Foundations of Supply-Side Economics: Theory and Evidence*. New York: Academic Press, 1983.

Debreu, Gerard. *Theory of Value, An Axiomatic Analysis of Economic Equilibrium*. New York: Wiley and Sons, 1979.

Fisher, Irving. *The Stock Market Crash—And After*. New York: Macmillan, 1930.

Frey, Bruno S., Werner W. Pommerehne, Friedrich Schneider and Guy Gilbert. "Consensus and Dissension Among Economists: An Empirical Inquiry." *American Economic Review* 74(December 1984): 986–994.

Friedman, Milton. "The Role of Monetary Policy." *American Economic Review* 58(March 1968): 1–17.

Galbraith, John K. *Economics and the Public Purpose*. Boston: Houghton Mifflin, 1973.

Hicks, John. "Mr. Keynes and the Classics: A Suggested Interpretation." *Econometrica* 5(April 1937): 147–159.

Keynes, John M. *The General Theory of Employment, Interest, and Money*. New York: Harcourt, Brace, and Co., 1936.

Kuznets, Simon. *National Income and Its Composition*. New York: National Bureau of Economic Research, 1941.

Lange, Oskar. "On the Economic Theory of Socialism: Part One." *Review of Economic Studies* 4(October 1936): 53–71.

Lange, Oskar. "On the Economic Theory of Socialism: Part Two." *Review of Economic Studies* 4(February 1937): 123–142.

Leontief, Wassily. "Input-Output Economics." *Scientific American* 185(October 1951): 15–21.

Lerner, Abba P. "Theory and Practice of Socialist Economics." *Review of Economic Studies* 6(October 1938): 71–75.

Lucas, Robert E., Jr., and Thomas J. Sargent. "After Keynesian Macro Economics." In *After the Phillips Curve: Persistence of High Inflation and High Unemployment.* Boston: Federal Reserve Bank of Boston, 1978.

Marx, Karl. *Capital: A Critique of Political Economy.* New York: The Modern Library, 1936.

Mitchell, Wesley C. *What Happens During Business Cycles.* New York: National Bureau of Economic Research, 1951.

Pasinetti, Luigi L. "Switches of Technique and the 'Rate of Return' in Capital Theory." *Economic Journal* 79(September 1969): 508–531.

Phillips, A. W. H. "The Relationship Between Unemployment and the Rate of Change of Money Wage Rates in the United Kingdom, 1861–1957." *Economica* 25(November 1958): 283–299.

Pigou, A. C. *Industrial Fluctuations.* London: Macmillan and Co., 1927.

Robinson, Joan. "The Production Function and the Theory of Capital." *Review of Economic Studies* 21(1953–54): 81–106.

Samuelson, Paul A. *Foundations of Economic Analysis.* Cambridge: Harvard University Press, 1947.

Simon, Herbert A. "Theories of Decision Making in Economics and Behavioral Science." *American Economic Review* 49(June 1959): 223–283.

Smith, Adam. *An Inquiry into the Nature and Causes of the Wealth of Nations.* Oxford: Clarendon Press, 1976.

Solow, Robert M. *Capital Theory and the Rate of Return.* Amsterdam: North Holland, 1963.

Thurow, Lester C. *Dangerous Currents: The State of Economics.* New York: Random House, 1983.

von Neumann, John, and Oskar Morgenstern. *Theory of Games and Economic Behavior.* Princeton, NJ: Princeton University Press, 1944.

CHAPTER 8

PROMOTING ECONOMIC LITERACY

Beverly J. Armento

The study of economics, or political economy, as this social science was originally called, can be traced in the United States to 1819, when John McVickar was made professor of moral philosophy and political economy at Columbia College, New York (Monroe 1911). While the economic problems surrounding the Civil War prompted some interest in the teaching of political economy courses at the college level, there was little demand for this course at the precollegiate level. However, the *Report of the Committee of Ten on Secondary School Studies* of the National Education Association in 1894 aroused the ire of those few advocates of precollegiate economics courses. The *Report* came out emphatically against formal instruction in political economy in the secondary school and recommended that "in connection particularly with United States history, civil government, and commercial geography, instruction be given in those economic topics, a knowledge of which is essential to the understanding of our economic life and development" (*Report* 1894, 181–183).

The study of political economy, though, had already made its way into high schools, particularly in the East and Midwest (Clow 1899). The growth of this course was further stifled by the NEA Committee on Social Studies' 1916 report, which proposed a 12th grade course called "Problems of Democracy" that would include social and political, as well as economic, content (Hertzberg 1981). No separate course on economics was recommended. And by 1922, a survey conducted by the U.S. Office of Education reported that less than 5 percent of high school students was enrolled in economic courses (Cummings 1950).

The early 1920s saw the growth of social science professional associations, many of which began to make claims for the legitimacy of their discipline in the school curriculum. The American Economic Association, for example, proposed an integrated conceptual economic curriculum for the junior high school as well as a number of economics and business courses for the high school (Marshall 1922).

The Depression prompted demands for more economics in the schools. In a 1931 article, "The Abolition of Economic Illiteracy," Shields called for a program of economic education from the early grades through the university levels. By 1938 the NEA and the American Association of School Administrators had published *The Purposes of Education in American Democracy,* which called for "economic efficiency" as a goal of schooling. Thorndike's 1939 proposal that *all* students in grades 7–9 take 90 hours of economics and business courses and that a fourth of all students should take an additional 180 hours in grades 10–12 seemed somewhat extreme. There was no widespread support for this recommendation.

From these beginnings of economic education to the current day, one can trace not only the advances and accomplishments, but also the persistent issues, topics and problems that have dominated the field. These major types of concerns occur throughout the literature of the last 50 years:

- Philosophical goal-oriented questions, including: What ought to be the focus of economic education? Why should economic education be included in the curriculum? Who should be involved in determining the content and scope of economic education?
- Pragmatic curricula concerns, including: Economic education for whom? Where should it occur in the curriculum?
- Instructional concerns, including: How should economic education be taught? Who should teach it? What materials should be used?

GOALS OF ECONOMIC EDUCATION

Over the last 50 years, there have been disagreements over why economic education should be included in the schools and over the proper approach that should be taken in teaching economics. Patriotic, life adjustment, and citizenship rationales have been offered to justify a place for economic education in the curriculum. Recurring questions on the proper emphasis that should be taken include: What is the proper balance between personal economics (consumer/career education) and citizenship economics (analytical, social science education)? Should economic education emphasize theoretical constructs or practical, concrete situations, or both; and how should this be done? And what should be the role of value judgments and controversial issues in economic education?

The economic problems of the Depression undoubtedly influenced the shift from a highly theoretical to a more practical approach to the teaching of economics in the schools. The 1938 Educational Policies Commission distinguished personal economic efficiency from economic literacy in citizenship, but viewed both of these as goals of education. Personal economic efficiency included (1) awareness of work satisfaction, (2) occupational information, (3) occupational efficiency, (4) occupational adjustment, (5) occupational appreciation, (6) personal economics, (7) consumer judgment and, (8) efficiency in buying and consumer protection. Economic literacy as a citizen included familiarity with broad economic issues, conditions, and procedures, and with important economic concepts such as supply and demand, investment, profit, and scarcity. "Only as a growing degree of competence and interest in these matters is diffused among the people can democracy function in the teeth of technological change," concluded the commission.

The participants in a 1939 Teachers College of Columbia University conference on "How Can Economic Illiteracy Be Reduced?" concluded that economic literacy meant the ability to proceed intelligently in the face of economic problems. The conferees recommended that the high school course should focus on economic problems in concrete life situations (Hunt 1940) and that controversial economic issues should be included at both the junior and senior high school levels. They reasoned that the school has an obligation to teach children the techniques of fact-finding and of objectivity and that students must learn to take responsibilities (Thorndike 1940). Hunt cautioned, however, that there were controversial topics that the

> public or influential sectors of the public would not allow to be explored. Teachers feel, in general, that if any economics is to be discussed, it had best be the safe, if arid, theory of the classical economists. (Hunt 1940, 584)

The 1940 Yearbook of the National Council for the Social Studies (NCSS), devoted to economic education, reflected this pragmatic tone and encouraged making economics more functional and more realistic. Gavian claimed that this movement to increase the teaching of economics lacked a name; some titles then being used were "thrift education," "consumer education" and "household education." Such names, she claimed, were not inclusive enough, while other titles such as "economic education" and "education for economic literacy" seemed to emphasize economic theory as ends in themselves. Gavian proposed "education for economic competence" as a good name for the movement and defined economic competence in terms of the skills needed for one's roles as a consumer, producer and citizen (Gavian 1942, 6–8).

Those persons favoring more economic education in the schools during the early 1940s tended to favor at least one of the following outcomes:

- A more favorable attitude toward the private enterprise system
- More intelligent use of income by consumers
- Better occupational adjustment and occupational distribution
- A clearer understanding of present-day economic issues.

The emphasis on practical and consumer-oriented economics was reflected by the Consumer Education Study (1942–1945), under the sponsorship of the National Association of Secondary School Principals and the National Better Business Bureau. The members of this group originally proposed to develop objective instructional materials, but actually found themselves analyzing the growing collection of teaching materials sponsored by business and special interest groups that had made their way into schools (Amberson 1945).

A shift in the practical versus analytical argument was set into motion when, during the fall of 1947, the School of Education of New York University sponsored a conference for various groups interested in economic education. G. Derwood Baker led discussions, which concluded that the public schools were not equipped to provide students with the necessary

> tools and skills for understanding our distinctively American economic institutions. The curriculum gives scant attention to economic institutions, problems, and issues. Appropriate materials of instruction are scarce and, most critical of all, the teachers in elementary and secondary schools have had little training in economic affairs. (Baker 1950, 391)

Funded by the Committee for Economic Development, a workshop was planned for the summer of 1948 that included economists and educators as well as representatives from business, labor, government and private research organizations. At this workshop, a conflict apparently arose between those who advocated that high school economics be taught primarily as an academic discipline, emphasizing analysis, models, and structure and those who advocated its continuing orientation as a consumer, personal-problems, institutional course. The issue was decided in favor of the "pure economics" emphasis, and the tone was set for the dominant approach the economic education movement was to take into the future.

Out of this workshop came the Interim Committee on Economic Education, which evolved in 1949 into the Joint Council on Economic Education, with G. Derwood Baker as its first Director (Baker 1950). The JCEE's early efforts were directed to the problems facing economic education in terms of poor teacher education, inadequate materials and outmoded instructional techniques.

In a 1954 JCEE-sponsored conference held in Riverdale, New York, economic understanding was defined as the "possession of a sense of 'what it's all about' as far as the economic phases of one's life in society are concerned; this understanding emerges from the study of the economic problem—scarcity." The Council decided that economic education should include (1) a method of analysis so that students will learn how to "frame assumptions, test hypotheses, identify sources, gather facts, and be able to use relevant and eliminate irrelevant variables," and (2) a body of economic understanding that enables students to "see factors in the economy in relation to a unifying structure." In addition, economic education should inculcate in students "a desire to participate in those activities in a democratic society which affect the common welfare" (Gemmell 1954, 12–17).

At the Riverdale conference, Lewis Wagner addressed the issue of the way in which value judgments should be embodied in economic education programs. Should economic education serve to perpetuate some "common beliefs" of society, or should it facilitate individual choice by making people aware of alternatives? He concluded that the latter approach was the only defensible stand, since

> economics cannot make ethical pronouncements and, at the same time, nestle snuggly under the protective wing of science and objective inquiry. Attempts to instill "wholesome attitudes," "correct habits," or to postulate any given set of values as basic or intrinsic is (1) to oversimplify; (2) to ignore contradictions in values; (3) to propagandize; (4) to focus attention away from economics as a science and toward it as an ethical system; (5) to encourage unquestioning acceptance of current values; (6) to preclude the objective examination of economic phenomena; and (7) to encourage attempts by individuals and groups to gain control over the process of economic education instruction. (Wagner 1954, 46–47)

Struggles over objectivity and the proper role of value judgments had been around for a long time and continue into the present day. In 1960 Baker stated that:

> Business groups want school to teach the virtues of free enterprise, but to say little about problems of inflation and unemployment while labor groups want you to be

sympathetic about labor issues but to say little about the responsibilities of labor to larger issues.

However, the schools "cannot champion the causes of particular interest groups"; if they are to command the respect of all the people, the schools must assume the responsibility for objectivity (Baker 1960, 399).

By 1960, however, there was a proliferation of materials supplied by various individuals and groups to influence the economic reasoning of students. As far back as 1929, the NEA had appointed a Committee on Propaganda in the Schools to assess the extent of the problem. This committee had recommended that state departments of education and local boards of education develop guidelines for the use of supplementary materials in classrooms. They recommended such general principles as favoring material that presents a pro and con discussion over material that presents only one side. In 1937, in a report by the Brookings Institution, Lyon recommended the involvement of professional economists in the preparation of educational materials as a defense against charges of propaganda in economic education material. "Most national organizations which call themselves educational are propaganda agencies for some particular point of view or interest" (Lyon 1937, 129).

The Bylaws of the then new Joint Council on Economic Education required representatives from business, labor, agriculture, and economic research organizations and specified that the Council would "not promote the special interest of any groups, engage in propaganda, nor attempt to influence legislation." This, however, did not inhibit other groups' efforts to influence economic education. Ayers (1953, 74) observed that

> trade associations, labor unions, newly created educational organizations, and other special interest groups, alarmed by trends in social change, disturbed by the lack of economic education in the schools, and gripped with a single idea of telling their story, have sought to provide educational leadership and perhaps even to dominate educational policy making, the content of instructional materials, and teaching practice.

There has been little change over the last several years either in the production and dissemination of materials and efforts by special interest groups or in the critique and counterefforts by educators and professional associations to curb the influence of these groups. In 1953 Briggs attempted to make a case for the National Association of Secondary School Principals as the "authoritative source which should be developing teaching/learning units in economic education for the schools." Baker estimated that U.S. business firms had spent some 50 million dollars in 1956 on free materials for school distribution; the Joint Council's contributions from 1949–1957 totaled about two million dollars. There were a number of observations: "Economic education has had more money than all the other Social Sciences combined" (Chamberlin 1979). Educators have "permitted the public schools to be supermarkets for special interest groups" (Boyer 1979, 17); all this material "is an injustice against children in schools" (Medsger 1976, 46).

> The JCEE, after a decade in existence, remained firmly committed to its charter policy that programs for economic education must be without regard to, and

independent of, special interests of any group . . . and that the responsibility for instituting and carrying out programs in Economic Education must always remain that of the schools themselves. (Fersh 1959, 47)

However, issues surrounding the proper role of special interest groups and the role of value judgments in economic education continue unresolved today.

The 1960s and Shifting Goals

The 1960s brought a new reform movement to social studies education in general and to economic education in particular. The reforms were partly in response to Sputnik, the changing social and political scenes, critical reviews of the schools, and reform movements already set in motion in mathematics and the natural sciences. This social science oriented reform emphasized the structures of the academic disciplines, inquiry, and conceptual learning.

A 1961 report of the National Task Force on Economic Education, funded by the Committee for Economic Development and cosponsored by the American Economic Association and the Joint Council on Economic Education, stressed a rational approach to economic problems. The report proposed that future citizens need to

acquire a modest amount of factual information about the economic world, but the primary obligation of schools is to help [students] develop the capacity to think clearly, objectively and with a reasonable degree of sophistication about economic problems. Mere description of economic institutions is *not* what we mean by economic education. (*Economic Education in the Schools* 1961, 13)

This Task Force report proceeded to outline what was thought to be the core of essential knowledge for economic understanding. This included emphasis on (1) concepts such as scarcity, opportunity cost, supply and demand, economic systems, markets, role of government, business organizations, international trade, money, and aggregate demand and supply; and (2) controversial issues such as those involving the role of the Federal Reserve System, labor unions, social security, the farm problem, and distribution of income. In addition, the Task Force recommended that more economic analysis be included in history courses. It was noteworthy in its endorsement of the teaching of controversial economic issues.

The "new economic education" was born! And, like the general reform movement known as the New Social Studies, the dominant approach to curricular development in economics had the following characteristics: identification of the structure or basic concepts of economics; discovery or inductive teaching and learning; use of the modes of inquiry of the economist; an attempt to build in cumulative and sequential learning; a proliferation of audiovisual material; and a degree of teacher involvement in the development and teaching of curricular materials. Numerous curricular projects manifested these characteristics. Most notable was Lawrence Senesh's *Our Working World,* which attempted to illustrate how the fundamental ideas or the structure of economic knowledge should remain the same for all grade levels while the illustration of these concepts changed in terms of their scope and complexity as children matured.

Built on the ideas of the 1961 National Task Force Report, the Joint Council on Economic Education's Master Curriculum Project served to give a new impetus to the teaching of precollegiate economics. A major part of this project was the defining of economic understanding as the synthesis of the following six elements: (1) identifying economic issues, (2) practicing a reasoned approach or a systematic way of thinking about economic issues, (3) possessing an overview of the economic system, (4) understanding basic economic concepts, (5) utilizing criteria for evaluating economic actions and policies, and (6) developing the ability to combine these elements and to apply them to the analysis of economic issues.

Current Issues Concerning Goals

The primarily social science, analytical approach tends to dominate current economic education curriculum development. It is the central focus of the JCEE's Master Curriculum Project, which includes a revised set of *Framework and Teaching Strategies* books for grades 1–12. These books include materials for the integration of economics into various other social studies courses at the high school level. Today, the Joint Council's network of professional educators is the largest nongovernmental teacher training system in the country, and it includes Economic Education Councils in each of the 50 states and at least 260 university Centers for Economic Education. The National Association of Economic Educators (NAEE) serves as the professional association for the economic educators who provide leadership at the various Councils and Centers. Additionally, there are at least 740 school districts participating in the Developmental Economic Education Program (DEEP), which emphasizes local decision making for economic education curricular improvement, K–12. The students enrolled in participating DEEP schools account for about 20 percent of the total K–12 population. The JCEE has set as its goal the expansion of the DEEP network to include 70 percent of the K–12 population by the end of the decade (JCEE Annual Report 1983–84, 3).

The "citizenship economics" versus "personal economics" question was re-examined during the 1970s and 1980s when considerable resources were devoted to support consumer and career education programs by public and private groups. Hansen argued that there was a mismatch in the market for economics education, with students more interested in short-term personal benefits that they might receive from a consumer-oriented curriculum and educators more interested in the longer-term benefits of a more analytical approach. The question was asked: How can we "find the right mix of personal and citizenship economics to promote greater student motivation and better match the supply side, or the willingness of educators to provide economic education?" (Hansen 1977, 66).

An even more serious question faces economic educators today as they assess the strengths and weaknesses of the "structure of the discipline" approach to the teaching of economics. The general aim of this approach is to help students learn subject matter and the inquiry methods of economists; if the approach is successful, students should develop comprehensive ideas for understanding social affairs and for interpreting human events. Does this, indeed, occur? Are

103

students able to synthesize their conceptual knowledge and analytical skills and apply these to personal and social issues?

As important, if not more so, is the issue of whether the interpretation of this social science approach to curriculum development has lost the element of free inquiry so important to the economist and to other social scientists. Often, scientific ideas are presented in curriculum materials and by teachers as immutable laws, rather than as tentative but vital theories (Popkewitz 1977). While the social sciences reflect many perspectives, curriculum writers have tended to focus on a singular perspective of society and thus to neglect the multidimensional nature of social inquiry. This approach presents one view of the world as morally correct without opportunity for critical analysis. Thus, the question of the proper role of value judgment and of social inquiry in the economic education curriculum has recurred in a new form. This question is complicated by the developmental question: When are students cognitively and affectively able to engage in social inquiry? Should the economic education curriculum encourage inquiry into multiple perspectives of the economic world? If so, how and when, developmentally, could this be done?

Concerns have also been expressed, particularly in the 1970s, about the goals of economic education for minority students and for women. Banks argued that the curriculum tends to present "an Anglo-American-centric" view of society:

> students are rarely encouraged to question the basic assumptions and practices of our economic system or to seriously examine how it systematically discriminates against powerless minority groups and perpetuates economic inequality. . . . Economic education should present youth with economic and social alternatives and help them attain the knowledge, skills, and attitudes needed to maximize their options. (Banks 1977, 124–127)

The same argument has been made concerning the treatment of women in the economic education literature. Ladd (1977) proposed that "all economic education materials must be purged of gender bias" to promote a maximum degree of individual economic and social choice for women. Lively debate surrounded the many empirical studies conducted during the 1970s and into the 1980s exploring gender differences in the "stock and growth" of economic achievement and motivation of men and women. This concern continues to draw the attention of economic educators.

PRAGMATIC CURRICULAR CONCERNS

If attention to economics is to be given in the curriculum, where shall this focus occur? Should there be a separate course in economics or should the economic content be integrated into other courses? Or both? If integrated, with which courses? Which students should be involved in programs of economic education? What should be the scope and sequence of instruction? These questions have recurred over the last 50 years, and new answers are being sought to these questions in the 1980s. Stoddard (1935, 27) proposed that

> economic education is not a matter of a semester or a year but must run through a considerable proportion of the elementary and secondary curriculum. Separate

courses in economics need not be taught in each of the grades, but there is a need for economic education in some form beginning with the kindergarten.

Calling also for a program of economic education for elementary school students, Gavian (1942) identified and responded to the typical arguments for *not* involving young children in economic learning. These arguments included: (1) Young children should not be exposed to adult problems before they are ready to cope with these issues. (2) The study of economics is unrelated to experiences of children. (3) The necessary skills, knowledge and understandings cannot be developed in young children and attempts to do so would result in mere verbalism. (4) Elementary school students do not (of their own accord) manifest much interest in economic aspects of life.

Gavian countered these arguments by observing that: (1) The economic activities observed or shared by modern children are fragmentary and require interpretation. (2) A life-centered curriculum must include a focus on economic aspects of life. (3) Any child's economic learning is occurring all of the time, and unless it is intelligently directed, it will not be suited to existing and emerging conditions. Further, she argued, the issue really revolves around the proper methodology of instruction, rather than focusing on the content.

The recommendation for a continuous program of economic education came also from the report of the 1961 National Task Force on Economic Education in the proposal that "economic understanding be emphasized at several points (in addition to the high school) in the entire school curriculum, from first grade on" (pages 70–71).

If there is to be a continuous program of economic education, K–12, what considerations should guide the development of a plan for scope and sequence? The extensive economic education curriculum development efforts of the 1960s were strongly influenced by the "expanding horizons" notions of Paul Hanna, the 1916 NEA report, the 1961 Task Force on Economic Education Report, and Jerome Bruner's hypothesis that any idea could be presented to a child of any age in some intellectually honest form. Thus, the same fundamental economic concepts have "spiraled" throughout the K–12 curriculum, with the illustrations of those conceptual ideas increasing in depth and abstractness as students mature.

As our knowledge of the developmental competence of students at various age levels has increased, some economic educators have questioned the appropriateness of the structure of the discipline approach, especially for younger students (Armento in press). Current efforts by the Joint Council on Economic Education and the Foundation for Teaching Economics to develop a rationale and scope and sequence recommendations call for input from developmental and learning theorists as well as from curriculum specialists, economists, economic educators and teachers. These efforts to systematically apply child development knowledge to curriculum efforts mark a turning point in economic education.

The question of whether or not a formal study of economics should occur in the K–12 curriculum has been answered for many school districts by the existence of a state mandate (often controversial) to that effect. By 1982 at least

22 states had required—either through state legislature or state board of education requirements—the teaching of a course in economics. The titles and descriptions of the mandated courses are far-ranging and, in themselves, illustrate the current existence of the persistent concern over the objectives of a "proper" study of economics. For example, in some states, consumer education courses are required, while in others the study of free enterprise or the U.S. economic system is required.

INSTRUCTIONAL CONCERNS

What skills and knowledge do teachers need in order to be effective economic educators? Who will provide the necessary teacher education? What materials and instructional methods are appropriate, relevant, stimulating and effective for different groups of students? As the field of economic education has matured, different answers have been proposed for these questions.

"Complexity and unreality" have been identified as the "two great barriers to vitalizing economic education" (Clark 1940, 399). These are barriers for both students and teachers. For teachers, part of the instructional problem has to do with understanding the analytical and inquiry elements of economics well enough to comprehend the discipline's simplicity, usefulness and relevance and to translate this understanding into meaningful instructional experiences. Teachers who fail at this complex set of tasks often are "prone to adopt the jargon of the professional economists," making the study of economics "abstruse and unreal" (Shields 1931, 316). Uninformed teachers, curriculum leaders, or administrators are also limited in their abilities to discern inadequate materials, bias, value judgments and other limitations in economic education curricular materials.

The minutes of the Interim Committee on Economic Education in 1949 reveal the group's priority concern for teacher education in economic education. Then, as now, few teachers were willing, confident and able to teach effectively a principles of economics course, or to integrate economic concepts and topics into other social studies courses. The 1961 Task Force on Economic Education reported that while economics courses in high schools were taught primarily by social studies and U.S. history teachers, fewer than half of these teachers had even one college course in economics. The Task Force recommended that: (1) teacher certification requirements in all states include a minimum of a one-year economics course for social studies teachers and business education teachers, (2) school boards and administrators encourage higher standards than these minimums, (3) there be more opportunities for teachers at inservice levels to improve their economic understanding by such means as summer workshops and nationwide educational television programs, and (4) colleges improve their economics offerings for teachers.

Today, a nationwide network of Councils and Centers for Economic Education affiliated with the Joint Council on Economic Education provides the majority of the inservice economic education for teachers. In 1983–84 over 100,000 teachers participated in at least one sponsored program. In addition to providing introductory workshops, many Centers and Councils sponsor specialized classes on such topics as integrating economic topics into U.S. history courses or improving the college undergraduate economics course. Through such inservice and preservice activities, contributions have been made to the improvement of teacher skills and knowledge. However, serious advances in this area can only be achieved through concerted efforts by teacher education institutions, school systems, and those organizations committed to the overall improvement of teachers and of schools. Recent guidelines for teacher education requirements in economics prepared by the Joint Council on Economic Education and the National Association of Economic Educators may contribute to further advances in this area.

Complexity and unreality may be perceived barriers for student learning if students view the means of instruction as contributing to that perception rather than as enabling them to construct useful meanings of their economic world. Over the last 50 years, major changes have occurred in the development of innovative instructional materials and dynamic teaching strategies. However, many students experience the traditional classroom fare of lecture and textbook reading.

While advances have certainly been made over the years in the ways in which the inquiry processes and conceptual knowledge are presented in written materials, there continue to be problems with dry, primarily descriptive material. Often study guides for high school economics courses present the instructional material as a series of definitions, rather than as a dynamic, interrelated, constructed inquiry into the economic world (Armento 1983).

Out of the New Social Studies reform movement of the 1960s came several economic education programs that illustrated clearly the characteristics of the structure of the discipline approach. These are some:

- A 9th grade inquiry course developed at Ohio State; the success of this program depended strongly on the teacher's skill of questioning and of helping students understand relationships among concepts.
- Econ 12, a one-semester course developed at San Jose State; this program used theoretical economic models as organizers.
- Chicago Elementary Program, consisting of units on exchange for 6th graders.
- Purdue Economics Project for elementary school social studies, which had an emphasis on teaching economic concepts.

It would be difficult to find any of these curricular projects in use in classrooms of the 1980s. One economic education project of the 1960s has not only remained, but today is stronger than ever and is playing a major role in the expansion and enhancement of economic education in the schools. That is the Developmental Economic Education Program, a partnership betwen school systems and the JCEE's affiliated network of state Councils and Centers (Calderwood 1970). A DEEP school district is one that has decided to engage in a process of curricular change aimed at the implementation of economic education from kindergarten to 12th grade. The DEEP program emphasizes a decision-making process model of curricular change, rather than a curricular products approach. Perhaps it is the DEEP process, whereby schools assume ownership for their own decisions, plans, and progress, that explains why it has persisted when almost all of the innovative curricular products of the 1960s have disappeared.

While the Developmental Economic Education Program stresses various processes of curricular change, there is also a rather extensive collection of innovative economic education products available today to facilitate curricular change in schools. The JCEE, in collaboration with other professional organizations or agencies, has continued throughout the last five years to facilitate the development of major educational products for the classroom. Included in these projects are three audiovisual programs: "Trade-Offs," for upper elementary school students; "Give and Take," a program for junior high school and high school students; and "Tax Whys," a program mainly for high school students. In addition, computer-assisted software and instruction in economic education are currently being developed.

The available materials for students and teachers offer innovative and meaningful ways for the modern-day teacher to make the inquiry into economic topics and issues interesting, relevant and appropriate for students of various age levels.

The problems of economic education today differ mainly in outer manifestations from those of the 1930s or even the 1960s. The current issues can be traced to their historical roots. The issues look very much the same, but variations in the theme have emerged. Economic educators today continue to search for answers to many of the same persistent issues that existed in the 1930s.

REFERENCES

Amberson, Rosanne. "New Yardsticks for Business-Sponsored Teaching Aids." *Printer's Ink* 211(April 1945): 21–23,102.

Armento, Beverly J. "Learning about the Economic World During the Elementary School Years." In *Elementary Social Studies: An Endangered Species,* NCSS Bulletin, edited by Virginia Atwood, in press.

Armento, Beverly J. "A Study of the Basic Economic Concepts Presented in DEEP Curriculum Guides, Grades 7–12." *The Journal of Economic Education* 14(Summer 1983): 22–27.

Ayars, Albert L. "A Frontal Attack on Economic Illiteracy." *The School Executive* 72(February 1953): 73–75.

Baker, G. Derwood. "Economic Education." In *Encyclopedia of Educational Research,* 3rd ed., edited by Chester W. Harris. New York: Macmillan, 1960, 398–403.

Baker, G. Derwood. "The Joint Council on Economic Education." *The Journal of Educational Sociology* 23(March 1950): 389–396.

Banks, James A. "Economic Education for Ethnic Minorities." In *Perspectives on Economic Education,* edited by Donald Wentworth, Lee Hansen and Sharryl Hawke. New York: JCEE, NCSS and SSEC. 1977.

Boyer, William Harrison. "Economic Miseducation." *The Education Digest* 44(March 1979): 17–19.

Briggs, Thomas H. "The Growing Demand for Unbiased Economic Materials." *The School Executive* 72(May 1953): 57–58.

Calderwood, James D., John D. Lawrence and John E. Maher. *Economics in the Curriculum: Developmental Economic Education Program.* New York: John Wiley and Sons, 1970.

Chamberlin, Don. "Should Business Support Economic Education in Our Schools?" *Minnesota Business Journal* 3(February 1979): 10–12.

Clark, Harold F. "Vitalizing Economic Education." *Social Education* 4(October 1940): 397–403.

Clow, F. R. "Economics as a School Study." In *Economic Studies.* New York: American Economic Association, 1899.

Committee on Propaganda in the School. *Report of the Committee on Propaganda in the Schools.* Washington, DC: National Education Association, 1929.

Committee on Social Studies, National Education Association. *The Social Studies in Secondary Education,* Bulletin 28. Washington, DC: U.S. Bureau of Education, 1916.

Cummings, Howard. "Economic Education in the Secondary Schools." *The Journal of Educational Sociology* 23(March 1950): 397–401.

Economic Education in the Schools. A Report of the National Task Force on Economic Education. New York: Committee for Economic Development, 1961.

Educational Policies Commission. *The Purposes of Education in American Democracy.* Washington, DC: National Education Association and the American Association of School Administrators, 1938.

Fersh, George L. "The Joint Council's Decade in Economic Education." *School and Society* 87(January 31, 1959): 47–48.

Gavian, Ruth W. *Education for Economic Competence in Grades 1–6.* New York: Teachers College, Columbia University, 1942.

Gemmell, James, Seymour Harris and S. P. McCutchen, eds. *Economics in General Education: Proceedings of the Riverdale Conference.* New York: Joint Council on Economic Education, 1954.

Hansen, Lee W. "The State of Economic Literacy." In *Perspectives on Economic Education,* edited by Donald Wentworth, Lee Hansen and Sharryl Hawke. New York: JCEE, NCSS and SSEC, 1977.

Hertzberg, Hazel Whitman. *Social Studies Reform: 1880–1980.* Boulder, CO: Social Science Education Consortium, 1981.

Hunt, Erling M. "Developing Economic Competence Through Public Education." *Teachers College Record* 41(April 1940): 573–586.

Joint Council on Economic Education 1983–1984 Annual Report, "Responding to the Challenge." New York: Joint Council on Economic Education, 1984.

Ladd, Helen F. "Male-Female Differences in Precollege Economic Education." In *Perspectives on Economic Education,* edited by Donald Wentworth, Lee Hansen and Sharryl Hawke. New York: JCEE, NCSS and SSEC, 1977.

Lyon, Leverett S. *Preliminary Analysis for a Program of Economic Education.* Washington, DC: The Brookings Institution, 1937.

Marshall, Leon C. "A Proposed Program of Social Studies in the Secondary Schools." *American Economic Review* 12(March 1922): 66–74.

Medsger, Betty. "The Free Propaganda That Floods the Schools." *The Progressive* 40(December 1976): 42–46.

Monroe, Paul, ed. "Economics." *A Cyclopedia of Education* 2(1911). New York: Macmillan, 387–392.

National Education Association. *Report of the Committee of Ten on Secondary School Studies.* New York: American Book Company, 1894.

Popkewitz, Thomas S. "The Latent Values of the Discipline-Centered Curriculum." *Theory and Research in Social Education* 5(April 1977): 41–60.

Senesh, Lawrence. "The Pattern of the Economic Curriculum." *Social Education,* 59(January 1968): 47–50.

Shields, Harold G. "The Abolition of Economic Illiteracy." *The Journal of the National Education Association* 20(December 1931): 315–316.

Stoddard, Alexander J. "Providing an Adequate Economic Education." *Nation's Schools* 16(September 1935): 27–28.

Thorndike, Edward L. "Increasing Knowledge and Rationality about Economics and Business." *Teachers College Record* 41(April 1940): 587–594.

Wagner, Lewis E. "Major Issues in Economic Education." In *Economics in General Education: Proceedings of the Riverdale Conference,* edited by James Gemmell, Seymour Harris and S. P. McCutchen. New York: Joint Council on Economic Education, 1954.

CHAPTER 9

SOCIOLOGY: FROM THEORY TO SOCIAL ACTION

J. Ross Eshleman

L
ike most fields of study, sociology as a discipline has undergone consistent change and modification in theory, method and substance. Yet, despite population shifts, technological innovations and societal transformations, continuities in issues, topics and problems exist. This chapter attempts to address a number of these continuities as well as changes in the study of sociology. Sociology is a young science with conflicting perspectives within the discipline. However, a convincing argument can be made that the spark for many new ideas and for selected unresolved issues, the major perspectives in contemporary sociology, and some of the changes that have occurred over the past several decades stem from our European ancestors.

UNRESOLVED ISSUES
FROM EUROPEAN ANCESTORS

A wide range of 19th-century European writers had a strong influence on what sociology is today. Many could be cited, but Emile Durkheim, Max Weber and Karl Marx were particularly profound and influential thinkers and writers. Although their ideas shifted in their own lifetime, their basic perspectives dominate contemporary sociological thought.

Durkheim (1858–1917), a French sociologist, devoted his life to making sociology a separate and unique science. To him, sociology was the scientific study of *social facts,* factors that are external to individuals but are coercive; that is, impose constraints upon them. Since the "social" represented a new order of phenomena, they could not be explained psychologically. When people get together in groups or institutions, something happens that differs from what happens to lone individuals. Questions such as what holds society together, why people form and abide by social relationships or conform to social norms, or what processes operate to maintain social order, he believed, do not have answers at the individual level.

Durkheim had an intense interest in group bonds and in factors that affect the cohesiveness and integration of social groups. These bonds, he argues, are important explanations for actions even believed to be highly personal or individualistic, such as suicide. Thus, to explain differences in suicide rates between Catholics and Protestants or the married and divorced, it becomes important to look at the social fact of the degree of integration in groups. His crucial idea, widely believed and tested by today's sociologists, is that social structure—that is, social facts external to the individual—can offer explanations for social behavior. Relationships and society are more than the sum of its parts; they are constraining on the parts. As will be noted later, these ideas are closely linked to the structural-functional perspective.

Another major contribution of Durkheim was the belief that the social world could be studied in the same way that we study the physical world or the biological world; that is, scientifically. His concern with what leads to social order was reinforced by a concern with the development of sociology as a science. He was one of the earliest, if not the first, to use systematic data collection and statistical analysis to test selected aspects of this theory. His research on suicide, for example, served as a model for later sociologists. It was done by studying existing data on suicide rates and relating suicide to a large number of traits such as nationality, religion, sex, age and seasons of the year. The methodology he established served as a model for many generations of sociologists that followed. But the controversy over whether or not sociology is a science or even whether social facts can be studied scientifically continues.

A second profound and influential writer on contemporary thought was a German sociologist, Weber (1864–1920). Whereas Durkheim analyzed society in terms of social facts and social structure—how the social parts are arranged— Weber focused on the individual as the basic unit of analysis. Religion, for example, viewed by Durkheim as a social fact central to social integration, was seen by Weber as only understood through the people who participate in religious life. Thus, the social scientist, according to Weber, needs to study people's motives for their behavior and investigate the subjective meanings that the people themselves attach to this behavior. Social interaction between two individuals occurs with each person defining and taking into account the perceived action of the other. Sociologists studying interaction, religion, families, power, bureaucracies, or other matters, therefore, need to be concerned with the subjective meanings that the interaction, religion, etc., has for its members. Reality is defined in terms of meaning. Contrast this with Durkheim's idea that interaction, religion, families and the like are social facts and realities in and of themselves and not explained by their parts; namely, individuals or their subjective meanings. This difference, whether reality is an objective fact or a subjective perception, remains with us today.

Another major contribution of Weber, like that of Durkheim, was a methodological one. Both Weber and Durkheim believed that social phenomena should be studied scientifically. But while Weber might agree with Durkheim that certain aspects of society can be understood by examining structures or facets of the social order external to people, Weber realized that many other aspects demanded an examination of internalized meanings, motives, feelings, values, goals, and other factors unique to humans. This method for studying social action Weber termed *Verstehen,* literally meaning understanding. This new approach toward studying human action involved an examination of the subjective meanings that people attach to their own behavior and that of others. Once values, motives and intentions were identified, Weber contended, sociologists could treat them objectively and scientifically.

How can sociologists gain this *Verstehen* or understanding? One way is to reproduce in themselves the purposive reasoning of the actor. Watching a student who is sitting in class with a note pad and pencil may lead one to conclude that the student is going to take notes of the lecture. A second way of understanding is empathy, putting oneself in the place of the actor and trying to see things as the actor sees them. Thus, to understand car theft, drug use, or prostitution, a sociologist could study existing records of these activities and could calculate gender, age and class differences. But to Weber this would be inadequate. The sociologist would need to find out the meanings of their actions to the people who steal cars, use drugs or engage in prostitution. To gain *Verstehen* the sociologist might get involved personally in these activities, might observe them without personal participation, might talk to the participants, or engage in any activity that enables him or her to be in the "shoes of the actor." To Weber, this approach was scientific and enabled the researcher to understand social action in a way impossible via external means. As will be noted later, these ideas are closely linked to the symbolic interaction perspective.

Weber also advocated the idea of value-free sociology. While values may inevitably influence the choice of problems studied, scientists and researchers should be value-neutral in their work. Personal moral concerns, for or against car theft, drug use or prostitution, should not influence their interpretation of data. As private citizens, we may abhor illegal activities, but Weber contended that social scientists can and must gather information and analyze it in ways that are not affected by their values. In addition, he believed that the scientific data obtained in and of itself do not tell the scientist what should be or what should not be done. Right and wrong, and good and bad, while legitimate personal and social concerns, are beyond science. Science may objectively study values but not prescribe them. Was Weber correct? As we shall note later, these issues are ongoing, persistent and unresolved a full century after Weber proposed them.

The third 19th-century writer who is still extremely influential in contemporary sociological thought was Marx (1818–1883). Unlike Durkheim and Weber, who were both concerned with creating a separate, distinct scientific discipline of sociology, Marx wanted both a science of society as well as a revolutionary program to change society. Unlike Durkheim or Weber, who are mostly claimed by sociologists, Marx is claimed by members of all the social sciences as one of their own. Within sociology his ideas were largely ignored before the middle of this century for political reasons. Since the 1960s he has gained widespread recognition with both claimers and disclaimers falling into highly polarized camps. Today few sociologists ignore him.

Marx contended that social conflict was at the core of society and the source of all social change. All of history and essentially everything that happens in society is caused by economic relationships. In time, society is divided into two basic economic classes that have interests antagonistic to the other—the bourgeoisie, who own the wealth and rule over its use, and the proletariat, who are the working class industrial workers who produce the wealth. The difference in power between these two groups of rich and poor, managers and workers, or privileged elite and exploited masses leads to feelings of alienation among the workers. The recognition among workers that they share the same plight leads to a sense of "class consciousness" and, ultimately, according to Marx, to revolution.

Revolution was viewed by Marx as essential for social change, since those with wealth and power will not voluntarily either share them or give them up. Since the bourgeoisie in capitalist societies own the land and the factories, the proletariat who sell their labor in order to survive become alienated and antagonistic. This eventually leads to revolution by the working class, which leads, in turn, to the means of production being socialized, with the ultimate result being a classless society. This idea is central to the social conflict perspective that is described later.

In sharp contrast to Weber, for whom science was value free, Marx's view of science was pragmatic. According to Marx, science should be used both to gain knowledge and to serve society. Durkheim, Weber and Marx believed that they were scientists and that society and its social components could be studied scientifically. What they meant by science, the general questions they posed about science, and the uses to which science should be put were vastly different. Marx's idea that scientists should use their knowledge to improve social conditions has had a tremendous impact on contemporary sociology, and sociologists today are greatly divided over this issue. It does, however, help us understand why many sociologists active in issues of inequality (class, race, gender) adhere to a conflict perspective.

To focus on selected ideas of three European writers is neither comprehensive nor value free. While others, particularly Comte and Spencer, could have been included, the three selected seem to best represent key issues that are unresolved in sociology a century later. In addition, Durkheim, Weber and Marx represent three contrasting theoretical perspectives in contemporary sociology. A brief discussion of these perspectives and their relevance follows.

MAJOR CONTEMPORARY PERSPECTIVES

By major perspectives in contemporary sociology, reference is made to what textbook writers frequently refer to as social theory. Theories within any discipline, whether natural or social science, are explanations offered to account for a set of phenomena. Social theories offer explanations of the social world—why people marry, attend sporting events or behave differently in different social situations. Theories may be likened to binoculars or to a pair of glasses that bring into focus selected phenomena while leaving other phenomena blurred or outside the field of vision entirely. Theories provide guides as to what to look for, questions to ask, propositions to explain, and variables for testing. That theories are different or even contradictory does not mean one must be wrong; they may be operating on different assumptions, asking different questions, and focusing on different dimensions of a similar phenomena.

To explain why sociology has had less acceptance in our secondary schools than history or mathematics, one theory may suggest focusing our lens on the history and philosophy of education in the United States, another may focus on teacher training, while others may focus on inadequate curriculum materials, a conservative political climate, or an economic system that provides few employment opportunities with low financial rewards for the sociology teacher. Theories may also explain this as being the will of God, as having a genetic or biological explanation, or as due to climatic conditions or the placement of the stars during this century. Is only one explanation accurate? Are all of them simply wild speculations that have no "correct" answers?

The determination of their accuracy or correctness depends upon our conception of science and the crucial linkage between theory and research. Science is a method of discovery that requires objectivity, replication and precision of measurement. Thus, certain theories, while hypothetically correct, fall beyond the realm of observation, repeated studies or precise measurements. A "good" theory should be testable, should be abstract, should have wide application, should be cumulative and should give grounds for prediction. The perspectives (theories) that follow, rooted in ideas of Durkheim, Weber and Marx a century ago, meet these conditions and provide insight into the topics dominating sociology today and the manner in which they are addressed.

Structural-Functional Perspective

The structural-functional perspective, many would argue, is the dominant theoretical view in sociology today. It is sometimes referred to as social systems theory, equilibrium theory, or simply functionalism. This perspective focuses on how the various parts of society fit together to maintain the equilibrium of the whole. It focuses on the parts themselves (organizations, families, teachers) as well as on the interrelationships among the parts. It analyzes social phenomena in terms of their functions or consequences for parts of society or society as a whole. It operates on the assumption so forcefully stressed by Durkheim that specific structures of society impose constraints on individual behavior. It stresses that the survival of a society is dependent on its members sharing common norms and values.

Among contemporary scholars, this perspective is most closely associated with the work of Talcott Parsons and Robert Merton. Parsons' *The Structure of Social Action* (1937), and *The Social System* (1951), and Merton's *Social Theory and Social Structure* (1949) set the contemporary stage for the analysis of society by focusing on society as a social system with interrelated parts, each of which has consequences for the whole. These parts can be functional if they meet the needs of the system and help contribute to the adjustment of the system, can be dysfunctional if they are harmful to the rest of the system, or can be nonfunctional if they are irrelevant to the system. For example, job discrimination against women and blacks may be dysfunctional for them, functional for white men, and seemingly nonfunctional for those retired. However, few parts are nonfunctional, since in functional analysis the parts of a system are interdependent and even retirement (mental health, social security, type and place of residence, occupational benefits) is affected by the discrimination faced by selected categories of persons in the work world.

Teachers at the high school or college level who, perhaps unconsciously, use this perspective in dealing with substantive topics in the classroom are most likely to focus on *one* key aspect of function or raise questions on the functions. What are the functions of employments? Sports? Religion? Education? In other words, what does each do for us, the community or society? Education, for example, is said to include basic functions of transmission of the culture, socialization of the young, preparation for employment and participation in civic responsibilities. It is also intended to help people reach their potential for personal fulfillment, expand intellectual horizons, and attain other goals. These are generally recognized as manifest functions of education; namely, those that are intended and generally agreed upon as things our educational system should do.

Teachers familiar with this perspective may analyze some of the school's latent functions. These are things that our educational system does that may be highly influential but are basically unrecognized, unintended, and not necessarily viewed as legitimate reasons for the existence of schools. Should tax money be used by our school system to provide a day-care service for mothers? Prolong adolescence by keeping teenagers in school longer when unemployment rates are high and jobs are not available? Help people find marriage partners? Segregate people by age, religion, race and class from the larger population? Weaken parental control and authority over the child? These are some of the latent functions of our educational system. These latent functions, as well as the manifest ones, can also be analyzed in terms of their dysfunctions.

In the past few decades, function has been used less by scholars and researchers to analyze what something does than to analyze the consequences associated with social structures. Rather than noting the functions of education, for example, the structural-functional perspective is used to determine the results associated with varying levels and types of education. How does education affect peoples' lives in terms of income, family size or recreational activities? What are the consequences of education in terms of gender roles for a society, of the effectiveness and types of governmental policies, or of increasing the likelihood of racial integration? Given the emphasis on social systems that suggest all parts are interrelated, renewed attention has focused on determining what structures are consistently related to others, the variability of these relationships when controls are placed on intervening structures, and the explanations that enable us to understand the particular relationships, generalize to similar situations and predict the probability of similar relationships existing in the future.

In the past three decades, methodologies and statistical tools, aided by a computer technology that permits the inclusion of nearly an unlimited number of variables and cases, have resulted in an increased body of knowledge about society and its interrelated parts. Much of this research, while not always explicitly defined as such, falls within a structural-functional perspective.

Social Conflict Perspective

Like the structural-functional perspective, the conflict perspective within sociology is generally used macrosociologically. Macro is used in sociology not merely to indicate the size of the unit under investigation but, like Durkheim's social facts, to refer to phenomena that exist independently of individuals or individuals in interaction. In other words, social conflict theory among sociologists is less likely to be used to deal with personal stress or antagonism between spouses or friends than to deal with how social structure affects these spouses and friends. It is assumed that individuals experiencing similar structures will behave in similar ways.

At this point the functionalists and conflict theorists abruptly part company. Whereas structural functionalism emphasizes integration, social stability and a stable social order, the conflict prospective stresses power differences, social instability and social change. While not all who follow a conflict perspective adhere to the class conflict and economic determinism associated with Marx, most follow his general thesis that conflict and change are always present in society. They share the general assumptions that in all societies some people have more power than others, that this differential power creates conflicts, and that this conflict is basic for change. Continual power struggles involve a broad range of groups or interests: young against old, female against male, one racial group against another, and, as Marx stressed, workers against employers. These conflicts occur because things like power, wealth and prestige are not available to everyone. They are limited commodities and the demand exceeds the supply. This perspective assumes, as indicated earlier, that those who have or control these desirable goods and services will defend and protect their own interests at the expense of others.

Conflict from this perspective does not mean merely the sort of event that makes headlines, such as war, violence or open hostility. It is the day-after-day struggle of people and groups to maintain and improve their positions in life. Neither should conflict be regarded as a destructive process that leads to disorder and the breakdown of society. Theorists like Dahrendorf (1951) and Coser (1956) have focused on the integrative nature of conflict and on its value as a force that contributes to order and stability. This is possible because people with common interests in terms of their shared position in society join together to seek gains that will benefit them all. Likewise, conflict between groups focuses attention on inequalities that might never be diminished without conflict.

Many teachers of sociology at the college level today personally adhere to a conflict perspective, and it is likely the vast majority use the perspective as a legitimate means of understanding and analyzing the contemporary social order. As indicated previously, the ideas of Marx, and this perspective in general, were largely ignored before the middle of this century.

It is likely that most secondary teachers of sociology have not, do not, and will not openly advocate this perspective in many school districts throughout the country. As Switzer indicates in his chapter on the teaching of sociology in this volume, a critical investigation of society is rarely the intent of high schools, there is a lack of teacher training in either new content or new teaching strategies, the social studies curriculum has been amazingly resistant to change, and probing into areas that question why things are structured the way they are frequently makes parents, school administrators and school boards uneasy.

117

Not many teachers can openly suggest, as conflict theorists do (Collins 1979), that our education system is used by the elite to maintain its social position; that students are taught to behave appropriately, to obey rules and to be unquestionably loyal to their superiors, the organization and the nation; that the rules, norms and tests that promote competition are those based on middle-class norms that many working-class ethnics and inner-city blacks do not experience in their daily lives; that this type of competitive educational system keeps the poor in poverty and at a disadvantaged position; or that the credentials, diplomas and degrees given by schools represent learning that is not essential to doing most jobs. While the basic functions of our school system center on learning and obtaining an education, what that education includes and excludes is highly controlled, as a conflict perspective would contend, by those in positions of power.

Symbolic Interaction Perspective
The dominant microsociological perspective in sociology today is that of symbolic interaction. The micro emphasis, like the macro, looks not only at size but, like Weber's stress on *Verstehen,* stresses the subjective meanings of individuals. From a micro orientation, social facts and social structures may exist, but their relevance exists only to the extent that people attach significance to them. For example, suppose you note the completion of a new school building. You may think, "Finally we will get the needed space and updated facilities for our students," or "Now we'll have to pay more taxes for a new building that wasn't needed," or "What beautiful architecture!" The point is that a new building does, in fact, exist, but meanings, perceptions and definitions differ. The responses to the school may be positive or negative, it may be seen as beautiful or ugly, and it may cause joy or despair. The relevance comes not in the building per se, but in the meanings people attach to it.

This idea of subjective meanings is central to a symbolic interaction perspective. Weber, with his emphasis on *Verstehen,* was an early pioneer on stressing the scientific investigation of subjective meanings. But the development of the interactionist approach is largely credited to George Herbert Mead at the University of Chicago and Charles Horton Cooley at the University of Michigan. They believed that society exists within every socialized individual and that its extended forms and structures arise through the social interactions taking place among individuals at the symbolic level.

The significance of the symbolic level in human interaction comes in noting that one person does not merely react to another's action (as a behaviorist perspective would suggest), but the response is based on the meaning attached to such actions. Interaction is mediated by the use of symbols. It is the ability to use symbols that sets us apart from animals and allows us to create social institutions, societies and cultures. According to an interactionist perspective, humans are unique among all forms of life in their capacity to symbolically represent themselves, ideas, and objects. Because humans can agree on and share the meaning of symbols (words, gestures, stop signs), they can communicate effectively. Since these meanings are learned in interaction with others and are not instinctive or strictly personal or psychological creations, they are necessarily social. In interaction with others, we learn (internalize) social expectations, a specific language, and social values. In interaction with others, we learn to share meanings and communicate symbolically through words and gestures. As humans we can interact at a physical level (a slap) or a symbolic level (showing a fist or making a verbal threat). Because we can relate symbolically, we can carry on conversations with ourselves, we can anticipate the responses of others, and can even imagine the viewpoint of another.

Taking the viewpoint of another is what Mead (1934) called *role taking*. For symbolic interactionists, role taking is the basic process by which interaction occurs. It enables us to take into account the feelings and intentions of others as well as to see ourselves from the viewpoint of others. It is the process by which we develop self-awareness and a concept of ourselves. Whether we see ourselves as popular or not, attractive or not, intelligent or not, our view develops in interaction with others and is dependent on our perceptions of how others think about us and treat us. Closely linked to this capacity for self-development is the interactionist assumption that humans are capable of examining and finding symbolic solutions to their problems. We think, plan, communicate, organize and do all sorts of things that are uniquely human through the process of symbolic interaction.

Of the three perspectives, it is likely that the symbolic level may find the greatest use and acceptance in the teaching of sociology at the secondary level. Social studies teachers in general tend to feel more comfortable in using the individual as the basic unit of analysis, rather than a social group, category, system or society. In addition, to deal with self-concepts, meanings, definitions of situations, language, symbols, roles and role taking appears less controversial than does dealing with critical analysis of our power structures and institutions.

The structural–functional, conflict, and symbolic interaction perspectives can be found within most of the issues, topics and problems in the study of sociology. They are not, however, the only ones of significance. Some would argue that an evolutionary approach, a macrosociological perspective associated with biological concepts and concerned with long-term change prevalent in the views of most of the early sociologists, is making a comeback.

Others may argue that it is unfair to deal with symbolic interactionism and make no reference to other microsociological approaches, such as ethnomethodology or exchange theory. The former is primarily concerned with understanding how people carry out the ordinary, routine activities of their daily lives and the way they construct, interpret and use rules or norms of conduct. The latter, exchange theory, emphasizes what individuals and human groups do in behaving with and toward one another. It suggests that behavior is determined by the costs and rewards of interactions. That is, people seek rewarding status, relationships, and experiences and try to avoid cost, pain and punishment.

The focus in this chapter is on unresolved issues from our European ancestors and on major perspectives in contemporary sociology, rather than on substantive topics such as labeling theories of crime and deviance, melting pot theories of race, or disengagement theories of the aging. Such a focus rests on the assumption that most, if not all, substantive topics can be analyzed by using these and related perspectives.

CHANGES IN THE STUDY OF SOCIOLOGY

In an editorial on continuities and discontinuities in sociology in the United States, Herman Lantz (1984) suggested that from the late 1930s into the late 1960s, American sociologists focused on such phenomena as alcohol and drug problems, predicting success or failure in marriage, understanding sociological basis and ecological distribution of mental illness, and understanding criminal and delinquent behavior. In race, the focus was on accommodation and assimilation. In stratification, the concern was with systems of classification and characteristics of classes in communities. Both pragmatism and a belief in empiricism merged because each was seen essentially as a problem–solving activity.

Lantz suggests several reasons for changes in the kinds of research done by sociologists since 1960. One was that society's problems could not be understood easily. Research results were frustrating and the limits of sociological analysis became increasingly apparent. The dramatic breakthroughs that would solve social problems with conclusive answers and would document the importance of sociology failed to appear. Often results were inconclusive. This disappointment among sociologists, he speculates, was one key factor responsible for a shifting orientation.

A second factor is rooted in the orientation of sociologists themselves. Many sociologists trained prior to the 1960s came from backgrounds with strong religious and moral overtones. They had a strong work ethic, wanted material success, and sought acceptance by the middle–class elements of their communities. Many, Lantz suggests, may have been ideologically incapable of developing a critical stance in their sociology. With events such as those involving the women's movements, the civil rights movement, and the war in Vietnam, a new generation was able to place less emphasis on community respectability and not be fearful of social rejection if they espoused the importance of critical writings about society and what they perceived to be the oppressive nature of macrostructures. A new community of sociologists emerged.

A third impetus toward change in the field came from within the discipline itself. Prior to the 1950s, theory and method were rigidly prescribed. Since then, particularly with the emergence of the critical or conflict perspective, sociologists became less culture bound. Multiple methods of studying the social order and social interaction became legitimate. Soft methodologies with no hypothesis testing and few quantitative techniques were supplemented with increasingly sophisticated hard–data analysis. Lantz speculates on the possibility of a shake-out in the future based on still newer theoretical and methodological positions.

Several changes in the study of sociology seem under way. Evident is the breakdown of barriers between academic disciplines and agencies of mass communication. Evident is the presence and growth of an applied orientation, not only in sociology but in many other academic fields such as agriculture and biology. Evident is the adoption by other disciplines of sociological perspectives and methods. These include education with all its branches, law, history, political science, nursing, social work, geography, psychology, human ecology, journalism and communication.

As witnessed by decreasing enrollments, today sociology seems to be perceived by most college students as having little importance. The 1980s are a period of increasing social conservatism. Students appear to be much more oriented toward goals of economic and material success. Advocation has been replaced by worries about vocation. Perhaps we are witnessing a shift from a protest generation to a prerequisite generation: a generation that views courses in terms of their relevance to pre-law, pre-business, pre-medicine, and pre-high-prestige careers. From this perspective sociology may seem quite irrelevant.

On the other hand, it is and will be increasingly impossible for most students to ignore the social world and context in which their vocations operate. Can students or we ignore the arms race, the safety of nuclear power or the health effects of pollution and industrial waste? Can we ignore injustices against women, minorities and the poor? Can we live without fear of crime, violence and discrimination? Do we not want and seek answers to the causes of suicide, mental disorders, alcohol and drug addictions, rape, marital discord, unemployment and terrorism? Do we not have questions about the processes of socialization; the functioning of schools, families, governments, businesses, and churches; and the changes occurring in our communities; the impact of a world population explosion; or the effects of working in a bureaucracy?

If we want to investigate these issues in depth, then sociology is here to stay. Sociologists have a diversity of perspectives and approaches that facilitate finding answers to interactional and organizational concerns.

In writing a brief handbook for students, one sociologist observes:

> In my moments of wild optimism, I see sociology like computer science was two decades ago—a discipline about to take off. There is a growing recognition that the scale of social problems and issues requires new kinds of professionals. Disillusionment with the simple promises of politicians and the failure of economists to manage the economy—to say nothing of the society—has forced the recognition that we now need professionals of a different sort. We require new technologies—not of the whiz-bang, mechanical variety but of the human measure. We need new and expanded knowledge and understanding of human behavior and organization. And, while we would not want to view sociologists as the new "programmers" and "technicians" of complex social patterns, we would appreciate their potential impact on human society. The understanding of the properties and dynamics of human organization and the knowledge of how to gather and interpret information about human affairs will be increasingly valuable, and to be blunt, marketable. (Turner 1985, 9)

What is the future of specific courses in sociology? As in the past, new courses will develop as new ideas, technologies and issues emerge. Prior to the 1960s, courses in gender roles, the sociology of aging or conflict theory were, for the most part, unknown. Today, computers are commonplace as both teaching and research tools. New courses are evolving in domestic violence, terrorism, women's studies, war, social conflict and the like. Internships, research and experiential learning courses seem to be gaining a renewed acceptance in many sociology departments for an increasing number of students. A widespread movement is taking place that emphasizes the applied aspects and policy implications of sociological thought.

At the college level, increasing numbers of students may take an introduction to sociology as their only course in a department of sociology. Social research methods and statistics courses may increasingly disseminate to fields of study outside of sociology. Substantive areas once taught exclusively within sociology may increasingly be integrated into the curriculum of other departments or into the content of other courses: medical sociology to schools of medicine and nursing; crime and deviance courses to law and criminal justice; family courses to social work and human ecology; urban and community courses to urban planning; economic sociology and labor relations courses to business; gender roles to women's studies programs; and others. These courses may or may not be taught by professors trained specifically in graduate programs in sociology.

These changes combined with factors such as declining enrollments may mean still fewer university positions for sociologists. But the future sphere of action for sociologists may rest in fields that need their knowledge and skills in collecting, analyzing and interpreting data on human populations. Advice may be sought from sociologists on how to resolve the countless number of organizational problems and dilemmas that confront our own and other societies. Turner suggests that we will probably be seeing sociologists as data analysts, office heads, sales directors, labor-management facilitators, eligibility workers in the welfare system, heads of adoption agencies, city planning directors, patrol officers on the police force, parks and recreation directors, liaison personnel in the various agencies of city government, redevelopment directors, community organizers, census bureau statisticians, management consultants, advertising executives, insurance agents and housing developers. Without exception, all these jobs require a knowledge of organizational dynamics, human behavior and cultural diversity.

In sum, the field of sociology has undergone consistent change and modification in theory, method and substance. Issues raised by our European ancestors lack consensus today: social facts versus subjective meanings, sociology as a science, the most appropriate unit to use for societal analysis, the extent to which sociology is value free, the role of social conflict, the extent to which science should be pragmatic, and the like. From this European heritage came a number of major perspectives that dominate contemporary sociology: structural-functional, social conflict and symbolic interactional. Each presents differing assumptions and views to account for, understand and analyze society.

Interrelated with the ideas of early theorists and the dominant perspectives of the discipline were many changes in the study of sociology. Shifts have taken place in substantive areas from focusing heavily on social problems and moral concerns to analyzing components of the social order. Changes have also occurred in the training and orientation of sociologists themselves to a more critical stance. The discipline itself has moved to a less rigidly prescribed theory and methodology. Barriers across disciplines have shifted as well, with many of the ideas and procedures of the sociologists moving to other fields of study and activity.

The recent movement toward social conservatism accompanied by student concerns about vocation and declines in student enrollments in sociology has led to further changes in courses and modes of instruction. Nevertheless, there is a need for sociological knowledge irrespective of vocational interests. Because sociology deals with society, human organization and social relationships, there is no escape for social beings from these persistent topics and issues.

REFERENCES

Collins, Randall. *The Credential Society: A Historical Sociology of Education and Stratification.* New York: Academic Press, 1979.

Cooley, Charles H. *Human Nature and the Social Order.* New York: Scribner, 1902.

Coser, Lewis. *The Functions of Social Conflict.* New York: The Free Press, 1956.

Dahrendorf, Ralf. *Class and Class Conflict in Industrial Society.* Stanford, CA: Stanford University Press, 1951.

Eshleman, J. Ross, and Barbara G. Cashion. *Sociology: An Introduction,* 2nd ed. Boston: Little, Brown and Co., 1985.

Lantz, Herman R. "Continuities and Discontinuities in American Sociology." *The Sociological Quarterly* 25(Autumn 1984): 581–596.

Mead, George Herbert. *Mind, Self and Society.* Chicago: University of Chicago Press, 1934.

Merton, Robert K. *Social Theory and Social Structure.* New York: The Free Press, 1949.

Parsons, Talcott. *The Structure of Social Action.* New York: The Free Press, 1937.

Parsons, Talcott. *The Social System.* Glencoe, IL: The Free Press, 1951.

Turner, Jonathan H. *Sociology: A Student Handbook.* New York: Random House, 1985.

CHAPTER 10

TEACHING SOCIOLOGY IN K–12 CLASSROOMS

Thomas J. Switzer

Very little from the formal discipline of sociology is usually taught in K–12 classrooms in the United States. Despite periodic attempts to develop curricular materials in the field of sociology and other efforts to infuse sociological concepts into the ongoing curriculum, sociological curricular materials and concepts generally do not reach our youth. Although there are many reasons for this lack of sociological content in our schools, two major factors stand out.

First, the structure of the curriculum in U.S. schools generally does not include sociology as a course of study. The social studies curriculum, the area in which sociology is generally placed, has been dominated by history and civics to the virtual exclusion of such social sciences as sociology. This social studies curriculum is the product of another era. As Smith and Cox point out, "For the most part, the curriculum structure proposed in the 1916 Report of the National Education Association remains intact." This recommended curriculum called for European history or geography at grade 7, U.S. history at grade 8, civics at grade 9, European history at grade 10, U.S. history again at grade 11, and government or problems of democracy at grade 12. The decision by the NEA committee that sociology was not appropriate for secondary schools and the decision to recommend a problems of democracy course had a major impact on the teaching of sociology in secondary schools.

The curriculum recommended in 1916 is generally the curriculum in place in 1986. Of course, some modifications have taken place, and exceptions exist within individual school districts. However,

> every era in the history of social studies education in the United States in the twentieth century has been dominated by variance of this 1916 model, which is a "traditional," basically conservative, narrative, expository, history-as-the-core approach to social studies education. This approach emphasizes the transmission of selected aspects of the cultural heritage which supports the views of the dominant group at the time and which fosters nationalistic loyalties. (Haas 1977, 52)

This model is hardly one to support the inclusion of sociology, which, by the very fabric of its discipline, raises questions about the nature of our society.

A second major factor accounting for so little sociology being taught in grades K–12 has been a general disinterest in precollegiate education by professionals in the field of sociology. Although numerous scholars have been interested in the sociology of education, a study of education as one of society's institutional arrangements, only a handful of academic sociologists have taken an interest in the teaching of sociology in elementary and secondary schools. As Hertzberg correctly points out, "Sociology, like Economics, developed modestly in the curriculum in the absence of, rather than as a result of, the interest or activity of professional associations." Two factors seem especially important in producing this lack of interest of professional sociologists in K–12 education. The first is a persistent belief that the subject matter of sociology is too difficult to be taught effectively before the collegiate level. This belief was held by Albion Small, founder of the American Sociological Association, and it continues to be held by many sociologists today. The general position is that an understanding of the interrelationships of the various components of society requires a level of abstraction that cannot be mastered at the secondary school level.

Second, the reward structure within the field of sociology does not take into consideration activities conducted on behalf of K–12 education. Most sociologists at the peak of their careers or on the cutting edge of the field simply cannot afford to spend time working on new curriculum materials or creating ways to teach sociology at the K–12 level. It is safe to say that few sociologists have achieved tenure within a college or university as a result of their efforts to promote the teaching of sociology in the secondary and elementary schools.

Given the nature of the structure of the curriculum for grades K–12 and the lack of interest in precollegiate sociology by professional sociologists, it is hardly surprising to find that sociology is not a major subject in most U.S. schools.

EXTENT OF SOCIOLOGY TAUGHT

Because of changing definitions of what courses should be counted as sociology in K–12 schools and differing research methods, it is somewhat difficult to get an accurate historical perspective on precisely how many schools offer a course called sociology or to determine how many students are actually exposed to the teaching of sociology. Accepting these limitations, it can generally be concluded that the number of students taking a course in sociology has increased considerably in recent years. The data in Table 1 reveal that not only has the absolute number of students enrolled in sociology courses increased throughout this century, but that this number represents an increasing proportion of the total enrollment, reaching 14.3 percent of grades 9–12 enrollment in 1981–82. The 1981–82 enrollment figures include courses labeled sociology/social organization, sociology/urban, social problems/criminology, and racial and minority problems. If only courses labeled sociology/social organization and sociology/urban are included, the enrollment figures would drop somewhat to 1.642 million, or 12.99 percent of the 9–12 enrollment for that year (National Center for Educational Statistics, 54–55).

In a 1965 study, the Survey Research Center of the Institute for Social Research at the University of Michigan asked 12th graders what courses they had taken in high schools. Only 11 percent reported taking a course in sociology, but another 25 percent had taken closely related "Problems" courses. However, 100 percent reported taking U.S. history, 54 percent world history,

TABLE 1
Sociology Enrollment, Grades 9–12, Per Selected School Year

Year	Years Elapsed	Sociology Enrollment	Total Enrollment	Percent	Percentage Difference
1934–35		111,718	4,496,514	2.48	—
	14				.96
1948–49		185,901	5,399,452	3.44	
	12				.08
1960–61		289,408	8,219,276	3.52	
	12				2.40
1972–73		795,860	13,438,263	5.92	
	9				8.38
1981–82		1,810,000	12,660,537	14.30	

and 47 percent U.S. government. The high percentages in these courses reflect the continuation of the 1916 curriculum reported earlier. Only 6 percent reported having a course in geography and 5.5 percent a course in psychology (Angell 1971, 308). There is generally a lack of current data on the number of secondary schools offering a course called sociology, but the number is probably in the 25–35 percent range.

Another way to assess interest in sociology at the precollegiate level is to examine the interest of commercial publishers in providing instructional materials for this market. The author recently surveyed 26 publishing houses to determine if they publish sociology materials for the secondary school market or if they intend to publish for this market. Of the 26 publishing houses included in our survey, 22 usable questionnaires (84.6 percent) were returned. Of these 22, it was found that only 15 companies actually produced any products for the secondary school market. Of these 15 companies, four companies (26.7 percent) reported that they currently published sociology textbooks and teacher's guides. Three of the textbooks were revisions of a previous book while one was an adaptation of a standard, college-level text. Although the information was not directly sought in the questionnaire, it was discovered that at least 2 of the 11 companies that did not currently publish sociology textbooks did so during the 1970s. Neither of these companies planned to renew publication of a sociology text. With regard to complementary sociology materials, no company reported publishing sociology serial booklets, audiovisual materials or microcomputer software.

Of 11 subject areas included in the questionnaire, sociology ranked eighth in the number of publishers who published textbooks for a subject area. Thirteen (86.7 percent) published textbooks for U.S. history, 10 (66.7 percent) for world history, nine (60.0 percent) for government, and eight (53.3 percent) for civics/citizenship. Additionally, 7 (46.7 percent) published for geography, 6 (40.0 percent) for economics, and 5 (33.3 percent) for psychology. General social science texts ranked eighth along with sociology. Three companies (20.0 percent) published for courses in anthropology/culture, while 1 (6.7 percent) published a textbook for a social problems course.

Eleven companies (73.3 percent) reported producing "other instructional materials" for use in U.S. history while only one company reported producing such materials for sociology courses. It is interesting to note that three companies (20.0 percent) published microcomputer software for U.S. history, world history, and geography, but none for sociology.

Factors that the publishers reported as influencing their decision to publish or not to publish a sociology text included market needs and size, curriculum trends, enrollments, competition, authors, product fit and budget/costs. An additional factor, the presence of good sociology textbooks already in the market, was also reported. As expected, market need/size was a common factor in the decision to publish or not to publish in the area of sociology. No publisher mentioned educational or national concerns as factors in reaching a decision on the publication of sociology material.

Finally, publishers perceived the importance of the publication of a sociology textbook within their publication series. Two (15.4 percent) deemed it to be very important, five (38.5 percent) considered it somewhat important and six (46.1 percent) considered the publication of a sociology textbook in their series of little or no importance.

These data suggest that publishing houses have only limited interest at best in providing instructional materials in the field of sociology for the secondary school market.

WHAT HAS BEEN TAUGHT AS SOCIOLOGY

To know the number of schools offering courses called sociology and the number of students electing these courses tells us nothing, of course, about what content is being taught under the label of sociology. We must also keep in mind that a great deal of what can be called content from the discipline of sociology can be taught in social studies subjects other than sociology, like history, geography or economics. Angell (1971, 308) reminds us that "sociological concepts creep in whenever the analysis of human action is a matter of central concern."

The content of what gets taught as sociology in the K–12 schools is, of course, subject to all of the factors that impinge upon curriculum-making in our schools in general and upon the making of the social studies curriculum in particular. Since the basic purpose of precollegiate education has been largely to transmit the dominant culture, a critical scientific investigation of our society is rarely the intent of subjects taught at that level. The intent has been to prepare citizens with the knowledge and skills necessary to deal with certain social problems and with the correct values to see that these problems are dealt with in a manner consistent with what is deemed good for the larger social order.

The "social problem" orientation in secondary school sociology can be illustrated in several ways. For example, Angell (1971, 309) reported that a survey of the most widely used textbooks in 1969 showed that these textbooks rarely focused on the systematic concepts of sociology. He reported that the texts generally dealt with problems of two sorts: problems of communities and societies, and problems of persons and small groups. Grier, in a 1971 study, conducted an analysis of textbooks and courses of study and concluded that although coverage or emphasis varied throughout the years, topics of the city, crime, education, economics, family, government, population and race remained of major concern.

Although the social problem orientation has remained the dominant theme in precollegiate sociology, it should be noted that *Inquiries in Sociology,* a one-semester sociology course developed by Sociological Resources for the Social Studies, a curriculum project of the American Sociological Association and published by Allyn and Bacon in 1978, focused on four sociological domains: socialization, institutional structure of society, stratification and social change. This inquiry-oriented course presented an opportunity for students to approach these topics from a more scientific perspective, and it represented a considerable departure from previous materials available for the high school market.

At the elementary school level, the expanding network or expanding communities model for development of the elementary curriculum has, in a sense, provided a fertile ground for the inclusion of sociological concepts. The sequential study of the family, the school, the neighborhood, the community, the state, the nation, and, finally, the world provides at least an opportunity for sociological concepts to be taught and has encouraged an interdisciplinary approach to the behavioral sciences in the elementary schools.

During the last 20 years, several efforts have been made to develop curricular materials for the elementary schools that drew heavily from the social sciences. The social science laboratory units developed at the University of Michigan by Lippitt and others; the Taba social studies program; *Our Working World,* developed by Larry Senesh; and *Windows on Our World,* conceived by Lee Anderson, are exemplars of materials with a social science emphasis.

Unfortunately, the back-to-the-basics movement, with its emphasis on mathematics, reading and writing, has placed increasing pressure on the elementary school curriculum and has been a major factor in reducing the amount of time in a school day devoted to the social studies and, indirectly, to the teaching of social science concepts. It is not clear, however, to what extent elementary teachers are including sociological concepts in their teaching of other subject areas, but it is reasonable to assume that such teaching is not as direct as when the social studies had a more prominent place in the elementary school curriculum.

INSTRUCTIONAL MODES

Given the generally conservative nature of our K–12 education with its emphasis on transmitting the dominant culture, it is hardly surprising to find that expository, narrative-type teaching has been the dominant mode in the social studies in general and in sociology courses in particular. It is, of course, very difficult to know what kind of teaching actually takes place behind closed classroom doors, but most specialists in the field agree that teacher-dominated and textbook-dominated teaching continue to be common practice (Brown, Goodall and Baer). For the most part, rote learning is the norm, with students as passive receivers of information. Based on their observations of high school sociology classrooms, Switzer and Wilson reported that teachers tend to teach as they were taught, with teachers dominating at least 70 percent of classroom time. They report a teaching pattern of teacher-and-textbook question followed by teacher-and-textbook answer, with minimal opportunity for student reflection on the question or for active student involvement in formulating the question.

Although expository teaching seems to be the dominant mode of instruction in sociology courses, there is, of course, a wide range of other instructional techniques used in sociology classrooms. It is beyond the scope and intent of this chapter to deal with each of these techniques. It is important, however, to discuss the major alternative to expository-textbook teaching, a set of instructional techniques that fall within the general category of inquiry teaching. It is especially important here to consider how inquiry teaching, as generally portrayed, has been reflected in curricular materials developed for use in sociology classrooms.

Inquiry teaching/learning has its theoretical foundations largely in the work of the perceptual psychologists and of educational theorists such as John Dewey, but its manifestation as applied to contemporary social studies teaching and to the social sciences in particular was stimulated to a great extent by publication of *The Process of Education* in 1960. In that short classic, Jerome Bruner laid down many of the principles that were to become the building blocks of the New Social Studies and which greatly influenced the nature of the teaching approach advocated in the curricular materials developed by the American Sociological Association for use in U.S. high schools.

The Process of Education reports findings from a 10-day conference called by the Education Committee of the National Academy of Sciences. The conference was to "examine the fundamental processes involved in imparting to young students a sense of the substance and method of science" (Bruner, viii). The four basic themes emerging from the conference were structure—as found in academic disciplines; readiness—especially as found in the work of Piaget and other developmentalists; intuition—especially as a "learned skill"; and motivation—including factors that are supportive (e.g., an exciting teacher) and those that are threatening (e.g., passive TV viewing).

These themes are of considerable importance when considering how inquiry teaching/learning has been applied to teaching the discipline of sociology. The best example of an effort to apply the principles of inquiry teaching/learning to secondary school sociology is in the materials developed by Sociological Resources for the Social Studies (SRSS), a curriculum project of the American Sociological Association, which operated from 1964–71. SRSS, with a grant from the National Science Foundation, produced a set of instructional materials (see next section of this chapter) designed to promote student inquiry while teaching good scientific sociology. In many respects, students were to take on the role of the sociologist: asking questions, forming tentative answers, examining or finding data, and drawing conclusions. In all cases, student questions were to precede those of teacher or text. The emphasis was on active student learning. The classroom was to present an open environment where students could question the workings of our society, where making mistakes was tolerated, and where teachers and students learned together.

While participating in this open inquiry–oriented environment, students were to discover the structure of the discipline of sociology, both its substance and its syntax. This effort to inquire into the structure of the discipline has led some critics to conclude that true inquiry (the free formulation of an intriguing question and the pursuit of an answer to that question unencumbered by the constraints of a discipline) could never take place. They concluded that students were simply being led down a path to predetermined conclusions through a rigid process employed in the science of sociology (Switzer and Wilson 1969, 348).

In some respects, true inquiry may not be possible within the teaching of a discipline such as sociology, for the discipline does have a structure to be conveyed and principles derived from past practice and research. The New Social Studies (and new sociology) really represented a blending of old and new with a resulting convergent form of inquiry more appropriate to inquiry within the structure of the discipline. Figure 1 displays one version of divergent and convergent teaching (Switzer 1974, 242). The model assumes that learning and interest are enhanced if students are actively involved in the learning process and that the process starts with some form of inquiry activity. With the divergent model (a more pure form of inquiry), students would move from their own problem or question (the generator of the inquiry) toward objectives that could include the discovery of new knowledge. In this case, inquiry is not constrained by predetermined outcomes. With the convergent model, the process still starts with a generator of the inquiry, but the question or problem is more likely posed by the teacher or textbook and is designed to result in the student learning some predetermined knowledge, generalization, or skill. The questions for investigation may be real questions without answers presented by teacher or textbook, and the students may be actively involved in the search for answers; but the outcome is still conditioned by the structure of the discipline being studied. This is the general form that inquiry teaching has taken when applied to the teaching of sociology at the secondary school level. Although this inquiry into the structure of the discipline may not represent pure inquiry, it allows teaching of the discipline of sociology in a form that promotes active student involvement in the teaching/learning process. Most experts agree that the teaching is more interesting and the learning is more meaningful with this approach than with expository teaching.

SOCIOLOGICAL RESOURCES

References have been made previously in this chapter to what has been called the New Social Studies and the involvement of the sociologist in the movement through a curriculum project, Sociological Resources for the Social Studies (SRSS). It is not the intent to recapitulate here the history of the New Social Studies or to present a history of SRSS. John Haas has provided an excellent

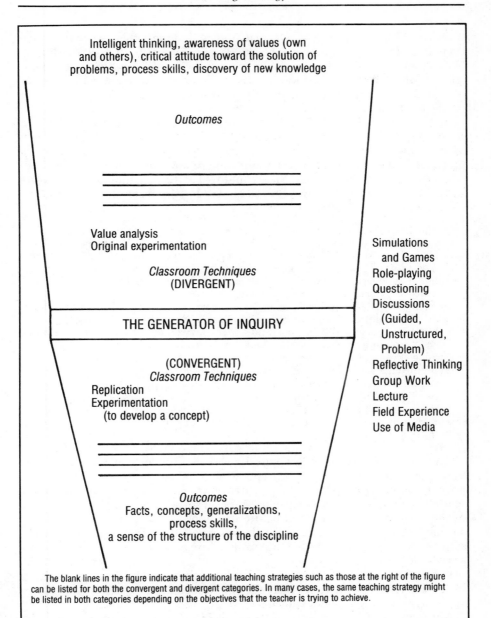

The blank lines in the figure indicate that additional teaching strategies such as those at the right of the figure can be listed for both the convergent and divergent categories. In many cases, the same teaching strategy might be listed in both categories depending on the objectives that the teacher is trying to achieve.

FIGURE 1

Intelligent thinking, awareness of values (own and others), critical attitude toward the solution of problems, process skills, discovery of new knowledge summary in his *Era of the New Social Studies,* and the activities of SRSS have been documented in various publications (Angell 1970, 1971, 1981; Haley; Switzer and Wilson). However, it is important to understand how this major effort of the American Sociological Association to produce innovative curricular materials for use in secondary school sociology courses has had an impact on the teaching of sociology, if indeed it has.

In 1962, the American Sociological Association appointed a committee to study the social studies curriculum in U.S. secondary schools. After a review of the status of the teaching of sociology at that time, the ASA submitted a proposal to the National Science Foundation to establish a curriculum project to prepare curricular materials that would reflect the best thinking of scholars and educators. The project was funded in May 1964, and continued in existence until the summer of 1971.

> One aim of the project was to introduce into existing social studies courses sociological analyses of specific topics of interest to high school students. To this end, a series of some 30 short units, called episodes, were produced, each written by a team of one sociologist and two high school teachers. The episodes have a strong inductive emphasis. Integral to each of them are exercises that require students to gather and manipulate sociological data. All the episodes are suitable for courses in social problems as well as sociology, and several are suitable for courses in economics, government, psychology, anthropology and history.
>
> A second aim was to develop a model sociology course. This too was collaboratively written by sociologists and high school teachers and strongly emphasizes learning through inquiry. It attempts to give a systematic understanding of sociology through topics of special interest to high school students.
>
> The third aim was to develop supplementary reading materials on such themes as city life and the population explosion. To this end, a series of six paperback books was produced, each containing about 20 papers based on the research of sociological experts but written in a style suitable for high school students. (Angell 1971, 310)

The initial emphasis on short episodes was an acceptance by the sociologists of the fact that if sociological concepts were to be taught in our schools, they must be infused into the ongoing curriculum. It was not likely that many schools would implement a separate course in sociology, given the persistence of the traditional curriculum structure mentioned earlier, but a one-semester sociology course was prepared for those schools that wanted to offer such a separate course. It also reflected the strong desire of the professional sociologist to present high school students with a more integrated approach to the subject than could be attained through use of the short episodes. The six supplementary paperback readers were to translate the best in sociological research into a form appropriate for high school students.

Throughout the episodes and the one–semester course, inquiry–type activities were written into the material as an integral part of the experience for students. Students were not just to read sociology; they were to do sociology. Student materials were written in such a way that it would be difficult for teachers to leave out inquiry activities. For the most part, these inquiry activities were typical of inquiry into the structure of the discipline (convergent inquiry) mentioned earlier in this chapter. There was a recurrent instructional pattern of question—data—analysis—and tentative answer, reflecting a strong inductive approach.

As was the norm with federally funded curriculum projects, after intensive trial testing and revision, the materials were let out for competitive bidding by commercial publishing houses. Only one publishing house, Allyn and Bacon, seriously considered publishing the SRSS materials and received an exclusive license to market the materials for six years.

The key question for consideration here is: What impact did these materials have on the teaching of secondary school sociology? How much did they get used? What long-term impact did they have on the nature of curricular materials available for use in sociology courses? Has the teaching of sociology changed as a result of having these models available?

It is difficult to determine the extent to which the teaching of sociology was influenced by the development and distribution of the exemplary instructional materials produced by SRSS. Most of the impact studies refer to the impact of the New Social Studies in general, with very few studies focusing specifically on sociology. Two studies conducted in the mid-1970s (Hahn, Marker, Switzer and Turner 1977) attempted to determine the percentage of high school sociology teachers who were using some of the SRSS materials in their courses. Both Turner and Switzer found that approximately 30 percent of the sociology teachers surveyed reported using some of the SRSS materials. The extent and nature of use was not considered in these studies.

Other studies conducted in the 1970s further suggest that the New Social Studies movement in general was having a desirable spin-off effect on the nature of materials produced by commercial publishers. In a study conducted for the National Science Foundation, BCMA Associates concluded that the projects had a major impact on the instructional materials developed by commercial publishers (BCMA Associates 1975, 166–167). And, in a study contrasting history books published prior to the New Social Studies movement with those marketed after the movement, Fetsko concluded that the newer commercially produced textbooks reflected the characteristics common to the New Social Studies movement more so than did the earlier textbooks.

However, as the New Social Studies movement began to decline (late 1960s and early 1970s) and the large federally funded curriculum projects began to fade from the scene, the apparent lasting impact of the New Social Studies and the new sociology also started to fade. In 1979 David Smith conducted a content analysis on widely used secondary level sociology materials existing before, during and following the reform movement with special attention to the SRSS materials. He concluded:

> The curriculum materials produced by this committee have had little lasting direct influence upon the teaching of high school sociology. The indirect influence of this project committee upon the more traditional textual materials is also negligible.
>
> The SRSS committee, like many of the new social studies projects, was a university-based alliance that did not effectively consider either the traditional function of social studies as citizenship education nor the realities of everyday life in the

classroom. This study should encourage curriculum designers to solicit more involvement from publishers, adoption personnel and classroom teachers before and during the construction of curriculum materials.

And Robert C. Angell, a past president of the American Sociological Association and the director of SRSS for most of its history, stated, "Though qualified judges pronounced the materials to be of high quality, their ultimate impact seems likely to be less than originally hoped. This would be unfortunate, since high school students would be missing the challenge of inquiry learning" (Angell 1981, 42).

Just why the SRSS project had little impact on the teaching of sociology is difficult to determine. Recommendations such as those suggested above by Smith are certainly worth considering in future curriculum design projects, but they reflect only a limited perspective on what happened to the new sociology and the New Social Studies. Irving Morrissett presents a more reasoned view of the decline of the New Social Studies.

> A few of the new materials were widely used in elementary and secondary schools, most received limited use, and some died in the pilot stage or in publishers' offices. Well before widespread dissemination could be expected or accomplished, national economic conditions, tightening school budgets, diminishing publishers profits, and lack of apparent and immediate success blunted and then stopped the thrust of the new social studies—as was also the case with "the new math" and the "new science." As of 1982, little is heard of the innovations of the 1960's and 70's.
>
> An important and neglected aspect of the decline of the new social studies is the decrease in concern for many social aspects of education. An important part of the educational reform movement of the 1960's and 1970's was an increased concern for portraying greater realism about nature and society. Value-laden issues—war, sex, economics, environment, and race—were introduced into many of the new curriculum materials, mostly in social studies. They reflected much of the concern with social problems of the broader society. With the exception of continuing and moderately effective concern for racial and sexual equity with respect to education and employment, most of these social concerns had been put on the back burner along with the new social studies. (Morrissett 1982, 8)

John Haas has also put the decline of the New Social Studies in a social context.

> The NSS began to decline as a movement during 1968, especially in the face of dire social upheaval. As it was aided by Lyndon Johnson's Great Society programs, so it was slowed by Nixon's new federalism and de-emphasis of social and educational reforms. The NSS quite accurately never expired, however, but gradually faded, and blended into other emerging interests and patterns. (Haas 1977, 78)

Switzer (1981) points to several factors contributing to the lack of impact of the new curricular materials. He cites the lack of teacher training in the new content and new teaching strategies proposed, the declining interest of professional societies when the big money grants were ended, the failure of publishing houses to fully understand the essence of the New Social Studies, and the lack of a carefully formulated dissemination plan for the new materials. He concluded that the greatest weakness of the movement was the failure to develop a comprehensive vision of the research, development, and diffusion process.

PROBLEMS IN TEACHING SOCIOLOGY

Most of the persisting problems facing the teaching of sociology today are, as might be expected, closely related to the past and have been touched on previously in this chapter. Four major persistent problems will be dealt with here.

First, the teaching of sociology will not be a major element in U.S. schools without a fundamental restructuring of how we conceive of the social studies curriculum. As stated previously, the social studies curriculum in place in our schools today still reflects the recommendations made in 1916, and it is dominated by history and political science. Despite major changes in the nature of our society, this curriculum has been amazingly resistant to change. And it does not appear that the current leadership of the social studies profession is prepared to propose major changes in this curriculum organization. A draft Scope and Sequence statement prepared by a task force of the National Council for the Social Studies (NCSS) in 1984, and currently being discussed by the NCSS membership, presents a very traditional view of social studies and continues to give little attention to the social sciences. Charles Smith points out that, without a recognized spot in the school curriculum, what does get taught from the discipline of sociology will continue to be pieced into other ongoing courses and will most likely reflect the social problems approach to sociology, instead of the more important establishment of a sociological perspective.

A second persistent problem has to do with how text materials for use in our schools are developed. There is no doubt that the great majority of teachers use a basic textbook as the principal source of information presented in the classroom. Instruction is organized around and dominated by the textbook. Textbooks are developed, however, by profit-making commercial publishing houses which must, understandably, make the pursuit of profit their primary objective. The materials marketed by these publishing houses must appeal to "what is" and not to "what ought to be." As long as the social studies curriculum in our schools continues to be dominated by history, with its traditional goal of transmission of the culture, it is unrealistic to expect commercial publishers to produce innovative, cutting-edge materials in sociology for which there is only a limited market. As noted earlier, only one commercial publisher seriously considered publishing the innovative SRSS curricular materials, and only four publishers in our recent survey published for the sociology market.

There are no easy solutions to the problem of how best to get high quality instructional materials into U.S. schools. Most experts agree that the federally funded curricular projects produced high quality instructional materials. But these materials did not have a major impact on the teaching of sociology and certainly did not have a major longstanding impact on the publishing industry. A partial answer to this lack of impact stems, of course, from the fact that when the materials were ready for large-scale distribution, they were given to a commercial publishing house that had not participated in the development of the materials, and understandably, was primarily interested in the sales aspects of the material.

Given that the great curriculum reform movement of the 1950s, 1960s, and early 1970s was not as successful as might have been hoped, there is some tendency to conclude that the federal government should not be actively involved in supporting curriculum development efforts. Quite the contrary; without federal dollars to support the development of new cutting-edge curricular materials, it is hard to see just how this would be done. Few school systems are able or inclined to mount such an effort, and the commercial publishing industry has little to gain and a lot to lose through support of too innovative curricular materials.

Good curricular materials are a necessary but not a sufficient condition for good teaching. A third persistent problem in the teaching of sociology is inadequate teacher preparation in both the discipline of sociology and in good teaching techniques appropriate for teaching sociology. Given the dominance of history and political science in the school curriculum and the fact that few teaching jobs are available strictly in sociology, few new prospective teachers pick sociology as their major area of concentration. In a study reported in 1984, Farmer asked teachers to rank in order the 10 subject areas that they felt most qualified to teach. Only 4.2 percent listed sociology as the area in which they felt most qualified, while 50.3 percent listed U.S. history, and 15.4 percent listed civics/government. At the other end of the scale, 32 percent listed sociology as their least qualified subject, whereas only 2.8 percent listed U.S. history in these categories.

There is also no reason to assume that instructors in social studies methods courses in colleges and universities are acquainting new teachers with new curricular materials and new teaching strategies. In a study of these methods instructors, it was found that the majority of them were not even aware of the existence of new curricular materials in social studies and that very few exposed their students to the new materials or used them to model instruction. (Switzer, Walker and Mitchell 1981).

For the teaching of sociology to become a more important part of U.S. education, a fourth persistent problem must be dealt with—the fundamental reason for being of K–12 education. As stated earlier in this chapter, the primary goal of K–12 education is to transmit and to perpetuate the ongoing social order. Further, the primary goal of the social studies curriculum is the development of good citizens prepared to carry on the society. The teaching of sociology, of course, can play a role in achieving this broad goal. But sociology is inherently a questioning discipline. It probes into our society and raises questions as to why things are structured the way they are and why they function as they do. It probes into areas of race and ethnicity, social class, deviant behavior, social change, and other matters that have been referred to as the "closed" areas in the social studies. Probing into these areas frequently makes parents, school administrators and school boards uneasy. Many people believe that if students inquire into these areas and are taught how to question, then they will surely challenge current ways of doing things and want to change the social order.

From this perspective, the teaching of sociology does not fit easily into the K–12 curriculum. But, one can argue, this is exactly the kind of education and teaching that is needed in a rapidly changing society where citizens are constantly asked to weigh evidence and to make decisions. In a sense, the essence of democracy and the essence of good citizenship within a democracy calls for an informed, questioning citizen who not only has a good understanding of history but also has a good understanding of our past, present and potential future societal arrangements. Achieving this, however, requires that the basic goal of K–12 education be broadened to include the development of such citizens and to encourage a place in the curriculum for the social sciences such as sociology.

REFERENCES

American Sociological Association. *Inquiries in Sociology,* 2nd ed. Boston: Allyn and Bacon, 1978.

Anderson, Lee F., and Charlotte Anderson, eds. *Windows on Our World.* Boston: Houghton Mifflin, 1976.

Angell, Robert C. "Reflections on the Project, Sociological Resources for the Social Studies." *The American Sociologist* 16 (February 1981): 41–43.

Angell, Robert C. "Sociology Instruction, Secondary Schools." In *The Encyclopedia of Education,* Volume 8, edited by Lee C. Deighton. New York: Macmillan, 1971, 308–311.

Angell Robert C. "SRSS in the Homestretch." Paper presented at the annual meeting of the American Sociological Association, Washington, DC, September 1970.

BCMA Associates. "Commercial Curriculum Development and Implementation in the United States." Pre-College Science Curriculum Activities of the National Science Foundation, Volume 11 and Appendix. Washington, DC: National Science Foundation, May 1975.

Brown, Lee, Robert Goodall and G. Thomas Baer. "The Sixties Social Studies Movement: Have Conditions Really Changed?" *The Clearing House* 55 (1981): 86–87.

Bruner, Jerome. *The Process of Education.* Cambridge, MA: Harvard University Press, 1960.

Farmer, Rod. "The Social Studies Teacher in the 80's: Report from a National Survey." *The Social Studies* 75 (July/August 1984): 166–171.

Fetsko, William. "Textbooks and the New Social Studies." *The Social Studies* 70 (March/April 1979): 51–55.

Grier, Lee W. "The History of the Teaching of Sociology in the Secondary School." Ed.D. diss. Duke University, 1971.

Haas, John. *The Era of the New Social Studies.* Boulder, CO: ERIC Clearinghouse for Social Studies/Social Science Education, 1977.

Hahn, Carole, Gerald W. Marker, Mary Jane Turner and Thomas J. Switzer. *Three Studies on Perception and Utilization of New Social Studies Materials.* Boulder, CO: Social Science Education Consortium, 1977.

Haley, Frances. "Sociological Resources for the Social Studies." *Social Education* 36 (November 1972): 765–767.

Hertzberg, Hazel W. *Social Studies Reform 1880–1980.* Boulder, CO: Social Science Education Consortium, 1981.

Lippitt, Ronald, and others. *Social Science Laboratory Units.* Chicago: Science Research Associates, 1969.

Morrissett, Irving. "Four Futures for Social Studies." Paper presented at Rethinking Social Education: A National Conference on Future Directions for Social Studies Education, Wingspread Conference Center, Wisconsin, August 1982.

National Center for Education Statistics. *A Trend Study of Offerings and Enrollments: 1972–73 and 1981–82* (Study A). Arlington, VA: Education Technologies, 1984.

National Council for the Social Studies: "In Search of a Scope and Sequence for Social Studies: Report of the National Council for the Social Studies Task Force on Scope and Sequence." Preliminary Position Statement of the Board of Directors. *Social Education* 48 (April 1984): 249–262.

Senesh, Lawrence. *Our Working World.* Chicago: Science Research Associates, 1964.

Smith, Charles W. "Sociological Insight and Imagination." *The Social Studies* 73 (September/October 1982): 203–206.

Smith, David W. "Assessing the Impact of the 'New Social Studies' upon School Curriculum: A Case Study of High School Sociology." (Ph.D. diss., Northwestern University, 1979) *Dissertation Abstracts International.* 40 (April 1980).

Smith, Frederick R., and C. Benjamin Cox. *New Strategies and Curriculum in Social Studies.* Chicago: Rand McNally, 1969.

Switzer, Thomas J. "Something Old and Something New: The Social Studies in Transition." *The High School Journal* 57 (March 1974): 240–249.

Switzer, Thomas J. "Reflections on the Fate of the New Social Studies." *Phi Delta Kappan* 62 (June 1981): 729–730.

Switzer, Thomas J., Ed Walker, and Gale Mitchell. "Undergraduate Social Studies Methods Instructors, Knowledge, and Use of New Curricular Materials." *Journal of Social Studies Research* 5 (Winter 1981): 9–18.

Switzer, Thomas J., and Everett K. Wilson. "Nobody Knows the Trouble We've Seen: Launching a High School Sociology Course." *Phi Delta Kappan* 50 (February 1969): 346–350.

Taba, A. Hilda. *Taba Social Studies Curriculum Project.* Menlo Park, CA: Addison-Wesley, 1969.

CHAPTER 11

COMING OF AGE IN ANTHROPOLOGY

Roger C. Owen

Modern anthropology has discovered the fact that human society has grown and developed everywhere in such a manner that its forms, opinions and actions have many fundamental traits in common. This momentous discovery implies that laws exist that govern the development of society; that they apply to our society as well as to those of past times and distant lands; that their knowledge will be a means to understand the causes furthering and retarding civilization; and that, guided by this knowledge, we may hope to govern our actions so that the greatest benefit to mankind will accrue from them. (Boas 1896)

"Did you see *Raiders of the Lost Ark*?" a young voice recently asked over my office phone. "I want to become an anthropologist," the caller went on, "so I can be like Indiana Jones in *Raiders of the Lost Ark*. What do I have to study so that I can do that kind of work?"

While I was heartened to speak about my field to an eager high school senior, that brief conversation gave me cause to reflect anew on the generally sorry state of precollege social science training. My young caller doubtless had a sense of how physicists, biologists, mathematicians, historians, and perhaps even economists work. He had no educational basis at all to judge whether or not that nonsensical film was really representative of how professional anthropologists spend their days. Public ignorance of the nature of anthropology brought about by the rarity of the subject in precollege curricula is to me the most pervasive challenge facing my profession now. What must we do to make anthropology an integral part of our nation's social studies curricula (Owen 1982)?

In contrast to the minimal role that anthropology plays in United States' schools, many college students have enrolled in anthropology courses and should be better prepared to judge the merits of contemporary media presentations such as *Raiders of the Lost Ark*. Introductory courses vary somewhat but all teach that anthropology (1) studies human culture, past and present, wherever it has developed; (2) has four major subfields: ethnology, archaeology, linguistics and physical anthropology; (3) is a unique blend of human biology, cross-cultural social science and the humanities, especially history, (4) is unified by a common concern with "culture" (or the social heritage of humans) in shaping behavior, language and even physical type, and (5) is practiced mainly by university-trained Ph.D.s who dedicate their careers to research and teaching.

Anthropology began to assume its present form around the beginning of this century, when Franz Boas, a German trained in the physical sciences, organized a department of anthropology at Columbia University. Here for more than 40 years, he educated and influenced many future greats in the field—Ruth Benedict, A.L. Kroeber, Margaret Mead, Melville Herskovits, to name a few. As the 1930s began, anthropological training was limited to aproximately a half dozen United States universities: Columbia, California (Berkeley), Chicago, Harvard, Yale and Pennsylvania. Students were required to be proficient in the four subdisciplines, to do original field research, and to write and usually to publish a doctoral dissertation. National meetings were attended by only a few hundred old friends and colleagues, all of whom not only knew each other but also knew what everyone else knew. Anthropology had many of the characteristics of a "folk" society as defined by Robert Redfield: small, isolated, homogeneous.

After World War II, returning soldiers by the thousands, many now familiar with foreign peoples and places, and possessed of the G.I. Bill of Rights, matriculated in the burgeoning colleges and universities. Very few of them knew of anthropology but, when freshman English classes closed, and physics, chemistry and biology required Saturday labs, more and more students wandered over to the registration desks with short lines in front of them. One of these was always anthropology.

Our subject matter was usually exotic people in exotic times or places (including modern Americans known to many as the "Nacirema"), generally romantically interesting (monkeys, pyramids, the alphabet, cannibalism, sex and marriage, "lost" continents, human sacrifice, and much more), and usually not especially demanding conceptually. This mix of subject matter, when combined with a few documentary films, personal fieldwork slides and anecdotes presented by the counterculture critics that many anthropologists believed themselves to be, ensnared students by the thousands. Today, there are nearly 10,000 anthropologists worldwide. Almost 6500 anthropologists are full-time teachers in over 500 U.S. colleges and universities; nearly 1,000,000 students enroll in our courses annually.

During the past 50 years, anthropology has undergone intense specialization as to topic and region. Today one might study diet or ritual, New Guinea wood carvings or blood proteins, chimpanzee communication or Inuit (Eskimo) grammar, the early Pleistocene ("Ice Age") in East Africa or a town's garbage dump. In fact, any topic relevent to human existence is fair game. Each topic and world region has its anthropological devotees, its own professional organization and probably its own specialized journal.

The annual national meeting of the American Anthropological Association today attracts 10,000 or more professionals and students, who may deliver more than 1,000 research papers on specialized topics. Most anthropologists can be acquainted with the work of only a relative handful of their national and international colleagues. Professional anthropology, no longer a folk society, has evolved to resemble more closely a transnational corporation with branches, affiliates and personnel worldwide; however, unfortunately, it is sadly lacking in working capital.

TYPES OF ANTHROPOLOGISTS

There are dozens of types of anthropologists and the number of specialties is growing rapidly. The basic division is that between physical and cultural anthropology, the latter including ethnology, ethnography, archaeology and linguistics.

Physical Anthropology

Physical anthropology poses two basic research questions: (1) What has been the course of human evolution? (2) What is the nature and significance of human physical variation?

Paleo-anthropologists, of whom the Leakeys—Louis, Mary, and Richard—are the most famous, study the course of human evolution. These scholars seek and analyze fossil remains of our ancient ancestors. When successful, they attempt to reconstruct the world in which the creatures lived. Their research often requires them to work in concert with paleontologists, climatologists, geologists, geochronologists and others. Despite being scarcely more then 100 years old, paleo-anthropology has achieved remarkable scientific maturity: it has outlined the major steps in human evolution for the past sixty million years.

The scientific study of human variation is older than paleo-anthropology, having interested the Greeks and Romans. An influential racial classification was published as long ago as 1775 by J.F. Blumenbach. In the contemporary study of human variation, researchers focus on its genetic basis as well as on the influence of evolution and culture in affecting human physical features; for example, the shape and form of our bodies, our skin texture and color, or blood groups and their distributions. Because of their expertise in human osteology and anatomy, especially concerning deceased remains, physical anthropologists sometimes become involved in forensic or legal matters. In 1985, one was a member of the team of scientists called to Brazil to study a burial that was thought to be that of a fugitive Nazi, Joseph Mengele.

During the past two decades, many physical anthropologists have come to specialize in the study of nonhuman primates. Jane Goodall's study of wild chimpanzees has received the most public notice, but many other primatologists have extensively studied other forms, including gorillas, chimpanzees, orang-utans and gibbons, as well as dozens of varieties of monkeys, both in the animals' native habitats and in primate research centers.

Cultural Anthropology

Ethnology and Ethnography. At the core of anthropology is ethnology, the systematic comparative analysis of sociocultural data on ethnic groups, present and past.

The data base for ethnology is drawn from the work of ethnographers, specialists who study living people by residing with them and participating in their lives usually for a year or more. Ethnographers generally learn the language of the people they study, take a census, and collect copious notes on most aspects of everyday sociocultural life. Their formal concerns include kinship and genealogical characteristics; socioeconomic activities; the material world; political structure and conflict resolution; religious beliefs and organization; the thought and dream world; and ecological relationships. Margaret Mead was ethnography's most famous practitioner during the mid-20th century.

The primary task of ethnographers is to attempt intellectually to enter behind the eyes and into the minds of their hosts and thus look out with them and share their vision of the universe. By this means ethnographers hope not only to discover the cultural directives to which their informants customarily respond, but also to lower or eliminate their own cultural biases.

In ethnography this search for the hosts' own understandings of their activities is referred to as the *emic* approach. If successful, an emic investigation may provide to the ethnographer a figurative cultural map employed by the society's members in dealing with everyday life. Simultaneously, the ethnographer, as foreigner and scientist, makes his or her own informed judgments as to what transpires. This level of analysis is referred to as the *etic*. For example, if one is told that a comatose man was possessed of a demon (a rather common belief worldwide) at the emic level, a blood sugar test (etic level) might indicate that diabetes was responsible for the person's condition. Good ethnography consists of a careful weaving together of both in order to understand the culture's adaptive system.

Most ethnographers also work through memory culture, or the recollective history of the people they live with, often an unreliable source of information. But for most of the world's tribal people, who usually lack written records, recollections provide the best available window through which to see into their past. Life histories, autobiographical accounts given by informants, are one good source of data, especially when correlated with genealogies, archaeological data and such historical data as may exist in neighboring societies.

Two specialized kinds of ethnologists are the ethnohistorian and the cross-culturist. Ethnohistorians rely heavily upon documentary resources and have much in common with historians, but with an important difference: historians have traditionally been concerned with the "big traditions" of our complex civilizations. On the other hand, ethnohistorians emphasize the "little traditions" of tribal people who formerly occupied so much of the world's surface but who came under colonial control during the past few hundred years.

Cross-cultural researchers rely upon the wealth of ethnographic data now in existence in order to test hypotheses regarding cultural variations and uniformities. Why, for example, do some cultures practice segregation of females, or scarify boys, or engage in pre-emptive warfare? Cross-culturists seek preliminary answers to questions like these, and many others, by reference to the existing ethnographic data in order to search statistically for possible correlations and other relationships between variables tested.

Archaeology. Today it is widely known that archaeologists excavate in the ground to uncover remains of past cultures. By this means, they attempt to obtain a record for the past million or more years of the world's nonliterate cultures. Archaeologists, thus, are responsible for telling the human story for over 99 percent of its duration and also for most of its tangled global route.

In their research, archaeologists commonly excavate on locations (sites) believed to harbor cultural remains located either by regional surveys or by consulting local experts. Artifacts (tools) and features (complex remains including architecture and burials) are carefully identified, mapped, and preserved for laboratory analysis. For every day spent excavating, a week or more of work in the laboratory may ensue. To maximize information recovery, archaeologists collaborate with many other scientists including geologists, chemists, geochronologists, botanists, and, for ethnographic comparisons, with ethnologists. As local site reports have increased in number, regional integrations have become possible, and today an outline of the prehistory of Earth has been written.

Linguistics. In the opinion of most anthropologists, the creation and use of language is the primary basis upon which the human adaptation rests. The study of language, begun by the ancient Greeks, Romans and Hindus, began to flower in 18th- and 19th-century Europe quite apart from those intellectual developments that would lead to anthropology. During the late 19th century, anthropologists joined the investigation and began to study and to classify tribal languages. Linguistics received a great boost when, during the 20th century, following the work of Boas and the British ethnographer Malinowski, the use of native languages became mandatory for ethnographers. Hundreds of previously unwritten languages were recorded in notebooks, thus making available to linguistic scholars a great wealth of data. The collecting of other linguistic material continues.

Descriptive linguists record speech by using an international phonetic alphabet that permits any spoken sound to be given a written symbol. These recordings are then analyzed for three structural elements common to all languages: significant signaling units (phonemes), meaning units (morphemes), and rules of arrangement (grammar). Descriptions of specific languages, when published, permit comparison with other described languages in order to establish similarities and possible relationships.

Historical linguistics examines the genetic relationships of described languages in order to study the history and change in language clusters. Languages that can be shown to be related to each other—English and German, for example—are grouped into families, and related families are then placed into *phyla*. The Germanic family, to which English belongs, is a member of the Indo-European phylum, one of about 40 phyla into which linguists have been able to group the world's thousands of languages. Other Indo-European languages, which are more distant relatives of English than German, include Indo-Iranian, Balto-Slavic, Greek, Albanian, Armenian, Romanic and Celtic. It is possible that all languages ultimately stem from one source, but we may never possess the means to know whether that is true.

Other linguistic specialists investigate how language is acquired by humans. Despite the great differences among languages, all possess certain structural features, such as actors, actions and descriptive terms. This has led Noam Chomsky, a leading linguistic theorist, to propose that basic language rules are inborn and part of our evolutionary, biologically based heritage.

Other linguists devote themselves to the study of the social functions served by language. Regional, class, gender and other dialects exist in all societies. Once learned, one's dialect becomes a mark of social membership. For example, in British society if you learn and speak the Cockney dialect, you can be marked for life as a member of the working class, unless, of course, good luck brings along a Professor Higgins.

Proxemics, the study of communication through space utilization and body movement, is yet another research interest of linguists. Edward T. Hall, in *The Silent Language* (1959), suggested that each culture teaches its members non-verbal means of communication: gestures, body position and movement, and others. The gestures one can make, whom one can touch and where, as well as the kind of regular body movements permitted, vary not only from one culture to another, but also by social categories within each culture. In the United States, anyone who fails to learn our proxemic "grammar," and persistently touches the wrong people the wrong way—pinching for example—might not only get a slap in the face but could even go to jail.

MAJOR PROPOSITIONS IN ANTHROPOLOGY

What would anthropologists want high school graduates to know about anthropology if the subject were well taught at the precollege level? As of the late 20th century, here are some of the cornerstones of the field.

Proposition 1. Anthropologists believe that the human species and human culture have evolved during the past several million years from earlier, simpler forms in response to natural processes that still operate.

Anthropology began its search for general theory in the 19th century with the speculative comparative method and general evolutionism of Herbert Spencer, Charles Darwin, Edward B. Tylor, Lewis Henry Morgan and others. Although empirically impoverished and often misguided methodologically, these 19th century intellectual giants produced major achievements. Today, new insights gained from research in human paleontology, archaeology, and studies of primates, as well as field research with recently surviving simple societies, provide many anthropologists with a more solid platform from which to speak of the past.

Experts in the field believe that our species, *Homo sapiens sapiens*, has evolved during the past four million years from earlier primate forms: *Homo sapiens neandertalensis, Homo erectus* and *Homo habilis (Australopithicus)*. They point out that, intertwined and simultaneous with physical evolution, shared human sociocultural behavioral characteristics began and grew: speech and language; tools; food-getting skills; social forms (probably including an incest taboo, kinship behaviors and specialized terms for relatives); belief in spirits and other supernatural forces; storytelling, song, and dance; and all the other cultural attributes that make us human. Prominent among these attributes are love, compassion, tolerance, dislike, hatred, violence and ambition.

These earliest cultural forms were developed in socially simple foraging societies of 50 or so people who obtained their livelihood by collecting plant and animal foods from their environment in ever more skillful ways. Scholars now refer variously to these kinds of societies as either hunters and gatherers or as bands. Band people, after a million years or more of existence, came to fill the habitable world about 12,000 years ago, when North America was first occupied by them.

Shortly thereafter, about 10,000 years ago, some band people began the climb to civilization when they started to cultivate plants in order to grow their own food. This appears to have occurred independently at about the same time in several places: Egypt and the Tigris-Euphrates drainage of the Near East, Southeast Asia, Central America, South America, and perhaps elsewhere. By investing their bodily energy through laboring in their fields, the people captured the far greater energy of the sun as well as the chemical power of the soil. They came to reap harvests on a predictable basis. Villages grew near the fields, population aggregates increased in size, and the first farmers became progressively more sedentary. A major revolution had evolved.

Possessed now of a sense of control gained by their growing knowledge of plants plus their ability to predict their food supply to a degree that hunters and gatherers had been unable to do, they could program their yields not only to supply themselves, but also to produce sufficient harvest so that an expanding number of domestic animals could also be fed. This adaptation is known as the horticultural or tribal stage of sociocultural evolution.

Band and tribal adaptations, few if any of which will survive the 20th century, lasted for a million years or more. They were among humankind's most enduring adaptations. Most of the structural features of our contemporary complex modern states, which are popularly supposed to be responses to ancient "human nature," were largely unknown on our planet until a few thousand years ago. These features include authoritarian political control, war and exploitive economic competition, as well as such social institutions as government, the military and churches.

Gradually some tribal societies came to control larger habitats, either by social, economic or military means. As the basis of sociality shifted from family to territory, some groups came to have facilities and power that others lacked. These privileged people formed the basis of the next stage of sociocultural integration: chiefdoms. Central to chiefdoms was some institutionalized inequality of membership, virtually unknown in tribes and bands. Big Men or chiefs were often the heads of powerful kinship groups with access to wealth. Redistribution of wealth was an expected function of the chiefs, who often lacked any real power to coerce other societal members to do their bidding. As some kinship groups accumulated wealth and prestige, their power grew. Territorial expansion over weaker neighbors was one common expression of this power, often motivated by a desire to ensure an ever-increasing need for food and other items for the privileged. As population pressure grew in some ancient chiefdoms, more efficient agricultural practices emerged, including irrigation, terracing and fertilization. Control of terrain and regional water resources became mandatory, and some expansionistic chiefdoms grew into proto-states. With this step, the cultural cornucopia from which our urban-industrial societies would flow was undammed.

In the mid-20th century, Leslie White, Julian Steward, Elman Service, Marshall Sahlins and many others have provided new and effective theory for understanding cultural growth and change. Anthropologists study "specific" evolution, that of specific cultures, as well as the intertwined and complementary process of overall or general cultural evolution.

Specific evolution operates locally on cultures, often independently of general evolutionary trends. General evolution refers to the accumulated specific changes that have occurred in all cultures. The results of general evolution have been (1) to bring about an ever-greater control of energy sources by humans, (2) to foster an ever-increasing complexity within cultural and social forms, and (3) to grant an ever-increasing capacity to manipulate the environment. General evolution has now joined all specific evolutionary traditions into an interdependent system of a few evolving global subsystems.

Perhaps the overriding cultural trend in operation today is modernization, which, for the most part, is often synonymous with Westernization. Western culture, often modern U.S. culture, has penetrated into every corner of the globe. Although modernization has often been imposed on the weak by the strong, it may also happen as a result of simple accident or through efforts of a receiving culture to obtain what it perceives as useful or advantageous. Members of traditional cultures often warmly accept and even seek foreign items such as guns, alcoholic beverages, medicines, foods, technological novelties and sometimes even new gods.

Interpenetration of a specific culture by others has been a normal occurrence since chiefdom times. Contemporary intercultural penetration is sometimes trivialized by its critics, who refer to it as producing Coca-Cola cultures or banana Marxism, but the results are not trivial. If we note but one donation of the Western world to less developed nations, the so-called Green Revolution, brought about by an often well-intentioned introduction of Western agricultural innovations to traditional economies, we can gauge the probable magnitude of future interventions. Thus, new food stuffs have fueled the greatest population explosion in human history. Simply in order to nurture their growing populations, whose growth is further accelerated by Western medical technology, many of the world's surviving traditional societies must adopt totally new economic and social philosophies, a requisite that will bring about changes in every sector of their cultural existence.

Proposition 2. The range of human cultural potential appears to be shared equally by all normal human societies, as well as by members of both sexes.

Exhaustive research by anthropologists for the past 100 years seeking to find significant variations in cultural capacity between human populations has disclosed no significant or major differences. In all important ways (linguistic, intellectual, sensory, artistic, mechanical, etc.), all normal human populations appear to share the same range of variation with respect to the capacity to speak, to think, to see, to create and to manipulate the environment. This conclusion regarding the apparent equality of cultural capacity of all human populations has been reached notwithstanding some acceptance in the early days by some anthropologists of existing notions of superior and inferior races. Research into the question continues.

Some of the earliest gender-behavioral research was done by Margaret Mead in the early 1930s, when she began to challenge the notion that "biology is destiny." Her work among Pacific islanders called to question the common acceptance of inherent male/female gender roles, when her ethnographic data indicated that gender roles varied sharply from culture to culture. More recently, anthropologists have been in the forefront of examining gender differences cross-culturally. Research results are similar to those achieved with respect to race: in most or all capacities that are culturally important, men and women are remarkably alike—any significant intellectual act that some men can perform, some women also can perform.

Proposition 3. Human behavior is not mandated by inborn biological imperatives; cultural learning is the major factor in determining human action.

Too often our actions are explained away popularly as being due simply to the operation of "human nature" or of instincts comparable to those possessed by homing pigeons, or by the territorially combative Siamese fighting fish, or by the natal stream-seeking salmonids. Were our human species possessed of such inborn behavioral directives, some human actions would have to be exhibited by all appropriate normal members of our species.

Commonly proposed as human instincts are ones with such labels as maternal, survival, acquisitive, territorial, reproductive or aggressive. But, if there is a maternal instinct in our species—that is, a biological directive that urges all females to reproduce—the "pill" and other effective contraceptives must have brought about a mutation in female genes. More and more otherwise normal women are choosing not to have babies.

There are many cultural rebuttals to the proposal that survival is an instinct which motivates all humans all the time. Cultural directives sometimes tell some societal members to seek their deaths. In the 19th century, Native American Sioux warriors, either because of some social embarrassment or simply because a vision or dream convinced them that their destiny was at hand, would vow to die at the next opportunity they had. And they did. In World War II, over 5000 Japanese joined the "Divine Wind" pilots, or *Kamikazes,* and flew their explosives-laden planes into United States warships. Today, in the Middle East, there seems to be no lack of Shiite Moslem youth willing to volunteer to ride to eternity in a four-wheeled political statement.

Cultural directives tell individuals what to do in nearly every circumstance likely to arise. These directives vary from one culture to another and thus defy simplistic biological explanations. Clifford Geertz, a leading anthropological ethnographer and theorist, makes the point in this manner:

> Men without culture would not be the clever savages of Golding's *Lord of the Flies* thrown back upon the cruel wisdom of their animal instincts. . . . They would be unworkable monstrosities . . . mental basket cases. (Geertz 1968, 152)

Proposition 4. Human cultures differ because of their particular history and ecology, but all possess similar structural and functional form.

In the early part of this century, Clark Wissler, drawing upon his wide ethnographic knowledge, proposed that all cultures possessed a set of core features. He believed that this universal pattern, which tended to give common form to all cultures, included speech, material traits, art, knowledge, society, property, government and war. We know now that most bands tend not to practice war or to permit private ownership of territory or scarce resources.

Later, a British "functionalist," Radcliffe-Brown, put forward a simpler, yet more inclusive, set of universal principles underlying sociocultural adaptation. They are (1) the ecological, or the ways in which the system interacts with the physical environment; (2) the social-structural, or the means developed to maintain an orderly and predictable social life; and (3) the mental, or ideological characteristics that provide a rationale for their ecological and social relationships.

Ethnographic research has shown that all cultures, from simple band societies of foraging people (now nearly extinct) to huge urban industrial states, possess highly symbolic, historically derived, ecologically relevent, ideological charters, often religious in nature, which define for the members a moral and ethical universe: good and evil, desirable and undesirable, possible or impossible. A good example of portions of a symbolic charter may be heard in the national hymns of the United States: "The Star-Spangled Banner," "God Bless America," and "America, the Beautiful." One need never read history, nor travel to Kansas, nor study the Bill of Rights to know what the United States, ideally, is devoted to. Just sing the songs; the younger the singer, the better for the system.

Families, often consisting of enduring collectives of several generations, shape new members to meet traditional expectations. Family ties initially organize individual actions but, as societies become more complex, other institutions such as clubs, schools, churches, industries and the military take over much of this function. The needs of these institutions come to override those of individuals and families and to give differential shape to the actions within their society's boundaries. As Marvin Harris puts it,

> cultures on the whole have evolved along parallel and convergent paths which are highly predictable from a knowledge of the processes of production, reproduction, intensification, and depletion. . . . Free will and moral choice have had virtually no significant effect upon the directions thus far taken by evolving systems of social life. (Harris 1977, xii)

Proposition 5. Human development and behavior can be carefully examined through the use of the statistical cross-cultural method.

"What is it to be human?" is perhaps the most pressing question before the members of our species. Were we created to be Jews or Christians, Moslems or animists? Are we to be capitalists, or socialists, or anarchists, or nihilists? Must we love and hate, create and destroy, dominate and submit? What is our potential? Is there somewhere we must go?

For the first time in human history, an "oracle" exists of which one may ask such questions. Data derived from the thousands of ethnographies compiled by scientists of U.S., British, French, and other national backgrounds have been collected into a single research resource. Named the Human Relations Area Files (HRAF), begun in 1937 at Yale University by George Peter Murdock and now widely available in university libraries, it contains ethnographic data on over 1200 world cultures. Its photoduplicates of published ethnographic sources as well as copies of other available descriptive materials, such as often obscure or rare documents and unpublished diaries, are organized under 88 standard anthropological categories.

By consulting HRAF, a researcher may make a bibliographic study of a single culture in greater depth than all but the finest research libraries would permit. Or one can examine a sample of cultures—those of tropical Southeast Asia and of tropical Central Africa, perhaps—in order to detect and explain similarities and differences. A great value of HRAF is that its availability and organizational format permit bibliographic research to be done in a fraction of the time it formerly would have taken.

There are many definitions of human nature but one particularly useful one is that contained within the etic premise: We are what we do. HRAF contains what may be the best promise for research into the worldwide range of actual human practices before the spread of modernization brings increasing homogeneity to most of the globe. A majority of the cultures described in the HRAF files are either extinct or greatly changed, so we are unlikely ever to possess better data about them. One completed project of general interest is described in *Sexual Practices: The Story of Human Sexuality,* a book in which the author nonjudgmentally presents the range of variation worldwide for one of humankinds favorite activities (Gregersen 1983).

Proposition 6. Anthropology is a humane science: its goal is to understand human development without reference to preconceived moral, ethical, aesthetic, or ideological convictions so as to enable humankind to reach its full potential, whatever that may be.

Anthropology cut its teeth on the study of conquered and oppressed tribal societies. Because participant observation, the ethnographer's mandated research technique, requires living closely with the people studied, as well as the adoption of a life-style consistent with the expectations of one's hosts, tough-minded research scientists have often come to know better than any other outsiders the problems experienced by the people they have studied. Most anthropologists are without economic or political resources to permit intervention in the course of events; however, intimate association with oppressed, underprivileged and exploited social segments has led to a profession-wide concern for the fate not only of tribal and former tribal people but of all humankind.

Imbued with the conviction that all cultures can represent valuable solutions to human problems (just as each species of life possesses valuable irreplaceable DNA), anthropologists cherish cultural variation and tend to fear the homogenization brought about when developed states engulf less complex societies. This attitude of esteem for the appreciation of cultural diversity is a key ingredient of cultural relativism. Relativists must view all specific evolutionary developments nonjudgmentally, regardless of personal feelings. For example, one may learn from and even esteem the long-enduring, if ended, band adaptation of the !Kung Bushmen of the Kalahari. On the other hand, the brief but significant adaptations fostered by Hitler and Stalin, however brutal and abhorrent, are of no less intrinsic interest. It is important to note, however, that both Hitlerism and Stalinism were eradicated or modified by the concerted efforts of people who opposed the inhumane character of those despots. Thus, the general response to these specific developments was to change them.

Cannot anthropologists, then, with their humane concern and understanding of cultural processes, achieve solutions to widespread contemporary human suffering, such as that brought about by the current worldwide food shortage? Are there not insights that anthropologists, through their sense of humaneness, might provide that would help? Such questions are difficult to answer. If we could know the route of future cultural evolution, then anthropologists might be able to smooth the road, perhaps even to shorten it. However, anthropology, of necessity, is dedicated to research; and so far it has developed few understandings that would permit widespread application and guaranteed success. As scientists, anthropologists know few laws. And, even if they could elaborate on means to achieve humane ends, how many people would listen to them? Many of the world's political systems are in the hands of demagogues devoted mainly to chauvinism, provincialism and militarism, as well as to perpetuating their power. Few, if any, are ready to begin to consider social science solutions to economic, ideological, ethnic and racial confrontations which underlie most of the social problems of our globe.

PERSISTENT QUESTIONS

Anthropology has a core of shared premises but, on the other hand, a number of controversies exist still. Key questions include:

Question 1. Is anthropology a science, a humanity, or both? Most anthropologists insist upon the empirical, inductive methods of the "harder" sciences that search for causes and natural laws. Others insist that deduction and even intuition are legitimate tools in an interpretive humanistic, holistic anthropology. Scientists seek major hypotheses that will explain both general and specific events, past and present. Humanists utilize personalized interpretations that may prove to be highly individualized and non–replicable, to be derived from the context of analysis rather than from general comparative theory. Characteristic of the scientific position, specifically that of cultural materialism, is the work of Marvin Harris; Clifford Geertz, on the other hand, represents the search for a more humanistic science. The former seeks explanation, the latter understanding. There is need for both.

Question 2. Do the subdisciplines of anthropology possess a sufficient shared core to hold themselves together as a single scientific discipline?

Commitment to the use of the concept *culture,* as well as to the cross–cultural method, not only unites anthropologists but also differentiates them from researchers in allied fields such as sociology, history or biology. Most anthropologists, regardless of specialization, can talk to each other on some common ground most of the time. Nonetheless, due more to the exigencies of survival and success within the academic environment than to any basic philosophical differences, some universities have established separate human biology and archaeology programs; and many have separate departments of linguistics. The problem of the relationships between the subdisciplines of anthropology continues to exist.

Question 3. Is it not true that anthropology is a product of colonialism and capitalism and is fairly characterized as the science of "white people studying oppressed colored people"?

That hurts, but the question is a justifiable one. In Great Britain and the United States—leaders in the establishment of anthropology—the earliest field studies that their scholars conducted were of conquered or colonial people. The British focused on Africa, Australia, and other of their then colonial areas; the United States' anthropologists emphasized the study of Native Americans and Filipinos. As more and more formerly preliterate people entered the world of their former conquerors, some took up a cudgel against anthropologists, their former friends. They believe that anthropologists, who spent many years studying them and, admittedly, personally profited in their careers by so doing, should now be of help in alleviating their current social problems. They are usually unaware that anthropology currently is primarily a research science, not an applied one. Thus, a recent "Nova" production on television, "Papua New Guinea, Anthropology on Trial," presented a very hostile one-sided view of this issue. The other side of the coin is indicated by the fact that hundreds of anthropologists are of Third World background, often dedicating themselves to the study of their own people. Perhaps best known of these was Jomo Kenyatta, Kenya's first president.

In 1972, a group of anthropologists founded Cultural Survival, Inc., a private corporation located in Cambridge, Massachusetts. It is dedicated to mobilizing assistance for endangered cultures. A similar agency, Survival International, was founded in London. Sometimes called the "conscience of anthropology," these organizations raise funds for and increase public awareness of band and tribal people threatened anywhere on the globe.

Question 4. Is it not true that as the tribal people of the world disappear, anthropology will wither up and die?

Not likely! Anthropology is concerned with far more than the study of tribal people. Ethnic groups now deserve the most serious and careful attention. Every nation on this planet is multicultural. Even such an apparently homogeneous land as Japan has an important ethnic population of Koreans, a remnant population of its native Ainu people, a hereditary outcaste group (Eta), plus outlanders such as Iwo Jimans and others. The Russians have their Ukrainians (and many more), the Swedes have their Laplanders, the French have their Corsicans, the English have their Irish, and the United States has an increasing number of Hispanic-Americans.

Indeed, the United States, once dedicated to the melting pot concept, has ethnic minorities increasing both in variety and in number. Native Americans, for example, who once were expected either to die out or to be assimilated, now number nearly two million, perhaps double the number that Columbus encountered in 1492. India alone has 15 major language groups divided into a variety of dialects, dozens of regional cultures, at least 20 important religious populations, and numerous local castes with varied customs. Cultural diversity is not going to disappear in the foreseeable future.

If leaders of countries are to establish the peace and harmony, internal and external, upon which political stability and cultural growth rest, then they must come to grips with the problems associated not only with multiethnic societies, but also with a world filled with billions of people who respond to different symbol systems. "Death before dishonor" has a thousand faces around the world, and tensions among peoples are worldwide. Anthropologists are uniquely positioned to work dispassionately to understand and to attempt to alleviate the conflict which results so often when different worlds meet.

National leaders, as well as the people who put and keep them in power, whether by vote or force, must soon realize that despotism, oppression, suppression, violence, terror and armed conflict breed instability. There must be alternative ways of viewing human relationships other than those that the 20th century has witnessed in application to Armenians, Jews, Tibetans, Vietnamese, Afghanistanis, people of South Africa and so many others. If the leading citizens of modern states were as familiar with the forces underlying sociocultural evolution as they are with the Periodic Table, the writings of Shakespeare, or the teachings of Karl Marx, perhaps they could appreciate the fact that there must be other ways. As Franz Boas noted nearly 100 years ago: If only we will become cognizant of the ways in which societies operate, then ". . . we may hope to govern our actions so that the greatest benefit to mankind will accrue from them."

REFERENCES

Boas, Franz. "The Limitations of the Comparative Method of Anthropology." (1896). In Franz Boas, *Race, Language and Culture*. New York: Macmillan, 1940, 270–280.

Geertz, Clifford. "The Concept Culture and the Concept Man." *Social Education* 32(February 1968): 147–152, 166.

Gregersen, Edgar. *Sexual Practices: the Story of Human Sexuality*. New York: Franklin Watts, 1983.

Harris, Marvin. *Cannibals and Kings: the Origins of Cultures*. New York: Random House, 1977.

Murdock, George Peter. *Outline of Cultural Materials*. 3rd rev. ed. New Haven: Human Relations Area Files (Co-author with C.S. Ford, A.E. Hudson, R. Kennedy, L.W. Simmons and J.W.M. Whiting, 1950).

CHAPTER 12

TRENDS IN PRECOLLEGIATE ANTHROPOLOGY

Thomas L. Dynneson

Although the concepts and methods of anthropology have been applied to the study of educational problems since before the beginning of the 20th century, the teaching of anthropology in the schools is a relatively recent phenomenon. Most of the recognition that precollegiate anthropology has received came in the 1960s with the advent of the New Social Studies movement. During the 1960s and 1970s, the social sciences gained the attention of social studies educators to the extent that new programs were added to the school curriculum.

PRECOLLEGIATE ANTHROPOLOGY EMERGES

Precollegiate anthropology emerged during the period from 1935 to 1985. Within this span of time we are able to identify three periods of development that have contributed to precollegiate anthropology.

1935 to 1957

It is difficult to state that precollegiate anthropology began on a specific day or year, for it was an inauspicious beginning without fanfare or great notoriety. It was the beginning of a recognition of something that always had been present but without a distinction of its own. Some social studies teachers began to teach or include anthropological materials in their courses following World War II because of the interest that had been aroused in non-Western cultures and peoples as a result of magazine articles and newsreel stories about exotic places. It was pointed out:

> Both teachers and students felt called upon to try to come to terms, not only with the West, as they had in the past, but also with the great non-Western nations and high cultures and with the smaller societies then emerging from the dissolving colonial empires. Existing social studies curricula provided few tools for this purpose. The hope was that anthropology would help supply the tools. (Fallers 1968, 105)

Despite the initial interest, anthropology did not find enough support among educators and the general public to lead to the development of textbook materials for teaching anthropology. With the exception of a few independent cases in which individual teachers began to develop their own materials for lessons, units and courses, anthropology was mainly excluded from the curriculum.

History, civics, geography and other courses had developed a tradition of support from professional societies such as the American Historical Association. History had been an important social studies subject before the American Historical Association was founded in 1884. It seems that anthropologists were slow in having their discipline included in the public schools. Jules Henry was one of the earliest anthropologists to consider teaching anthropology in the public schools. In 1939 he proposed its introduction as either a supplemental part of the current curriculum or as a separate course of study similar to the courses that were taught in colleges and universities. In 1955, E. Adamson Hoebel expressed doubt that anthropology would ever become part of the public school curriculum, and, if it did, he thought that it would play only a minor role when compared to history, geography and the other standard subjects.

During this same period, colleges and universities were adding anthropology faculty and departments. College students began to enroll in these courses as degree majors or minors, while some students took anthropology courses on an elective basis. Prospective teachers usually did not find anthropology on the list of approved courses for elementary or secondary teaching. Despite this limitation, anthropology began to attract a number of students who eventually would become social studies teachers and who would be more likely to include anthropology in their established social studies courses.

In the 1950s, educational literature began to report instances in which individual teachers had developed instructional materials or courses that included anthropological concepts and activities. Anthropology courses were treated as a sort of curriculum oddity that aroused the curiosity of teachers and educators who were looking for fresh ideas that might appeal to students. In 1957 Hayden reported on his 5th grade class that "took a crack" at anthropology. But most classroom teachers were not willing to teach subject matter unfamiliar to them. This was especially true when the subject was not identified as suitable for precollegiate students, or was considered a subject in which teachers had no formal college course work. Some felt that anthropology might cause controversy because of evolutionary theory or because of the implications of subject matter when viewed in the light of the dominant culture. Thus:

> Experimental courses for the precollegiate level of instruction were difficult to organize. This was due mainly to the lack of teaching materials designed for elementary or secondary schools. In addition to this complication, there were no guidelines to help teachers design units or courses of instruction in anthropology. Each teacher had to improvise a course based upon his or her own experiences. (Dynneson 1981, 304)

1957 to 1972

After 1957, federal support for curriculum reform and revision affected the social studies by promoting the teaching of the social sciences. Congress moved to create agencies through which funds could be channeled to revitalize the mathematics and science curricula. Private funds also became available to develop educational programs. Large sums, both public and private, were used to overcome the perceived weakness in the existing curricula.

During the New Social Studies curriculum movement of the late 1950s and 1960s, six social studies curriculum projects made significant use of anthropology:

- Anthropology Curriculum Project (ACP)
- Man: A Course of Study/Education Development Center (MACOS/EDC)
- Anthropology Curriculum Study Project (ACSP)
- Materials and Activities for Teachers and Children (MATCH)
- Project Social Studies/University of Minnesota
- High School Geography Project

Three of these curriculum projects developed materials that were organized around a specific anthropological orientation. They were the Anthropology Curriculum Project; *Man: A Course of Study,* developed by the Education Development Center; and the Anthropology Curriculum Study Project.

Anthropology Curriculum Project

The Anthropology Curriculum Project was funded in 1961 by the U.S. Office of Education. Located in the Social Science Education Department of the School of Education at the University of Georgia, it was directed by Professor Marion J. Rice, a social science educator, and anthropologist Wilfrid C. Bailey. As a result of this project, materials in anthropology were developed reflecting a cross-cultural perspective on human behavior. Two types of materials were developed in an experimental form: a sequential set of materials for grades K–7, and some junior and senior high materials that were outside the sequential program to meet some special instructional needs. All these materials were designed as self-contained units of study to supplement existing social studies programs. Although the materials were widely disseminated in the 1970s, they were never published commercially.

Man: A Course of Study (Education Development Center)

The Education Development Center was founded in 1958 as the result of a grant by the National Science Foundation. It was directed by Peter Dow and located in Cambridge, Massachusetts. *Man: A Course of Study* was developed as an upper-elementary/middle school course focusing on the life cycles of animal and man. Among the outstanding scholars and educators associated with the design and development of this course were Jerome Bruner, Douglas Oliver, Irvene DeVore, Asen Balikci and Frances Link. A unique feature of this program was the establishment of 85 regional teacher-training centers for those who were planning to teach the course. A distinctive feature was the extensive use of nature and ethnographic films that depicted the life and behavior associated with the life cycle of salmon, gulls, baboons and the Netsilik Eskimo.

These films were not narrated and allowed the pupils to make their own observations and to draw their own conclusions. The course did not include a textbook, but printed content was available in the form of booklets. *Man: A Course of Study* became available from Curriculum Development Associates. Unfortunately, this program became controversial for several reasons, among them being the so-called "inappropriate" nature of the content, which included the butchering of hunted animals, the emphasis on communal living within the Netsilik culture, and an inferential support for the theory of evolution. Community and national reaction to these materials caused the discontinuation of the program in the 1970s.

Anthropology Curriculum Study Project

The Anthropology Curriculum Study Project was funded by a grant from the National Science Foundation in 1965 and was sponsored by the American Anthropological Association, making it the most recognized program specifically for the teaching of anthropology in high schools. This project was directed by Malcolm Collier and her associates at the University of Chicago. They developed a one-semester course entitled *Patterns in Human History* designed to be taught in conjunction with the 10th grade world history course. The purpose of this program was to refocus the teaching of world history by providing an anthropological perspective on the development of man and the role of behavior in the transmission of culture. In addition, ACSP developed two units for junior high school entitled *The Great Tree and the Long House: The Culture of the Iroquois* and *Kiowa Years: A Study of Culture Impact.*

Patterns in Human History contained four units that introduced the student to various aspects of anthropology. *Studying Society* provided students with an orientation for the units that would follow with special emphasis on cultural anthropology. *Origins of Humanness* emphasized physical anthropology so that students learned to apply its concepts and methods to the investigation of human origins. *The Emergence of Complex Societies* emphasized societal developments covering a period of 10,000 years. Students learned about the activities of hunters and gatherers and studied the origins of complex civilizations. *Modernization and Traditional Societies* emphasized the study of traditional societies, such as peasant societies, that have dominated much of the world for the past four thousand years.

Because this program was supported by both the National Science Foundation and the American Anthropological Association, and was marketed by the Macmillan Company, it reached a wider audience than many other project materials. Despite these early successes, the program was discontinued after only a few years of distribution.

Three curriculum projects contained significant amounts of anthropologically oriented instructional materials within their total program. They were the Materials and Activities for Teachers and Children, Project Social Studies/ University of Minnesota, and the High School Geography Project.

Materials and Activities for Teachers and Children (MATCH)

The Boston Children's Museum received a grant in 1964 to develop a number of MATCH units, which were widely used in the upper elementary and junior high schools. The units, prepared by the museum, contained great quantities of materials reproduced from museum specimens from specific cultures. Included was an archaeological unit on ancient Greece, *A House of Ancient Greece.*

Students simulated an excavation of a site containing a house that existed during the classical period. The unit was designed for use with 25 to 35 students who would be divided into archaeological teams. Frederick H. Krese served as director.

Among the instructional materials were reference books on ancient Greece, artifacts, pictures and maps. The students were expected to gain insights into this ancient culture and into the daily lives of people who occupied the home. The units developed by MATCH were activity-centered and encouraged direct interaction with artifacts, rather than relying primarily on the printed text. This approach was unique for most pupils. The units added variety, interest and excitement to the social studies classroom. They were especially helpful for pupils who were poor readers but had average and above average ability to reason and to make inferences.

Project Social Studies/University of Minnesota

Project Social Studies, under the direction of Edith West at the University of Minnesota, was funded in 1963 to develop social studies units for grades K–12. Included in this program were unit kits based on anthropological content. Some of these materials, edited by Charles Mitsakos, became commercially available from Selective Educational Equipment in the late 1960s and 1970s. The materials that were developed for grades 1 and 2 contained a strong anthropological emphasis. Eight units were developed for these two grades based on the study of family life in various cultural settings: Hopi Indian Family, Ashanti Family, Japanese Family, Family of Early New England, Kibbutz Family in Israel, Soviet Family in Moscow, Quechua Family of Peru, and Algonquin Indian Family.

The units were designed in kit form with a teacher's guide, artifacts and selected reading books for children. The teacher's guides were of exceptional instructional quality, while the artifacts were inexpensive. The entire K–12 curriculum continued to use anthropological perspectives. As a consequence, anthropology was given equal consideration along with history and the other social sciences. Some of the materials from this project were marketed for use as independent kits or as courses for the lower elementary grades. These materials sold well for a few years and then were no longer available from the commerical publisher.

High School Geography Project

The High School Geography Project, located at the University of Colorado, was funded in 1961 for the purpose of developing a one-year, six-unit course for high school students. Nicolas Helburn and William Pattison were the project directors. The course, entitled *Geography in an Urban Age,* was developed under a grant from the National Science Foundation. The third unit was devoted to the study of culture and emphasized such key concepts as cultural relativism, cultural diffusion, culture change and the cultural regions of the world. While the unit was designed as a geography unit, it also could be used to teach major anthropological concepts and perspectives. The Macmillan Company published the course in commercial form. This program had the support of the Association of American Geographers. The Macmillan Company marketed *Geography in an Urban Age* for only a few years.

In addition to the funded projects that were specifically designed for anthropological instruction and projects containing appreciable anthropology components, there were many projects that included anthropology as a supplemental subject. Anthropology was also incorporated into area study programs, cultural studies, world history multiethnic studies, multicultural studies and world cultural studies. Greater Cleveland Social Science Program, Providence Social Studies Curriculum Project, Taba Curriculum Development Project, Michigan Elementary Social Science Education Program, Asian Studies Inquiry Program and Project Africa all contained some anthropological aspects.

1972 to 1985

After 1972 most funds for the development of innovative curriculum programs for the social studies disappeared. As a result of the decline of the New Social Studies, the status and support for the continued development of precollegiate anthropology would rest in the hands of commercial publishers, professional organizations, and individuals who would continue to support anthropology education.

Many of the projects that promoted the teaching of anthropology were no longer in operation after 1972. The curriculum programs that were developed either remained in the form of experimental instructional materials or they were published by textbook companies that hoped to market them for a profit. Those that were marketed remained in print for a relatively short period of time. Beginning in the 1970s, various commercial publishers introduced a relatively large quantity of anthropology materials for the schools. For example, Holt, Rinehart and Winston produced a K–6 social studies series with a separate course in anthropology. In addition, anthropology textbooks, kits, filmstrips, packets, pamphlets and a host of other materials were marketed by several publishing firms (Dynneson 1977).

Holt, Rinehart and Winston also developed a K–6 social studies program in 1972 called *The Databank System*. The 4th grade course, *Inquiring About Culture*, was developed by Roger C. Owen, an eminent professor of anthropology. *The Databank System* included a teacher's guide, a student textbook, and resource materials in the form of databank boxes. This course began with the study of anthropology and the work of anthropologists. It presented information about people, places and cultures from an anthropologist's perspective. The study began with the hunters and gatherers and ended with the study of industrial urban centers. *The Databank System* was so well designed, developed and illustrated with supplemental materials and activities that it was also relatively expensive.

In 1973 Bantam books published a kit entitled *Anthropology: A New Approach.* The materials, intended as a high school program, consisted mainly of paperbacks and a few cassettes. The teachers received a teacher's guide, student evaluation cards and a reading log. In 1974 the Globe Book Company published a junior high textbook entitled *Exploring Civilization: A Discovery Approach.*

The text made use of many anthropological concepts and methods through an area study approach.

In 1973 Harcourt Brace Jovanovich published a paperback entitled *Anthropology*. This book, which could be used as the basis for a one-semester course for high school students, was a study of man and nature, and man and culture. In 1976 the Globe Book Company published a one-semester textbook for the junior high entitled *Inquiry into Anthropology*. The textbook was organized around several subfields of anthropology. By the 1980s several kinds of anthropological materials continued to be published for use in the schools, including textbooks, films, cassettes, kits and numerous other supplemental materials.

The department of anthropology of Saint Mary's University, located in Halifax, Nova Scotia, began in 1981 the publication of the *Teaching Anthropology Newsletter*. Circulated throughout Canada and the United States, it contains articles and resources for the teaching of anthropology in grades K–12, information on conferences in precollegiate anthropology, reports of teaching experiences, and precollegiate anthropology activities in other nations. This publication demonstrates the commitment that some departments of anthropology have made to the teaching of anthropology in the schools.

In 1984 a new anthropology magazine, entitled *Faces,* began publication for elementary school pupils. The November 1984 issue was dedicated to the Pueblo Indians. It contained articles on history, myths, puzzles, ceremonies, kachinas, recipes, poems, teaching ideas and activities. The magazine, a product of Cobblestone Publishing Company, located in Peterborough, New Hampshire, is published in cooperation with the American Museum of Natural History in New York.

ORGANIZATIONAL SUPPORT

Organizational support for the teaching of anthropology in the schools is growing. This support has been reflected in the attention that precollegiate anthropology has received in various journals, at conferences, and as the recipient of institutional financial support.

The National Council for the Social Studies has helped to support the teaching of precollegiate anthropology by including it as a topic of interest in its journal, *Social Education,* and in its special publications. During its annual meetings, anthropology sessions are included in which papers are presented, teaching ideas are shared, and programs and materials for the teaching of anthropology are distributed.

During the 1960s and 1970s the Social Science Education Consortium collected all kinds of social science instructional materials, including anthropology materials. It began to publish a *Databook* that described the rationale and characteristics of the project materials. The Consortium has contributed to the development of anthropology education by providing workshops and written reports on the nature, use and effectiveness of these unique materials.

Educational Resources Information Center/Clearinghouse for Social Studies/ Social Science Education (ERIC/ChESS) specializes in documents and materials pertaining to the social studies, including anthropology. In 1974 Robert Fox provided an ERIC grant for the writing of a monograph on precollegiate anthropology. The monograph, *Precollegiate Anthropology: Trends and Materials,* was published by the Anthropology Curriculum Project under the direction of Marion J. Rice in 1975 (Dynneson 1975). In addition, ERIC/ChESS continues to catalog and house most of the major documents and articles pertaining to precollegiate anthropology, an important activity in light of the fact that many of these early efforts were lost with the closing of the projects.

The American Anthropological Association has supported the teaching of precollegiate anthropology to the extent that it helped to sponsor the development of the Anthropology Curriculum Study Project in the 1960s. In addition, the AAA has expressed some concern about teacher training and the need for anthropologists to share in that responsibility.

The AAA has expanded its interests in education by helping to promote the combined interests of anthropologists and educators through a related organization, the Council on Anthropology and Education, formed in 1968.

A concern for the teaching of precollegiate anthropology was reflected in the committee structure of the organization. The Council on Anthropology and Education publishes the *Anthropology and Education Quarterly,* which contains articles on the status and teaching of precollegiate anthropology. It also provides a meeting ground where educators and anthropologists can share common interests. At the same time, it has the capability of becoming the liaison organization between the National Council for the Social Studies and the American Anthropological Association for issues and interests pertaining to the social studies and the teaching of anthropology.

The Smithsonian Institution in Washington, D.C., has been interested in the teaching of precollegiate anthropology for many years. Because the Smithsonian contains vast collections of materials that have anthropological relevance, it is a natural precollegiate teaching institution. It also has an anthropology department and staff. In 1979 George Washington University and the Smithsonian Institution's Anthropology for Teachers Program began to publish *Anthro-Notes: National Museum of Natural History Newsletter for Teachers* for those interested in precollegiate anthropology. Funded by the National Science Foundation, this program includes teacher development programs for social studies teachers in the Washington metropolitan area. It represents one of the strongest programs of institutional support for the teaching of anthropology at the precollegiate level in the United States.

Anthropology Curriculum Project, located within the Department of Social Science Education in the School of Education, at the University of Georgia, has continued to support the development of precollegiate anthropology. Professor Rice and his colleagues have sponsored the publication of instructional, reference and research materials. While ACP has not had the financial resources that have been available to many of the other centers, it has done a remarkable job in promoting the development of precollegiate anthropology.

RESEARCH ON THE STATUS
OF PRECOLLEGIATE ANTHROPOLOGY

Among the earliest research on the status of precollegiate anthropology was a study begun in 1971 and designed to attempt to measure the extent to which anthropology was being taught in the public schools before and during the time that the New Social Studies was still influencing the curriculum. It consisted of survey research in which a questionnaire was sent to social studies specialists in each of the 50 states (Dynneson 1972). This same research was replicated in 1978 and in 1985.

The Status in 1971

The 1971 survey attempted to measure the status of precollegiate anthropology at both elementary and secondary school levels in all 50 states. The results of this first survey, mailed to state social studies specialists, reflected the lack of knowledge that existed regarding the teaching of precollegiate anthropology. Only 20 questionnaires were returned and many of them simply did not have any information regarding the status of precollegiate anthropology in the public schools (Dynneson and Taylor 1974).

The states that did report instructional programs provided a most interesting patch-quilt of activity. For example, Alaska reported a very strong interest in anthropology because of its large indigenous population of Indians and Eskimos. Fifty-three of the 355 school districts in California, a relatively high percentage, had some type of program in anthropology. Several northeastern states had school districts that offered some anthropology courses. Delaware had developed a course on the archaeology of Delaware. Rhode Island had recommended the teaching of anthropology as one of the integrated disciplines. In the Southeast, most of the states, with the exception of Georgia, did not respond to the questionnaire. The influence of the Anthropology Curriculum Project at the University of Georgia was quite pervasive in promoting the teaching of anthropology in Georgia. In Missouri, only 3 school districts out of a total of 460 had a course in anthropology. The study revealed similar situations in Idaho, Vermont, Wisconsin, Wyoming and New Jersey. Some states, such as Texas and Tennessee, reported that the teaching of anthropology was directly tied to the New Social Studies projects and materials that were being promoted at the time, especially *Man: A Course of Study.*

The teaching of anthropology as a separate instructional area within the social studies curriculum is a very small part of the curriculum when compared to history, government, geography and even sociology and psychology. But the state specialists seemed to express a willingness to expand the role of anthropology in the social studies curriculum. This survey did not measure the extent to which anthropology had made inroads on the social studies curriculum in the form of cultural studies in the elementary schools and in the form of integrated and supplemental studies at the high school level. It can be reasonably inferred that the study of cultures and the supplemental role of anthropology expanded considerably in the 1970s. The supplemental role of anthropology coupled with the concern for multiethnic/multicultural studies and area studies introduced an appreciable anthropological emphasis into the social studies.

The Status in 1978

A follow-up to the 1971 study was conducted seven years later. The revised questionnaire reflected a greater awareness of the contemporary trends in curriculum development in the social studies. In addition, the researchers were much more tenacious in their determination to obtain responses from each of the curriculum specialists.

The year before the second survey was sent out to the state specialists, Rice attempted to determine the number of social studies teachers teaching courses and units in anthropology. He approached the problem by inserting a questionnaire in the October 1976 issue of *Social Education*. At that time the journal had a circulation of about 20,000 readers, mainly elementary and secondary school social studies teachers—a minority when compared to the actual number of social studies teachers in the United States. Unfortunately, only 50 of the responses that he received were usable (Rice 1977). His research attempt illustrates the difficulty that lies in trying to measure accurately the extent to which curriculum areas are taught. As a result of these difficulties, the 1978 replication study focused on the state social studies specialists because their position represents a focal point for this type of information.

The 1978 survey netted responses from all 50 of the state social studies specialists; from their responses the researchers were able to piece together the following picture:

- Anthropology had moved from a largely unrecognized or hidden aspect of the social studies curriculum to a more recognized instructional component. This transition occurred during the 10-year period from 1965 to 1975.
- The curriculum materials produced during the New Social Studies were mainly responsible for the new role and status of anthropology in the curriculum.
- Educators throughout the United States tended to view anthropology as an integrated part of the social studies curriculum, rather than as a separate subject matter offering such as history.
- Anthropology was not viewed as having much chance of becoming a required course similar in curricular standing to such courses as United States history and United States government. It might be taught as an elective, but its main role would be to supplement ongoing subjects that dominate the curriculum.
- Separate and elective courses in anthropology were most likely to be offered in large urban centers with diverse populations and cultures. They were less likely to be taught in small and rural schools.
- Anthropological content generally was *not* viewed as controversial, and there seemed to be an overall willingness to teach anthropology, especially in light of the interest in cultural studies and human behavior. This was a strange result considering the controversy caused by *Man: A Course of Study*. It seemed that public rejection was aimed at specific programs and not at entire subject areas, although anthropology, like biology, was disliked by segments of the population for ideological reasons.
- The future of precollegiate anthropology will depend on the availability of well-planned instructional materials, and these materials must come mainly from commercial publishers (Dynneson 1981). A survey of social studies instructional materials in the 1985 catalog from *Social Studies School Services* indicates that the catalog contains a surprisingly large offering of materials

under the heading of culture and anthropology; however, the mainline text-book companies are the ones that will have the most control over the future of anthropology education.

The Status in 1985

At the time that this chapter was being written, this author and Fred L. Coleman were in the process of conducting a third survey of curriculum specialists. The latest research instrument is more sophisticated than the first two; it attempts to measure the following aspects of precollegiate anthropology:

- The role of anthropology in the collegiate preparation and state certification of social studies teachers.
- The status of anthropology in the school districts of each state, including data on the extent to which anthropology is seen as a separate subject or as supplemental instruction.
- The nature and source of precollegiate anthropology instructional materials, including data on the extent to which textbook publishers are influencing the teaching of anthropology and the extent to which teachers are using improvised materials.

LOOKING TO THE FUTURE

Despite its late start and meager beginnings, anthropology will survive to become an important ingredient in the social studies curriculum. Its importance will depend on the development of appropriate instructional materials for each grade level. In time, the classroom teachers will come to recognize the potential of anthropology as more than that of just another discipline. They will come to recognize that while anthropology can and should stand on its own as a social science discipline for the schools, its strongest appeal may be to serve as the integrating core for the social studies curriculum of the future.

REFERENCES

Dynneson, Thomas L. *Anthropology for the Schools: An Analysis of Selected Anthropological Projects and Units with Content Ratings by Professional Anthropologists.* Boulder, CO: ERIC/ChESS, 1972.

Dynneson, Thomas L. *Pre-collegiate Anthropology: Trends and Materials.* Athens, GA: Anthropology Curriculum Project, 1975.

Dynneson, Thomas L. "The Status of Pre-collegiate Anthropology: Progress or Peril?" *Anthropology and Education Quarterly* 12(Winter 1981): 304–309.

Dynneson, Thomas L. "Review and Update: Pre-collegiate Anthropology Materials." *Anthropology and Education Quarterly* 8(February 1977): 28–30.

Dynneson, Thomas L., and Bob L. Taylor. "The Status of Anthropology in Schools." *Pennsylvania Council for the Social Studies Journal* 3(Spring 1974): 54–57.

Faces: The Magazine About People. Peterborough, NH: Cobblestone Publishing Co.

Fallers, Margaret C. "Anthropology: Introduction." *Social Education* 32(February 1968): 105–106.

Hayden, Robert I. "Fifth Graders Take a Crack at Anthropology." *Instructor* 66(May 1957): 85, 91, 97.

Henry, Jules. "Anthropology in the Secondary Schools." *Progressive Education* 16(November 1939): 509–510.

Hoebel, E. Adamson. "Anthropology in Education." *Yearbook of Anthropology.* New York: Wenner-Gren Foundation for Anthropological Research, 1955, 292.

Owen, Roger C. *Inquiring About Cultures.* New York: Holt, Rinehart and Winston, 1976.

Rice, Marion J. "Teaching Pre-collegiate Anthropology: The Results of a Survey and Recommendations." *Anthropology and Education Quarterly* 8(August 1977): 193–195.

Teaching Anthropology Newsletter. Department of Anthropology, Saint Mary's University. Halifax, Nova Scotia. Quarterly.

CHAPTER 13

PSYCHOLOGY:
SOCIAL SCIENCE, NATURAL SCIENCE AND PROFESSION

Michael Wertheimer, James Brodie, David Fendrich, Suzanne Mannes, Chie Okuda, Matthew Sharps and James Weisberg

Psychology in 1985 was partly a natural and partly a social science, and a set of applications of the knowledge gained from both strategies in the improvement of human welfare. As was true in 1935, psychology was still occasionally confused by some lay people in 1985 with psychiatry, psychoanalysis, parapsychology, "pop" psychology and psychopathology. But organized psychology in 1935 was somewhat different from how it appears today.

Fifty years ago, most psychologists were natural scientists doing research on or teaching about "general experimental psychology," by which was meant the problems of perception, learning and motivation; but the social science approach was also already reasonably well established, although applied psychology was in its infancy (primarily in the form of industrial and clinical psychology).

During the next half century, experimental psychology grew, but the social science aspects of psychology grew even more rapidly. The greatest growth, in terms of numbers of people engaged in such activities, though, was in professional/practicing psychology. In 1935 most of the approximately 2,000 members of the American Psychological Association (APA) were identified with the research/academic orientation; this had reversed during the 1950s, and today the 60,000-member APA has far more psychologists reflecting the professional/practicing orientation than the research/academic orientation.

Almost all psychologists see their field as a research-oriented discipline that bases its conclusions (and all conclusions are viewed as tentative) upon empirical evidence; that is, that uses the methods of other natural sciences and of other social sciences to study a broad range of problems of human (and animal) behavior. Unsupported personal opinion, unfounded assumptions and superficial interpretations about the underlying causes of behavior play essentially no role in this endeavor.

Amateur psychotherapy, the encouragement of "growth" experiences by poorly trained leaders, and other forms of psychotherapy or psychological counseling by ill-prepared practitioners are explicitly prohibited by the APA's *Ethical Standards of Psychologists*. Thus, the public image of psychology occasionally displayed in the media, in the form of personal advice columns in newspapers or in fanciful tests purporting to provide instant personality diagnoses in national magazines, does not match the image that the field has of itself.

NATURE OF THE DISCIPLINE

An overview of how contemporary psychologists see their field is provided by the more than 40 "divisions" or special interest groups within APA. Among those representative primarily of the professional/practicing emphasis are divisions of clinical psychology, counseling psychology, psychotherapy and consulting psychology. Divisions representative of the research/academic orientation can be broken down into fields that use primarily the methods of the natural sciences (such as the divisions of experimental psychology, physiological and comparative psychology, health psychology, and psychopharmacology) and those that use primarily the methods of the social sciences (such as the divisions of personality and social psychology, community psychology and psychology of women).

The chief difference between the natural and the social science strategies, to oversimplify somewhat, is that the natural science method typically involves manipulation of one or more variables and observation of the effect of the manipulation on various other variables (that is, performance of an experiment in the technical sense), while the social science method usually involves assessment of a number of naturally varying attributes without manipulating any of them, and observing the extent to which they are correlated (typically using survey or questionnaire techniques).

Psychology Is Fragmented but Empirical

The diversity of the various APA divisions shows that modern psychology is a loosely knit conglomerate of a wide variety of disciplines. Indeed, this diversity is even greater than that sample suggests; there are, for example, also divisions on the teaching of psychology, on psychology and the arts, on military psychology, on engineering psychology, on population and environmental psychology, on the history of psychology, on state psychological association affairs, and on psychology and law. It is widely held that psychology is not a unified field, but that it would be more appropriate to speak of "the psychological disciplines" (Koch 1959–1963). These disciplines are so heterogeneous that specialists in one subfield may find it difficult to communicate effectively with specialists in other subfields.

Yet almost all psychologists have two major perspectives in common beside their interest in some aspect of human or animal behavior: an evidential, empirical orientation and a conviction that all psychological concepts must be measurable if they are to be taken seriously.

Fifty years ago, experimental psychology was synonymous with general psychology. In the interim, the experimental method has spread to many fields other than perception, learning and motivation; those fields in which experimentation is not technically or ethically feasible typically use an empirical, quantitative social-science methodology nevertheless. Speculation is considered acceptable only if it leads to concrete, empirically testable hypotheses. To repeat, data, not mere opinions, are used throughout psychology as the basis for reaching conclusions. Characteristic of all areas of psychology is a high level of sophistication about inferential statistics, a set of mathematical tools that are used for drawing inferences about populations of people or animals from data on samples which have been systematically selected from those populations for close observation or experiment.

This strategy for obtaining knowledge means, of course, that psychological questions must be stated in a form that permits observation and measurement of specific dimensions. Such measurements may be very precise, as in the number of trials required for the first perfect recitation of a list of material to be memorized, or quite crude, as in a judgment about whether or not an individual displays a particular psychological trait or personality characteristic. Yet, most psychologists agree that if you can't measure something, or can't tell whether something is present or not, then that something is not worth considering seriously. Progress in psychology often comes in the form of the discovery of a new way to measure a significant variable that previously was unmeasurable or could only be assessed very crudely.

Tens of thousands of reports of the results of empirical research in psychology are published in hundreds of journals every year, with the consequence that it is almost impossible for any individual to keep up even with the major findings in any relatively broad area. Another consequence of this volume of output is that there are often many slightly different studies of similar phenomena or the same phenomenon, occasionally with conflicting findings. A frequently voiced need until a decade or so ago was for a reasonably objective method for efficiently integrating the findings from diverse studies within a common field. Glass, McGaw and Smith (1981) succeeded in devising precisely such a technique, meta-analysis, which systematically combines the results from a large number of controlled studies of the same phenomenon to yield a single rational conclusion; this technique has been productively applied to such research areas as the effectiveness of psychotherapy (Smith and Glass 1977) and the effect of class size on the achievement of elementary-school pupils (Glass and Smith 1979).

External Influences Shaped Psychology

Psychology, like all other academic disciplines, is substantially affected by its social, intellectual and political context; it is inevitably a product of its time and place. This process has been as evident during the last half century as during psychology's history before that time. Among the differences in place, for example, European psychology tended to emphasize the influence of genetic determinants of behavior, including psychopathology, while psychology in the United States emphasized the role of learning.

World War I had helped launch psychological testing, as psychologists devised measures for helping to decide which potential recruits were suitable, and which were unsuitable, for military service. World War II helped to establish applied experimental psychology, with such fields as human factors research (designing equipment so that human beings could interact with it appropriately with a minimum of errors) and training research (comparing the effectiveness of various forms of training programs), and to expand differential psychology, which was used to help place people into jobs which best fit their abilities and interests. World War II also provided a major impetus to clinical psychology, as the Veterans Administration tried to cope with the mental health needs of returning veterans.

Largely for complex political reasons, federal funding for research and training in psychology increased dramatically during the 1950s and 1960s, but declined rather steeply again during the 1970s. Biological psychology, social psychology, experimental psychology, clinical psychology and other fields flourished and declined with these changes in funding patterns, and the kinds of problems studied by psychologists fluctuated with changes in national priorities about research on gerontology, on poverty, on learning to read, and on other foci as the shifting winds of politics made massive funds available to study them but then withdrew them again several years later.

Community mental health centers were the recipients of substantial infusions of federal monies during the Kennedy administration; soon concern about the effectiveness of such intervention programs led to the growth of a new field focused on the measurement of program effectiveness, namely, evaluation research, which obtained further impetus from the national concern with accountability during the 1970s.

External influences on psychology have also included the needs of business, industry, and the educational establishment, which have had a profound impact on psychological testing, on industrial/organizational psychology, on clinical psychology, on social psychology and on the psychology of learning and memory, as people outside the field came to realize that some specific psychological knowledge could be applied productively to the solution of concrete problems that they faced in their everyday work.

The recent advent of the computer has also had a substantial effect on psychology, especially on the field of cognition, as will be elaborated below; indeed, it has been suggested, only partly in jest, that the computer tail may be wagging the psychology dog.

Psychology Addresses Ethical Issues

Both external and internal forces have led to extensive concern during the last half century with ethical issues in psychological research and in the practice of psychology. Codes were developed for the protection of the participants in psychological research projects, of psychology students, and of clients receiving the services of practicing psychologists. APA created a Committee on Scientific and Professional Ethics in 1938, and major boards or committees within APA have been charged ever since with overseeing ethical issues that might arise in any facet of psychological research or practice. Over the years, APA has generated a variety of codes and other documents, most of which have undergone revisions several times and are under continuing scrutiny. They deal with such topics as the conduct of research with human participants and the care and use of animals, standards for educational and psychological tests, standards for providers of psychological services, and ethical guidelines for high school psychology teachers. Further, during the last half century, each of the separate states in the United States has enacted laws for the licensure or certification of practicing psychologists. The American Board of Professional Psychology was established several decades ago for national certification of specialists in clinical psychology, industrial/organizational psychology, and other applied fields.

Active Models of Human Nature Complement Passive Ones

The dominant theoretical orientations of the mid-thirties, behaviorism and psychoanalysis, viewed human beings implicitly as passively molded products either of environmentally controlled learning or conditioning, or of uncontrollable unconscious forces and early childhood experiences. Since then, more proactive models of human nature have dominated the field. Partly due to the research of the Gestalt psychologists (a third school of psychology that flourished early during this period), it came to be recognized that perception and cognition are not just a passive registration of sensory input, but involve the active construction of cognitively meaningful representations of the perceptual world. Further, animal research by such workers as Bitterman showed that the kind of organism studied profoundly affects the kinds of learning phenomena that are observed. A "systems approach" has come to characterize many fields of psychology. Such an approach normally stems from a comprehensive model that depicts the interrelationship and interdependence of an organism and its environment in such processes as development, perception and cognition.

In developmental psychology, the highly influential constructivist work of Jean Piaget has shown that the child and its surroundings act together to produce the complex phenomena of development. The child is not a passive learning device, but an active agent in its own development, operating in different ways at different times in its own physical and psychological growth. Such an "organismic" perspective has emerged in a variety of developmental areas. Cognitive and emotional processes are no longer regarded as necessarily developing toward better functioning, but as changing with the needs of the organism. The infant, once regarded as imprisoned in a world of buzzing confusion, has been demonstrated to be a complex, capable organism. The newborn is highly competent in some behavioral functions, such as perception, but less able in other areas, such as motor skills; this pattern appears to be commensurate with the growth and survival needs of the infant.

In a comparable fashion, modern ethological theory (Lorenz 1965; Tinbergen 1951) evaluates animal behavior and behavioral development within the context of the natural environment and ecological needs, leading to substantial new insights into such matters as patterns of aggression, sexual relations and rearing of the young. Animals are now recognized as complex organisms that are active participants in their interaction with the environment, rather than as simple, reactive, instinct-driven robots; the parallel with the current conception of infancy is striking. Further, developmental psychology in the last fifty years has turned its focus across the lifespan, to study the development of mental processes in adulthood and old age as well as in childhood, yielding greater awareness of how processes change, and therefore how they operate.

Another instance of the more "active" orientation is Festinger's cognitive dissonance theory, which provided a powerful perspective for the study of human motivation. The theory holds that an individual will attempt to minimize dissonance between viewpoints: if you pay dearly (in effort, funds, or commitment) for something, you will value it more than if you obtain it cheaply. This theory has broad applicability in many areas, including professional development and marriage counseling. The social learning theory of Bandura has also had a substantial impact in its demonstration that individuals will imitate others as a function of those others' perceived power and reward for action. This theory has major implications for such matters as the understanding of effects of the media on children. Heider's ideas about attribution, which have grown into the large modern research field of "attribution theory," have proven significant for the understanding of persons' perceptions of each other, and of what factors influence these perceptions.

By contrast, and more consistent with a "systems approach" that draws from both the active and the passive views, Milgram has provided frightening insight into such phenomena as the development of totalitarian movements, in demonstrating that individuals will tend to follow orders with very harmful consequences if the orders are given by an authority figure. Comparably disturbing findings were obtained in widely cited studies by Rosenhan, showing that sham patients in psychiatric hospitals are seen by the staff as psychotic even if, after admission to the hospital, they exhibit no symptoms of psychological disturbance; and by Zimbardo and others, who found that research participants asked to fill the roles of prison guards and prisoners readily and convincingly adopt attitudes and behaviors consistent with these roles.

B.F. Skinner has been perhaps the most visible psychologist in the last half century. His orientation, which views human and animal conduct as almost totally determined by the environmental consequences of that conduct, represents the passive perspective on behavior. His work, which has often been misunderstood as implying a George Orwellian society, has led to many successful applications of the principles of instrumental or operant learning to behavior modification, to programmed instruction, and to control of inappropriate behavior in classrooms, penal institutions and mental hospitals. Skinner has proposed not that we *should* control people's behavior to some political end; but that since environmental consequences *do* control behavior, we should try to set up environmental contingencies in such a way as to maximize fulfilling, productive, constructive behavior and the actualization of each individual's, and the society's, positive potential.

NEW DEVELOPMENTS

In sharp contrast to Skinner's thoroughly objective behaviorism, a new area focused on *subjective* processes emerged during the 1950s and has been flourishing ever since: cognitive psychology (Neisser 1967).

The Emergence of Cognitive Science

Two relatively independent forces led to this development: a growing dissatisfaction with the behavioristic approach, and the computer revolution. Behaviorism was widely viewed as too narrow to provide an account of the richness and complexity of human behavior. Technological advances produced the modern computer, which was eagerly adopted throughout society and which appeared to psychologists to be a system that could serve fruitfully as an analogy or metaphor for human cognition. Computers and people can be considered similar in that both receive information from their environments, store it and incorporate it with other information in a memory, and produce some response or outcome based on rules or strategies. Using what has come to be called an information-processing paradigm, cognitive psychologists have attempted to answer questions concerning perception, memory, language, reading, problem solving and decision making, among other cognitive processes.

In addition to the computer's function as an analogy for cognition, it is also used as a tool for its study in two significant ways. First, computers are used to simulate cognition. A computer can be programmed to perform a cognitive task in a particular way proposed by a psychologist. If the pattern of output of the computer is similar to the behavior of a human being given the same problem, then it may be that people are actually solving the task in the manner proposed by the psychologist and built into the computer program. It is, however, recognized that caution must be exercised in such inferences, since it is possible that a given solution may be arrived at in a number of different ways, and thus the computer's method may after all be quite different from the human's method.

A second use of computers in the field of cognition is in the generation of artificial intelligence (AI). Research workers in AI write computer programs that display intelligence as a goal in and of itself, without necessarily being concerned with whether or not the process or output of the program resembles the process or output of a human solution. AI programs have been written to play chess and other complex games, to construct mathematical proofs and derive scientific laws from experimental data, and to diagnose diseases and machinery failures, to predict the weather, and to discover oil.

Computers cannot, of course, perform such tasks "from scratch," but must start with strategies and raw information provided by people. A problem with older AI programs was that they could work only when they were provided with a great deal of specific information before they started on the task they were to solve. Such a technique was criticized as not demonstrating genuine intelligence. Consequently, a later goal of AI researchers has been to write programs that provide the computer with a general strategy and the capacity to learn. Such programs (e.g., the General Problem Solver of Newell, Shaw and Simon 1958) come closer to what is generally considered intelligence than did the earlier versions.

An unanticipated by-product of the computer revolution is that it has forced those concerned with information processing to reconsider the issue of difficulty. That is, when psychologists attempt to program computers or build machines to do what humans do, they soon realize that the things we take for granted—or do automatically—can be difficult to mimic with computers and machines. For example, it is extremely difficult to develop programs which comprehend sentence structure, but playing chess with computers has not been as difficult. Considering the difficulty problem has, in turn, forced psychologists to deal with the issue of representation (how information is coded) and the organization of representations.

The new cognitive science is not only a result of a revolt against behaviorism and of the computer revolution, however. Some early research on text comprehension, an area of major research concern in modern cognitive psychology, was conducted by Bartlett, who was interested in answering questions about the reconstructive nature of text recall. The idea of a *schema,* which he used to explain recall, has recently re-emerged in cognitive psychology. Now it is well accepted that we do not remember prose verbatim exactly as it is presented, but that we use our knowledge of the world and remember the material in an organized, more abstract, fashion. Experimental results that support such ideas have culminated in an influential general theory of text comprehension, the van Dijk-Kintsch model. This model has survived many tests and appears likely to prove useful for both psychologists and educators in the future for, among other purposes, assessing the readability and difficulty of text.

Cognitive psychology was also affected by the new field of psycholinguistics, which deals with language and the development of language skills from a psychological point of view. Osgood devised a technique, the semantic differential, for measuring subtle, complex aspects of the connotative meaning of words, and helped to launch the field. Chomsky argued that language structures are hierarchical, not sequential, that the capacity to develop linguistic communication is innate, and that more important than how people produce language (language performance) is how people know what they know about language (language competence) and language rules.

Problem solving has been a major focus of research at least since the early 1940s (Luchins 1942; Wertheimer 1945, 1982). A series of principles of problem solving are now accepted by a large part of the cognitive community. One such principle is that problem solvers use a hierarchical organization to structure their attempts at solution. For example, a distinction has been made between problem solving as an algorithmic, rule-following process as opposed to a heuristic, rule-of-thumb process. Most prople tend to use a heuristic, semi-structured process. Nobel Laureate Herbert Simon has used heuristics as a model for highly successful computer simulations of human problem-solving behaviors (Newell and Simon 1972). Kahneman, Slovic and Tversky have extended Simon's work by demonstrating how heuristics and biases influence judgments made under uncertainty, and decisions under risk (Slovic 1982).

Other Natural Science Fields of Psychology

While the emergence of cognitive science has perhaps been the most visible change in psychology during the last few decades, other subfields have enjoyed substantial progress as well. Since they are not as directly relevant to psychology as a social science, it is not appropriate to elaborate upon them here in detail. Suffice it to mention, however, among many specific trends and discoveries that deserve attention, a few representative ones that truly stand out. The electron microscope has been used successfully in the study of minute structural changes within nerve cells that accompany such behavioral processes as habituation or learning. Contrary to the centuries-old belief that human sensory experience is of elemental colored patches of particular brightness, and the like, Hubel and Wiesel found what they called complex and hyper-complex cells in the cortex of the brain that respond only to lines at particular angles to the horizontal moving across the visual field at a certain rate; their discovery demonstrated that what were assumed to be complex learned perceptual organizational processes are instead built directly into the nervous system. Olds discovered brain centers the stimulation of which is rewarding, bringing us closer to an understanding of the physiological mechanism of reinforcement. Seligman and others found that repeated exposure to a situation in which the organism has no control over aversive stimulation may lead to learned helplessness, that is, inability to learn avoidance of or escape from a new unpleasant situation even if avoidance or escape is possible. Maier and his co-workers discovered that animals with learned helplessness are more susceptible to physical disease and have poorer immune reactions than animals that have received the same aversive stimulation but had control over it. Studies by Roger Sperry and others of animals and of people with split brains—that is, individuals whose corpus callosum (the large bundle of fibers connecting the left and right hemispheres of the brain) has been severed—have produced such findings as that one half of the brain may functionally not know something that the other half of the brain has learned, and that the two halves of the brain, to some extent, serve slightly different functions. This work won Sperry the Nobel prize in physiology in 1981. Perceptual processes, fundamental mechanisms of motivation, neural correlates of learning, and many other psychological functions are now better understood than they were 50 years ago.

Psychological Testing Is More Sophisticated and Responsible

Another major focus of psychology, both as a natural and as a social science, the effort to develop accurate tests for measuring individual differences, has had a profound effect not only on psychology as a discipline but upon society at large. During the last 50 years, psychological tests have pervaded the United States to such an extent that major steps in the course of most individuals' educational and professional careers are typically preceded, and not infrequently altered, by standardized psychological tests. Used ubiquitously are achievement tests in elementary schools, admissions tests for colleges and for graduate and professional schools, as well as licensing and certification examinations for trades and professions.

The technology of the measurement of individual differences, as mentioned earlier, received a substantial impetus from both World Wars. While many early tests were individually administered, later tests were primarily devised for group administration. Methods for measuring, and for enhancing, how well tests perform their intended purpose (i.e., their reliability and validity) became far more sensitive and sophisticated, as test construction and test evaluation became highly technical specialties. These developments occurred not only in intelligence or aptitude testing, but in tests of interests, personality and psychopathology as well.

Among tests that stand out in the history of psychology during the last 50 years are the Rorschach inkblot test of personality, which enjoyed wide popularity until the late 1950s, when empirical studies raised serious questions about its validity, resulting in a precipitous decline in its use since that time; and the Minnesota Multiphasic Personality Inventory, or MMPI, a questionnaire on which there is probably more substantial empirical information, including carefully derived statistical norms, than any other.

An effort has persisted during the last 50 years to make aptitude and ability tests "culture free," that is, to construct the tests without any cultural biases. That goal has continued to elude test construction experts; it appears to be impossible to write a test item without implicitly including in it a host of unintentional cultural assumptions. Largely as a consequence, various subgroups within the United States have, on average, scored differently on particular widely used tests, raising the question of whether it is fair and equitable to use such tests in decisions about who will receive a particular job, be admitted to a particular training program, or be excluded from such privileges. The issue had sufficiently massive potential social consequences that uniform guidelines on employee selection procedures were adopted by the United States Equal Employment Opportunity Commission in 1978, to the effect that no test can lawfully be used for selection purposes if it discriminates against identifiable subgroups of the general population, unless performance on the test can be demonstrated to be significantly related to actual performance on the task or job for which the selection is being made.

Professional Psychology

In part as a result of improved techniques for assessing individual differences and in part because of the emergence of new techniques for evaluating the outcomes of interventions in problem situations in the real world, the last half century has witnessed a rapid expansion of applied or professional psychology. Clinical psychology, counseling psychology, consulting psychology, school psychology and industrial/organizational psychology have all flourished. While each of these specialties differs from the others, they have in common a dedication to the enhancement of human welfare through the application of psychological knowledge.

Clinical psychology, which has undergone the most dramatic growth among all the applied fields of psychology, can serve as an example of the institutionalization of applied psychology during the last 50 years. As mentioned earlier in this chapter, World War II helped catalyze the growth of clinical psychology. In an effort to serve veterans' needs, various branches of the government and the Veterans Administration, in collaboration with university departments of psychology, developed training programs to prepare clinicians. Substantial amounts of government funding catapulted the profession of clinical psychology into national prominence.

A series of conferences was held to standardize curricula among training programs; the Ph.D. was recommended as the entry level degree for professional psychologists. A 1949 conference in Boulder, Colorado, developed a series of recommendations, called the "Scientist-Practitioner" training model, which emphasizes a curriculum that combines a solid grounding in the knowledge base and methodology of empirical psychology with substantial practical training in clinical skills (Raimy 1950). During the 1960s and 1970s clinical psychology solidified its identity as a helping profession with clearly defined roles and functions. Meantime, state governments passed licensing or certification laws governing the practice of psychology. During the 1970s and early 1980s, a new training plan that diverges significantly from the Boulder model, leading to a Psy.D. degree rather than to the Ph.D., was instituted at several universities and free-standing professional schools of psychology; this program diminishes the emphasis on research while increasing the amount of practical clinical training.

Two difficult issues have plagued clinical psychology in recent decades, raising serious questions about how well clinical psychology can, in fact, perform the tasks it is intended to perform. In 1954, Paul Meehl compared actuarial (statistical) with clinical prediction of such matters as the number of sessions of psychotherapy that would be required by particular clients and found that clinicians typically perform less well than simple actuarial formulas. Eysenck reviewed the entire literature on the effectiveness of psychotherapy, surveying all reports of studies that had used a control group, and came to the disquieting conclusion that the findings did not support the assertion that people with emotional problems who receive psychotherapy are more likely to improve than such people who do not receive treatment. A study by Smith and glass in 1976, using the complex and sophisticated statistical technique of meta-analysis, came to a more reassuring conclusion: the results of almost 500 studies indicated that, on the average, 75 percent of clients who received psychotherapy did better than 50 percent of controls–but it made no difference whether the psychotherapy was some form of behavior modification (typically, based on Skinnerian or conditioning principles) or psychodynamic (based on Freudian approaches). The question of the effectiveness of clinical practice, in assessment, intervention, psychotherapy and counseling, has continued to be a major focus of concern during the last decades.

Health Psychology—a New Field

Distinct from clinical psychology, and recognized as a speciality by creation of a new division within APA as late as 1978, is the rapidly expanding area of health psychology. It is not devoted to psychological assessment, psychometric testing, or psychotherapy, but studies the relationships between life-style or other behavioral features and susceptibility to physical illness. Health psychologists investigate such questions as social, biological and psychological correlates of cancer, heart disease, and stroke. Among the better known findings, for example, is that tense, strongly motivated, and highly competitive individuals (sometimes classified as Type A) are more prone to coronary problems than more relaxed and less ambitious people (Type B) (Friedman and Rosenman

1974). Among behavioral issues dealt with both in research and in practice by health psychologists are salt consumption, cholesterol intake, exercise, and smoking, all of which are apt to have health consequences. Psychological techniques, such as biofeedback and behavior modification, are also being used to help patients with chronic pain cope more effectively with their disability. By the mid–1970s, it was possible to demonstrate that, on a statistical basis, inclusion of psychologists in the health delivery system significantly reduced the mean number of times that individuals visit a physician, as well as the cost of medical services both to individuals and to carriers of health insurance. Clearly, psychological factors can contribute substantially to physical health.

Humanistic Psychology Protests Injustice to Human Nature

In contrast with almost all of the rest of psychology, a small but growing subgroup of psychologists during the last three decades argued that the scientific method, with its emphasis on determinism, objectivity, and concern with mechanical cause-and-effect analyses, gives insufficient recognition to the dignity, value and essential goodness of human nature. Humanistic psychology emerged as a self-conscious rebellion against the passive, reactive image of humanity implicit in psychoanalysis and in behaviorism. Prominent humanistic or existential psychologists such as Carl Rogers, Abraham Maslow and Rollo May have pleaded for recognition of the validity of the subjective interpretation of individual experience, and of such phenomena as choice, responsibility, autonomy, self-transcendence and self-fulfillment. They argue that human beings are free and capable of determining their own destinies, and that psychology should devote attention to such human qualities and potentialities as love, creativity, growth, being, becoming, spontaneity and the search for meaning. A journal, *Humanistic Psychology,* has been published since 1961, and an Association of Humanistic Psychology was founded in 1962. The APA recognized this orientation as the focus of a significant number of psychologists by establishing a Division of Humanistic Psychology in 1971.

Psychologists outside the humanistic movement claim that various humanistic therapies and techniques of education such as encounter groups, self-enhancement procedures, and growth groups have been used too uncritically, and that humanistically oriented research remains a program or a proposal for the future, having accomplished very little to date. Understandably, mainstream psychologists are disturbed by humanistic attacks on verifiability and objectivity, and in turn accuse humanistic psychology of being so vague that its assertions are not verifiable and cannot be objectively tested, that is, that they are outside the scope of the generally accepted scientific method. Nevertheless, few psychologists object to humanistic psychology's admonition that we should be careful not to forget what is distinctively human when engaging in psychological research or theory construction.

Diverse, Growing and Flourishing Discipline and Profession

Psychology, then, is a sprawling, fragmented field that encompasses a wide variety of problems, issues, trends, aims and methods. Its foci are so varied that different subfields may have very little in common with one another. There are tens of thousands of psychologists, some of whom do research with the methods of the natural sciences, others of whom do research with the methods of the social sciences, and most of whom try to apply psychological knowledge to solving the problems of industry, the classroom, the military, intergroup tension, and the clinic. The number of psychologists, and the number of subfields of the discipline of psychology, have grown enormously over the past half century. There has been substantial progress in some problem areas, while other problem areas have remained intractable. But almost all psychologists today, as 50 years ago, are convinced that the dispassionate evidential approach to issues of human and animal behavior will help alleviate suffering and can be useful in promoting the public welfare.

REFERENCES

American Psychological Association. *Ethical Standards of Psychologists.* Washington, DC: APA 1953, 1959, 1963, 1965, 1972 and 1977.

Bandura, Albert. *Social Learning Theory.* Englewood Cliffs, NJ: Prentice-Hall, 1977.

Bartlett, Frederic C. *Remembering: A Study in Experimental and Social Psychology.* Cambridge: Cambridge University Press, 1932.

Bitterman M. E. "Toward a Comparative Psychology of Learning." *American Psychologist* 15(November 1960): 704–712.

Chomsky, Noam. *Syntactic Structures.* The Hague: Mouton, 1957.

Eysenck, Hans-Jurgen. "The Effects of Psychotherapy: An Evaluation." *Journal of Consulting Psychology* 16(1952): 319–324.

Festinger, Leon. *A Theory of Cognitive Dissonance.* Stanford, CA: Stanford University Press, 1959.

Friedman, Meyer, and Ray H. Rosenman. *Type A Behavior and Your Heart.* New York: Knopf, 1974.

Glass, Gene V, et al. *Meta-analysis in Social Research.* Beverly Hills, CA: Sage, 1981.

Glass, Gene V, and Mary Lee Smith. "Meta-analysis of Research on the Relationship of Class-size and Achievement." *Evaluation and Policy Analysis* 1(1979): 2–16.

Heider, Fritz. *The Psychology of Interpersonal Relations.* New York: Wiley, 1958.

Hubel, D. H., and T. N. Wiesel. "Receptive Fields, Binocular Interaction and Functional Architecture in the Cat's Visual Cortex." *Journal of Physiology* 160(1962): 106–154.

Koch, Sigmund, ed. *Psychology: A Study of a Science,* 6 vols. New York: McGraw-Hill, 1959–1963.

Lorenz, Konrad. *Evolution and Modification of Behavior.* Chicago: University of Chicago Press, 1965.

Luchins, Abraham S. "Mechanization in Problem Solving." *Psychological Monographs* 54(1942): 248.

Maier, Steven F. "Learned Helplessness and Animal Models of Depression." *Progress in Neuropsychopharmacology and Biological Psychiatry* 8(1984): 435–446.

Maslow, Abraham H. *Motivation and Personality.* New York: Harper and Row, 1954.

May, Rollo. *Existential Psychology.* New York: Random House, 1969.

Meehl, Paul E. *Clinical vs. Statistical Prediction: A Theoretical Analysis and a Review of the Evidence.* Minneapolis: University of Minnesota Press, 1954.

Milgram, Stanley. "Behavioral Study of Obedience." *Journal of Abnormal and Social Psychology* 67(October 1963): 371–378.

Neisser, Ulric. *Cognitive Psychology.* New York: Appleton-Century-Crofts, 1967.

Newell, Allen, et al. "Elements of a Theory of Human Problem Solving." *Psychological Review* 65(1958): 151–166.

Newell, Allen, and Herbert A. Simon. *Human Problem Solving.* Englewood Cliffs, NJ: Prentice-Hall, 1972.

Olds, James. "Physiological Mechanisms of Reward." In *Nebraska Symposium on Motivation,* vol. 3, edited by M. Jones. Lincoln, NE: University of Nebraska Press, 1955.

Osgood, Charles E. "The Nature and Measurement of Meaning." *Psychological Bulletin* 49(May 1952): 197–237.

Raimy, Victor C., ed. *Training in Clinical Psychology.* Englewood Cliffs, NJ: Prentice-Hall, 1950.

Rogers, Carl R. *Client-centered Therapy.* Boston: Houghton Mifflin, 1951.

Rosenhan, David L. "On Being Sane in Insane Places." *Science* 179(January 19, 1973): 250–258.

Seligman, Martin E., and Steven F. Maier. "Failure to Escape Traumatic Shock." *Journal of Experimental Psychology* 74(May 1967): 1–9.

Skinner, B. *Science and Human Behavior.* New York: Macmillan, 1953.

Skinner, B. *Beyond Freedom and Dignity.* New York: Knopf, 1971.

Slovic, Paul, ed. *Judgment Under Uncertainty: Heuristics and Biases.* Cambridge: Cambridge University Press, 1982.

Smith, Mary Lee, and Gene V Glass. "Meta-analysis of Psychotherapy Outcome Studies." *American Psychologist* 32(September 1977): 752–760.

Tinbergen, Niko. *The Study of Instinct.* Oxford: Oxford University Press, 1951.

Van Dijk, T. A., and Walter Kintsch. *Strategies of Discourse Comprehension.* Orlando, FL: Academic Press, 1984.

Wertheimer, Max. *Productive Thinking.* New York: Harper & Row; Chicago: University of Chicago Press, 1945, 1982.

Zimbardo, Philip, et al. "The Mind is a Formidable Jailer: A Pirandellian Prison." *The New York Times Magazine* (April 8, 1973).

CHAPTER 14

TEACHING PSYCHOLOGY IN HIGH SCHOOLS

John K. Bare

In the early 1930s, enrollment in a college course in psychology required sophomore status, presumably on the grounds that studying both normal and abnormal characteristics required a certain level of intellectual maturity or an ability to be able to view one's self with at least some objectivity. At the same time, psychology courses were being offered at the high school level in 13 states, with almost half of the principals surveyed replying that they either did not offer the course or were opposed to doing so (Pechstein and Broxon 1933).

The National Center for Educational Statistics reported that in 1982 psychology courses were offered in 58.7 percent of the high schools in the United States, a percentage of social studies offerings exceeded only by sociology/social organization, world civilization/history, and career education/occupational guidance. The data from several sources suggest that the growth in the number of high schools offering the course has been steady linear since 1950.

Despite this rather remarkable growth, there have not been the concomitant developments that one would expect. In 1973 only 29 states had provisions for certification in psychology that were separate from those for the social studies (Johnson 1973). Most high school teachers have come to psychology *de nouveau,* most often with majors and several years of teaching experience in the social studies but frequently from other fields entirely. Of several studies that report on teacher preparation, the highest mean figures are 13.9 undergraduate semester hours and 19.8 graduate semester hours of course work in psychology (Bare 1973). When psychology is offered in the secondary schools, fundamental disagreements occur about what the course content should be.

THE DEMANDS OF SOCIETY

Society has a history of expecting too much from education. Among the demands made on the schools is the expectation, sometimes explicit and sometimes implicit, that in preparing the student for life there must be some provision for teaching morality and learning ways in which one can live a satisfying, productive, personal life and realize both one's own goals and those of society.

Horace Mann, in the mid-19th century, expected that the effective teaching of poetry should

in sentiment . . . inculcate all kindly and social feelings; the love of external nature; regard and sympathy for domestic animals; consideration and benevolence towards

179

every sentient thing . . .; all filial, all brotherly and sisterly affections; respect for age; compassion for the sick, the ignorant, the destitute and for those who suffer under a privation of the senses or of reason; the love of country and that philantropy which looks beyond country; . . . [and] a passion for duty and a homage for all men who do it. . . . (Quoted in Church and Sedlak 1976, 89)

Sixty-three years later, the Commission on the Reorganization of Secondary Education, appointed by the National Education Association, concluded in its 1918 report:

In order to determine the main objectives that should guide education in a democracy it is necessary to analyze the activities of the individual. Normally he [*sic*] is a member of a family, of a vocational group, and of various civic groups, and by virtue of these relationships he is called upon to engage in activities that enrich the family life, to render important vocational services to his fellows, and to promote the common welfare. It follows, therefore, that worthy home membership, vocation, and citizenship demand attention as three of the leading objectives. (Commission 1918, 10)

After another 23 years, the Educational Policies Commission, created by the National Education Association and its Department of Superintendence, in its 1938 report entitled "Purposes of Education in American Democracy," chose four central purposes for education: self-realization, human relations, civic efficiency and economic competence. (Church and Sedlak 1976, 403). Only partially buried in these long-term goals there appears to be recognition of the need for psychology.

Major events in history can impose demands upon education that are specific. In 1936, in the midst of the Great Depression, an article in *Education* put some of the burden to satisfy society's demands explicitly on a course in psychology:

In this age of specialization and experts, of relief and insecurity, when the whole force of circumstances seems to combine to convince the average man all too often of the futility of initiative, ambition, and self-control, such a course as described above in psychology should act as an excellent counter-irritant. It offers the average citizen the means whereby he may organize and direct his life so as to maintain his self-respect. The most attractive feature of the whole situation is that in so doing he may, as his forefathers so often did, act independently. (Salisbury 1936, 621)

Three years earlier Pechstein and Broxon, in the survey described above, found that those educators favorable to psychology as a high school course saw personality adjustment as the most important topic to be included.

In the bleak days of World War II, Geisel wrote about the need for psychology, in what he called mental hygiene in the high school curriculum.

The importance of education for personal and social adjustment has been enhanced of late by the recognition of a need for morale on the home front. For what is morale but the ability and the will to carry on under more than usually trying circumstances? Wartime for youth is a time when grief, fear, and anger inhibit or distort behavior—a time when, if ever, they must be well adjusted if they are to meet not only the usual frustrations, but many more serious difficulties as well. In many schools mental hygiene programs of one sort or another have been set up to cope with the problems of adjustment. Some have stressed its subject matter aspects, and others method. But all are coming to feel a deeper concern as the dislocations of war present added difficulties of adjustment to our young people. (Geisel 1943, 82)

Implicit in these demands were society's perceptions of the knowledge contained in the discipline and the assumption that psychology was ready to meet the demands. The perceptions were limited, if not erroneous, and the assumption was only partially true.

THE NATURE OF THE DISCIPLINE

Psychology in 1935 was reveling in the success it had achieved by adopting from John Dewey the functional psychology that gave rise to behaviorism. Behaviorism has several characteristics: an emphasis on methodological rigor, a goal to develop an objective science in imitation of the established sciences like physics, an insistence on operational definitions, and an espousal of a philosophy of science that proposed that only those questions that imply how the answer might be measured were meaningful in science.

Learning was behaviorism's central topic, with enough data already accumulated to lead to theories of learning that competed for verification. It rested on the assumption that learning would provide for an understanding of all behavior—individual and social, moral and immoral, normal and psychopathic (Hull 1943). Adjustment, as used by those proposing the topic for high school psychology, was the prototypical case of learning. In his introductory text, Guilford included the following chapters in the section entitled Acquiring New Adjustments: Conditioned Responses, Other Ways of Learning, Memorizing, and Remembering.

As Wertheimer points out elsewhere in this volume, in 1935 psychology had a passive model of the organism that emphasized reactions to the environment rather that its active manipulation. Psychologists said little about cognitive processes. They had turned away from the study of consciousness and assumed that the principles of behavior discovered in lower animals were common to humans. Guilford expanded the psychology topics deemed suitable for high school students by including sections on sensory action, motivation of behavior, symbolic activity, and individual differences. Psychology's primary concern was the understanding of human organisms in terms of the principles of behavior that governed their lives; and psychologists assumed that if these principles were known, the understanding of a particular individual would be inevitable. Physics, after all, had discovered the laws governing the fall of *any* object, and to make predictions about a particular case one needed only to specify the conditions under which the prediction was to be made.

The pragmatism that was also part of John Dewey's legacy made society expect immediate results. But educators who were more knowledgeable about psychology than the general public were saying such things as:

Quite often a mass of monotonously and laboriously learned facts about sensations, perceptions, memory, and such material forms the basis of psychology. In many instances, these facts are not associated with the needs of everyday life. . . . [Psy-

181

chology is a] useful subject provided it is taught in its general aspects. (Geisel 1943, 85)

Why did this very large discrepancy between the expectations of society and the nature of psychology come about? There are at least two reasons.

First, nearly all of us, by our very nature and not as a consequence of any formal training, see ourselves as psychologists. We have lived in close, immediate contacts with the consciousness, the thoughts, the desires, the emotions, the dreams, the sorrows, the ecstacies, the frustrations, the perceptions, the idiosyncracies, and even the occasional abnormalities of one human being. We have also lived in close contact with a large number of other human beings, and with them we have struggled to adapt ourselves to the environment that includes them, just as Darwin had said that all organisms were destined to do. We grew wiser in the process, wished we had known then what we know now, recognized our inadequacies, and applauded the adjustments of others.

But what we failed to recognize was that our view of psychology was limited by that very experience. We do not experience directly how we learn, how our senses operate, what determines our perceptions, why we are motivated, how our nervous system modifies the information that we receive from the environment, what impressions we create in others, how our personalities develop, or even how we make adjustments. The list could be lengthened.

Second, we fail to realize that we are asking psychology to provide the understanding for a unique self, when at best it can provide only the principles of behavior that apply to all selves. Psychology, given those principles and the conditions under which the individual developed, can then make all individuals understandable.

To complete the context for understanding the history of teaching of psychology in high schools, those who teach the subject must be satisfied that what is being taught to students at any level adequately reflects the knowledge in that discipline. The knowledge almost always goes beyond the understanding of the students and sometimes beyond the understanding of the teachers. The findings of Pavlov, Piaget and Freud, among others, stand as examples.

The discrepancy between society's demands and the nature of the discipline influences the teaching of psychology at all educational levels.

TEACHING RESOURCES

Textbooks

The Psychology Teacher's Resource Book (American Psychological Association 1979), described more fully below, reviews 68 of some 200 textbooks in introductory psychology now on the market. Twenty of those reviewed are either written or judged appropriate for a high school course. The books range from Tallent and Spungin, *Psychology: Understanding Ourselves and Others,* to Wrightsman and Sanford, *Psychology: A Scientific Study of Human Behavior.* If these two books represent the demands of society on the one hand and the nature of the discipline on the other, the remaining 18 texts represent mixtures of nearly all possible blends. The variety of texts available makes possible the teaching of quite different courses.

The most frequently used text, Engle and Snellgrove's *Psychology: Its Principles and Applications,* demonstrates that over time there can be differences in approach. In its fourth edition (1964) the seven units were entitled "The Science of Psychology, Learning, Patterns of Human Behavior, Why We Have Varied Patterns of Behavior, Mental Health, Love and Marriage, and You and Society. The seventh edition (1979) has 20 chapters on 20 subtopics that range from heredity to social interaction. It would appear that the pressures from the discipline could no longer be turned aside.

Given the comparatively large size of the market, it is not surprising that books continue to be written expressly for the high school student. Two fairly recent examples are Ragland and Saxon (1982) and Kasschau (1980). A reviewer describes the first as " . . . a careful balance between presenting psychology as a discipline and as a vehicle for learning about one's self," and the second as " . . . an excellent text for the traditional survey high school psychology course" (Cameron 1982, 6–7).

Teaching Aids

The American Psychological Association (APA) has had a continuing interest in psychology at the secondary school level at least since 1935, when it appointed a committee to study problems connected with the teaching of psychology in high schools and junior colleges. Not only has the committee continued, but the APA established the Clearinghouse on Pre-College Psychology and began publishing a newsletter entitled *Periodically* in 1970, which has become the *High School Psychology Teacher.* In 1970 the APA also obtained a grant from the Office of Education to begin the first phase of a curriculum development project, and in 1973 it received a grant from the National Science Foundation to develop curriculum materials intended for national use. Out of those efforts it published the *Psychology Teacher's Resource Book* (1979) and the *Activities Handbook for the Teaching of Psychology* (1981); in cooperation with ERIC/ChESS it also published the short booklet *Psychology, Where to Begin* (1971) and the monograph by Kasschau and Wertheimer, *Teaching Psychology in the Secondary Schools* (1974). The Association's Division of Teaching of Psychology began a newsletter in 1964 that contained brief articles on the teaching of psychology. That publication became the journal *Teaching of Psychology* in 1974.

The *Psychology Teacher's Resource Book* contains reviews of introductory psychology textbooks, books of readings, and laboratory manuals; provides information on periodicals appropriate for the high school; has annotated bibliographies of supplementary readings and reference materials; includes brief descriptions of film series, television courses, slides, and transparencies; has a topical listing of films and filmstrips; lists commercial sources of instruments and supplies (with addresses); and provides addresses of national organizations that might furnish teaching materials and other useful information.

The *Activities Handbook for the Teaching of Psychology* was an outgrowth of the newsletter *Periodically,* which had included suggestions for 88 activities, demonstrations, and experiments appropriate to both high school and college classes. These, along with newly written suggestions, were incorporated into the *Activities Handbook.*

Psychology, Where to Begin briefly describes 10 topics that might be attractive and interesting to high school students. The monograph by Kasschau and Wertheimer is the most comprehensive treatment of the teaching of psychology in the secondary schools currently available.

CURRICULUM DEVELOPMENT EFFORTS

Two major curriculum development efforts affected high school psychology courses: Mosher and Sprinthall's *Psychological Education in Secondary Schools* (1971), and the American Psychological Association's *Human Behavior Curriculum Project.*

Mosher and Sprinthall describe their curriculum as a course in individual and human development to be taught to high school juniors and seniors. The core of the course, intended for all students, is essentially cognitive and presents materials from the discipline pertinent to understanding individual and human development. They continue:

> A special focus of this material is on three stages in individual development: early childhood—the first five years of life; adolescence—both white and black—in this culture; and adulthood. The "theme" here is personal history, which we selected from a number of alternate themes or issues vital, in our view, to adolescents. These include the nature of authentic relations with people (e.g., parents, peers, minority groups); personal history; competence and the future; and authority relationships and personal values. But the issue of personal history—Who was I as a child? Who am I now? Who am I becoming?—is the intellectual focus for the course. (Mosher and Sprinthall 1971, 917)

Resource material for this part of the course includes excerpts from stage theorists such as Erikson, Kohlberg and Piaget, units on intelligence and personality testing, contemporary novels and biographies on adolescence, a study of films, and the examination of case studies.

The Mosher and Sprinthall curriculum requires that the students personalize their learning of psychology. To accomplish this task they developed five "laboratory" activities from which the students choose one: Theater Improvisation and Communication, the Psychology of Interpersonal Behavior (a discussion group that examines behavior in a group), Teaching (and a discussion by the students of their teaching experiences), Activities Associated with Counseling, and Communications and the Art of Motion Pictures. All these activities reflect a continual concern for the integration of the cognitive and the experiential.

The authors are specific about the constraints under which the course was developed. They do not believe that the teacher of the course need be a psychology major, since a number of the techniques can be learned in the process of teaching. They do believe that a single course can make a difference in the lives of students. Data from six such courses (Sprinthall 1980) indicate that both ego development and moral maturity show improvement following this "deliberate psychological education."

The *Human Behavior Curriculum Project* was supported by a grant in 1970 to the American Psychological Association by the National Science Foundation. Given the source of the funds, it is not surprising that principles of behavior are emphasized. It was, however, the explicit goal of the project to make those principles relevant to the lives of the students. The rationale for the materials to be developed was stated by the project director:

> Signal detection can be esoteric unless you would like to improve the reading of chest X-rays for malignancies; operant conditioning can lead you to think about rats and monkeys unless you would like to see how much an autistic child or a child with Down syndrome can learn; attribution theory can be academic until you wonder if personality characteristics are a figment of your imagination; the role of the nervous system in behavior can be dull until you have a stroke patient at home; the expression "rots of ruck" can make you feel superior until you know something about phonemes and speech perception. (Bare 1977, 4)

The curriculum materials were originally developed by a team consisting of a psychologist, two teachers and two students. The materials dealt with topics selected by a steering committee consisting of psychologists, a sociologist and an anthropologist—all distinguished in their respective fields. A module format was designed for the materials so that each module could be taught for a period of two to three weeks. The teachers had the choice of selecting the modules to be taught in the classroom. The modules were reviewed by the Steering Committee and were closely examined by members of the Advisory Committee, a group of educators and parents familiar with the contemporary world of students and education. The modules were tested locally by the development teams, revised as necessary, and tested nationally before being submitted to the publisher (Columbia Teachers College Press). Thirty modules were planned.

The module on *Conditioning and Learning* can serve as an example of the way in which principles of learning are introduced and how such principles can be applied by students to their own lives. After introducing a particular kind of learning with the procedures by which the behavior is changed, the authors describe the applications. Thus, classical (or respondent or Pavlovian) conditioning is followed with a description of studies of the way that attitudes may be conditioned, Wickes' description of the treatment of enuresis, Wolpe's description of the way in which conditioning principles might be used in the treatment of fear, and Lang and Lazovik's experimental demonstration of their use with a phobic patient.

For operant conditioning, an excerpt from Holland and Skinner's programmed text is a must. Also included are: Azrin and Lindsley's study on the reinforcement of cooperation in children; the description of the training of Dicky, the autistic child, to wear glasses that would keep him from going blind (Wolf, Risley and Mees 1964); and the reinstatement of verbal behavior in a psychotic by Isaacs, Thomas and Goldiamond. It was impossible to omit the Brelands' success in training animal acts and some of their difficulties ten years later when the training seemed to go awry (Breland and Breland 1961).

For the topic of imitation and observational learning, some of the studies by Bandura and his associates on avoidance behavior are summarized, as is O'Connor's study of the modification of social withdrawal in a child by symbolic modeling. The module closes with a consideration of the moral issues involved in behavior change. The students are asked *who* is attempting to change *their* behavior, *whose* behavior *they* are attempting to change, and *to what ends* these attempts are being made.

Unfortunately, when the National Science Foundation decided to get out of the curriculum development business, the grant was discontinued. Only 8 of the 30 modules were completed.

TEACHER ASSISTANCE AND INSERVICE TRAINING

The American Psychological Association continues to be very active in its support for high school teachers of psychology. Through its Clearinghouse on Pre-College Psychology it publishes the newsletter *High School Psychology Teacher*. The APA has established the G. Stanley Hall Lectures, intended for teachers of the introductory courses (the lectures are presented yearly at the national convention of the Association and then are published); it sponsors workshops for high school teachers at its convention; and, through its Committee on Psychology in the Secondary Schools, it sponsors workshops at regional meetings. The APA presents awards for outstanding projects in psychology at the annual International Science and Engineering Fair, recognizes excellence in high school teaching by presenting yearly awards, and has established a writing competition for high school psychology students.

The National Science Foundation at one time sponsored at various colleges and universities Summer Institutes for High School Teachers, Summer Institutes for High School Students, and Summer Training Programs for High Ability High School Students, but in recent years has eliminated psychology from the last two. In its programs for teachers, NSF stressed the principles approach for the high school psychology course.

Members of the National Council for the Social Studies have formed a Psychology Special Interest Group that shares materials, strategies, and ideas for teaching psychology in the high school through a newsletter and sponsored sessions at the NCSS annual convention.

CONCLUSIONS

It is clear that the teaching resources, the curriculum development efforts, inservice teacher training, and assistance to high school psychologists by the American Psychological Association and the National Council for the Social Studies have not produced a general course in psychology that is widely taught in high schools. There is still no agreement on the certification requirements for high school teachers of psychology, and the fact that nearly half of the states do not have certification requirements separate from social studies comes as no surprise.

Instead, teachers with varying amounts of formal preparation will, with considerable ingenuity and no less effort, continue to teach a variety of courses that range from attempts to produce self-understanding to attempts to produce an understanding of one another in terms of the principles of psychology.

As the knowledge in the discipline grows, the probability becomes smaller and smaller that what is known about human behavior will be included in our required education. At the heart of this failure is society's limited perspective of the breadth of knowledge in the field of psychology.

REFERENCES

American Psychological Association. *The Psychology Teacher's Resource Book: First Course.* Washington, DC: APA, 1979.

American Psychological Association. *Activities Handbook for the Teaching of Psychology.* Washington, DC: APA, 1981.

Azrin, Nathan H., and Ogden G. Lindsley. "The Reinforcement of Cooperation Between Children." *Journal of Abnormal and Social Psychology* 52 (1956): 100–102.

Bandura, Albert, Joan Grusec and Frances L. Menlove. "Vicarious Extinction of Avoidance Behavior." *Journal of Personality and Social Psychology* 5 (January 1967): 16–23.

Bare, John K. *Psychology: Where to Begin.* Washington, DC: American Psychological Association; Boulder, CO: ERIC Clearinghouse for Social Studies/Social Science Education, 1971.

Bare, John K. "High School Psychology: Principles or Applications." Paper delivered at the annual convention of the American Psychological Association, San Francisco, 1977.

Breland, Keller, and Marian Breland. "A Field of Applied Animal Psychology." *American Psychologist* 6 (June 1951): 202–204.

Breland, Keller, and Marian Breland. "The Misbehavior of Organisms." *American Psychologist* 16 (November 1961): 681–684.

Cameron, Samuel M. "In the Reviewer's Opinion." *High School Psychology Teacher* 13 (September 1982): 6–7.

Church, Robert L., and Michael Sedlak. *Education in the United States: An Interpretive History.* New York: The Free Press, 1976.

Engle, Thelburn. *Psychology: Its Principles and Applications,* 4th ed. New York: Harcourt Brace Jovanovich, 1964.

Engle, Thelburn, and Louis Snellgrove. *Psychology: Its Principles and Applications,* 7th ed. New York: Harcourt Brace Jovanovich, 1979.

Erikson, H. Erik. "Identity and the Life Cycle." *Psychological Issues* 1 (1) Monograph, 1959.

Geisel, John B. "Mental Hygiene in the High School Curriculum." *Bulletin of the National Association of Secondary School Principals* 27 (May 1943): 82–88.

Guilford, Joy Paul. *General Psychology.* New York: D. Van Nostrand, 1939.

Holland, James G., and B. Skinner. *The Analysis of Behavior: A Program for Self-Instruction.* New York: McGraw-Hill, 1961.

Hull, Clark L. *Principles of Behavior.* New York: Appleton-Century, 1943.

Isaacs, Wayne, James Thomas and Israel Goldiamond. "Applications of Operant Conditioning to Reinstate Verbal Behavior in Psychotics." *Journal of Speech and Hearing Disorders* 25 (February 1960): 8–12.

Johnson, Margo. "Certification Requirements for Teaching Psychology in United States Secondary Schools, Spring, 1973." *Periodically* 4 (October 1973): 3–4.

Kasschau, Richard A. *Psychology: Exploring Behavior.* Glenview, IL: Scott, Foresman, 1981.

Kasschau, Richard A., and Michael Wertheimer. *Teaching Psychology in Secondary Schools.* Washington, DC: American Psychological Association; Boulder, CO: ERIC Clearinghouse for Social Studies/Social Science Education, 1974.

Kohlberg, Lawrence. "State and Sequence: The Cognitive-Development Approach to Socialization." In *Handbook of Socialization: Theory and Research,* edited by David A. Goslin. Chicago: Rand McNally, 1969.

Lang, Peter J., and A. David Lazovik. "Experimental Desensitization of a Phobia." *Journal of Abnormal and Social Psychology* 66 (June 1963): 519–525.

Loevinger, Jane. "The Meaning and Measurement of Ego Development." *American Psychologist* 21 (March 1966): 195–206.

Mosher, Ralph A., and Norman A. Sprinthall. "Psychological Education in Secondary Schools: A Program to Promote Individual and Human Development." *American Psychologist* 25 (October 1970): 911–924.

National Center for Education Statistics. *Contractor Report: A Trend Study for High School Offerings and Enrollments: 1972–73 and 1981–82.* Washington, DC: Government Printing Office, 1984.

O'Connor, Robert D. "Modification of Social Withdrawal Through Symbolic Modeling." *Journal of Applied Behavior Analysis* 2 (Spring 1969): 15–22.

Pechstein, Louis A., and John A. Broxon. "The Determination of a Course in Psychology for the High School." *School Review* 41 (May 1933): 356–361.

Ragland, Rachel G., and Burt Saxon. *Invitation to Psychology.* Glenview, IL: Scott, Foresman, 1981.

Salisbury, W. Seward. "Vitalizing the Social Studies in the High School." *Education* 56 (1936): 618–621.

Sprinthall, Norman A. "Psychology for the Secondary Schools. The Saber-Tooth Curriculum Revisited?" *American Psychologist* 35 (April 1980): 336–347.

Tallent, Norman, and Charlotte I. Spungin. *Psychology: Understanding Ourselves and Others.* New York: American Book, 1977.

Wickes, Ian G. "Treatment of Persistent Enuresis With the Electric Buzzer." *Archives of Disease in Childhood* 33 (April 1958): 160–164.

Wolf, Montrose M., Todd Risley and Hayden Mees. "Applications of Operant Conditioning Procedures to the Behaviour Problems of an Autistic Child." *Behaviour Research and Therapy* 1 (1964): 305–312.

Wolpe, Joseph. *Psychotherapy by Reciprocal Inhibition.* Stanford, CA: Stanford University Press, 1958.

Wrightsman, Lawrence S., and Fillmore H. Sanford. *Psychology: A Scientific Study of Human Behavior,* 4th ed. Monterey, CA: Brooks/Cole, 1975.

CHAPTER 15

LOOKING BACKWARD
2035—1985

Stanley P. Wronski

The setting is November, 2035 A.D. in New York City. The National Council for the Social Studies is holding its 100th anniversary meeting. Gathered in a hotel room are three teachers who are to be the major presenters at a general symposium on "Social Studies: The State of the Subject," which is scheduled on the program for the following day. The three are:

Terry, high school teacher from Peoria, Illinois, who was selected "teacher of the year" by the NEA-AFT.

Lee, middle school teacher from Eugene, Oregon, and current president of the Pacific Northwest Council for the Social Studies.

Kelly, elementary school teacher from Storrs, Connecticut, who is coauthor of a leading textbook series published by American Venture Press, a subsidiary of Upright Oil Company of New Jersey.

TERRY: I'm glad you both were able to make it. I was worried that the strike of the computer maintenance union might prevent your obtaining air and rail tickets, but Lee tells me that AMFLITE resurrected some old IBM laser-controlled equipment and averted a shutdown in their scheduling and automatic ticket delivery system. At any rate, I thought it would be a good idea if we could meet before our presentations tomorrow and chat with each other to get a notion of the territory we intend to cover.

KELLY: Good! I like the idea of our getting better acquainted before we mount the speaker's podium tomorrow and face a largely unknown crowd. Besides, I have some questions that came to my mind during the one-hour trip from Storrs to New York. You know, that new magnetic propulsion highway frees you of a lot of the drudgery associated with driving and gives you time to reflect.

LEE: Let's get with it then. And I hope we can avoid whatever fluff and fuzz we intend to throw at them tomorrow and talk about the real state of affairs in social studies today.

TERRY: Well, since I suggested that we have this get-together, let me start by briefly outlining the essence of my presentation. And no, Lee, I don't intend to throw in either fluff or fuzz. Quite the contrary! As a teacher of history, I'm going to take a long-term view of where we now stand in social studies. To start with, I remind you that the National Council for the Social Studies had its first independent meeting in 1935. Do you know what kinds of topics were on the program then? Listen:

The keynote address by Carlton J. H. Hayes was on "History and the Present." The section meeting presentations focused on the following topics: "Social Problems in Present Curricula"; "The Status of Testing in the Social Studies"; "Adjusting Tests to a Changing Curriculum"; "The Condition of Freedom in Teaching"; "Organizing for Curriculum Revision"; and "Sequences in the Social Studies Program"—no mention of "Scope."

LEE: Sounds pretty contemporary to me.

TERRY: That's my point. To reinforce it, let me now quote from the 1985 program of the NCSS annual meeting in Chicago. Although the length of the program has expanded enormously, here are some titles of either section meetings, or workshops, or major addresses: "Getting Hooked on History"; "Problems, Solutions, Consequences: A Method of Learning"; "Custom-Made Tests"; and "Fifty Years After: The Status of Indoctrination in the Social Studies." And just to bring the story up to date, I have thumbed through the program for our 2035 meeting and find every one of these topics appearing—the role of social problems in the curriculum, the status and impact of testing, freedom of teaching, curriculum revision, and scope and sequence studies. Furthermore, I have talked with several recently retired teachers in our school district, some of whom began teaching as long ago as 1985. Their comments, plus my own observations and conversations with my present colleagues, lead me to the major conclusion of my remarks: the social studies of 2035 are more similar to the social studies of 1985 than they are different.

KELLY: That's going to be quite a letdown for the audience, isn't it? Besides I'm not so sure that I agree with such a conservative assessment. At least, I'm not so sure that it applies to social studies in the elementary schools.

TERRY: Well, of course, this is just one person's opinion. I'm sure I'll get plenty of contrary views during the discussion period after our remarks. But let me try to reinforce my position by some observations on what is going on in three subject matter areas in our school—and, I am sure, in many other schools nationwide. You all know about the AP program. Many years ago it was known as the Advanced Placement program, but now it has the more appropriate title of Accelerated Progress. Largely because of student pressure—which, in turn, was frequently stimulated by parental pressure—this program has expanded significantly. For those enrolled in the program, the transition from secondary school to college is almost imperceptible. In terms of subject matter it can hardly be called a radical departure from the traditional social studies curriculum.

In the 1960s and 1970s there were some faint efforts to infuse the AP program with some content that had more relevance to both the student needs and the societal needs of that time. But the back-to-basics movement of the 1980s and beyond pretty well squelched those efforts. The fact that we still refer to the social studies curriculum in high schools mainly in terms of separate subjects attests to the impact of the AP program, the back-to-basics movement, and many other societal influences that are conservative in nature. This is not to imply that no significant learning can occur within traditional curricular framework. It can, and in the classes of many dynamic and dedicated teachers some remarkable student achievements have occurred.

This is one of the dilemmas of social studies in our times. We have generated interest and genuine respect among students, the public and administrators. But there is still sharp disagreement on the purpose for which social studies exists in the curriculum. Most lay people still see social studies as an avenue for inducting our youth into the traditional values of the social order—even if it has to be done by rote indoctrination. Academicians mainly see it as a means by which students acquire what is perceived as intellectually indispensable background knowledge as preparation for further study. Some, but not all, social studies teachers—and I count myself among these—view our job as providing not only significant content but also developing modes of thinking and strategies for using data in such a way that these will enable us best to cope with societal and personal decisions.

KELLY: That last category—the one in which you place yourself—sounds rather utopian to me. Are you suggesting that, through the social studies, we can educate all youth to become philosopher-kings?

TERRY: No, not at all. In fact, one of the problems with practically all Utopias that have been proposed by social dreamers or novelists is that they are too utopian. Have you read Edward Bellamy, for example? In his *Looking Backward,* published in 1888, he describes a utopian society in the United States by the end of the 20th century in which the social machinery works practically to perfection. There is no unemployment, all individuals share equitably in the earthly goods of the society, and no injustices are inflicted upon one human being by another. There is liberty, equality and a sense of common concern about others—or fraternity.

The reality, of course, was that the United States of America in the 1980s did not achieve anything approaching such a utopian society. More significantly, the fundamental premise upon which Bellamy's novel was based—that citizens by their collective action through the instruments of governmental policies could institutionalize a fraternal society—was precisely the opposite direction from which U.S. society had actually moved in the 1980s.

Now, why do I introduce all this talk about Utopias, the social order and contemporary society in a discussion of the social studies?

LEE: I presume you're doing it to stress the point that the social studies do not exist in a social vacuum. That, since the establishment of formal educational systems, schools have become a reflection of the larger social order of which they are part. We all remember this from our educational philosophy courses taken as undergraduates.

TERRY: Yes, but remember what John Dewey said over a hundred years ago—theory may be more practical than practice. With that in mind, I intend to stress that what goes on now in social studies cannot be divorced from the philosophical underpinnings of our present-day society. All we have to do is look around us to see some of the manifestations of those underpinnings. At the national level, there is the "New Realism" promoted by the administration in power. Among its tenets is the claim that the hidden hand of the market is and ought to be the guiding force of our economic system; that the large underclass of socially deprived citizens that emerged after World War II is, for all intents, a permanent part of our society and any government attempts to ameliorate their condition is not only futile but counterproductive; and that collective citizen action to introduce rational social planning at the national level is not only undesirable but doomed to failure. Given these and other elements of the New Realism, it is not surprising to me that we now have a social studies program that deals more with "safe" topics than with such controversial questions as "How can we best deal with the problem of our permanent underclass?" Similarly, in the case of our economics course, you can see why we recently changed our textbook. It was one that devoted more than half its space to the operation of the international economic order and less than half to the role of the United States economy within that order. We now have a text that reverses these emphases.

LEE: Your comments both intrigue and disturb me. I'm intrigued because, even if I don't have as much history background as you, I still can piece together in a broad way a historical panorama that blends both the social studies and the social order. For example, the mid-1930s was a period of great social upheaval and social experimentation. Simultaneously, in the social studies we witnessed the appearance of probably the most radical textbook series ever to be used in U.S. schools—the series authored by Harold Rugg. Similarly, in the 1960s we had widespread social protests against traditional life-styles and numerous experimental social studies programs that encouraged not only inquiring into social issues but also questioning conventional values. By the 1980s the wave of political reaction was paralleled by a back-to-basics movement in the schools. The pendulum began moving again to the left around 2010. You will recall that then we reached the depths of the global depression, with widespread unemployment, starvation, and rioting in many of the less developed nations. It was also when we came the closest to a global holocaust, with the ultra nationalists' actual use of nuclear weapons in an attempt—precariously close to successful—to gain their demands for national recognition in the Middle East.

I can still remember my high school teacher at the time inserting various new units of work into the regular curriculum—units centered on such problems as "Should we adopt a world government now?" and "How can the United States best meet the economic and moral challenge of a more equitable distribution of the world's goods?" Those were fearful days. Now we have regressed to the right again.

TERRY: That certainly is an intriguing analysis. But I couldn't help thinking that the various swings to the left and right that you describe have moderated noticeably over the past century. We seem to have in both society and the social studies something like what the statisticians call a regression toward the mean. Take a look at both the curriculum and the textbooks we now have. There's not much rocking of the boat in either direction.

Sure, we have such things as our computerized data banks, which have made encyclopedias almost extinct, and our problem-solving simulations in which students compete with the artificial intelligence of computers. But we don't very often ask the students to back off, as it were, take a wide-angled view of our society, and devise some fundamental structural changes within it. In those rare instances when teachers have indeed tried this, they have had to buck overwhelming pressure at the local, state and national level. This has led to an insidious acquiescence on the part of most teachers to go along with the game and, for all intents and purposes, to censor themselves through inaction—or at least through a lack of radical experimentation either to the left or the right. Harold Rugg would be dismayed.

KELLY: You know, a lot of this talk so far sounds rather negative and even depressing to me. Can't we come up with a more positive picture of the state of our subject? I'm sure that we in the elementary schools are doing a lot of things that are right and that make our pupils feel good about doing social studies.

LEE: OK, Kelly. What are you going to be telling the crowd tomorrow that will make them stand up and cheer?

KELLY: Well, for starters, I'm going to describe the individualized learning centers that we have set up in our school. I know the concept of learning centers is not new, but we have taken it several steps forward. The basic equipment at each pupil station consists of a computer terminal and video screen. We have already referred to data banks to which all our computer terminals have access. This has enormously reduced the amount of time that we teachers have to spend on just transmitting information to the pupils. In the 2nd grade, for example, we don't have to list all the community helpers on the chalkboard and tell what each does. The pupil can simply give a voice command to the computer and such information appears on the video screen. If more detailed information is wanted about any one of these—for example, about the police— the computer will direct the video unit to display a five-minute tape that shows the police performing their duties. Similarly, during the study of our neighbors to the south in the 5th grade, the data bank, upon command, will produce in pictorial, graphic or written form as much or as little up-to-date demographic data as the pupil needs for the study of any one of the South or Central American countries.

There are other, not as obvious, advantages to these individualized learning centers. As we all know, elementary school children often have personal problems they are hesitant to reveal even to their parents or teachers. The individualized stations enable them to ask whatever personal questions they wish via their own individual and secret access code, and they can be assured of an anonymous response from a qualified school counselor, psychologist or psychiatrist.

TERRY: This all sounds good, but most of what you have described so far puts the pupil in a pretty isolated setting. After all, we're talking about *social,* not individual studies. How do these pupils learn about interacting with other individuals and with groups?

KELLY: You mean our SOCON classes? Yes, we have a separate room for social conditioning. A few years ago our entire staff participated in an inservice workshop during which we identified the behaviorally defined objectives we expected the pupils to achieve during their socialization activities. We relied heavily on the principles of operant conditioning to achieve these objectives. For example, most of the pupils no longer hold on to the centuries-old idea of a free will. In fact, their very concept of freedom is being modified—some would say muddied. You won't see in our SOCON rooms any of those quaint 20th-century world maps in which nations were naively divided into two categories, the free and the non-free.

LEE: Is this your main way of socializing your pupils?

KELLY: No, paradoxically the electronics revolution plus demographic developments have combined to produce a resurgence of the one-room schoolhouse. With a greater dispersion of population from urban centers and the prohibitive cost of transporting pupils via autovans, it has been desirable and feasible to build relatively small neighborhood satellite schools accommodating anywhere from 10 to 30 pupils of all elementary grade levels. Besides, having the kinds of electronic facilities I have already mentioned, these schools have the added advantage of providing a wider age range of social contacts for the children enrolled there. No longer do children go through elementary school with their main social contacts limited to cohorts. Satellite one-room schools broaden their social maturity and enhance their sense of fraternity and community.

TERRY: All this talk about socialization may be OK for you teachers at the elementary and middle school levels, but as a high school teacher I'm still interested in what kind of cognitive learning takes place there.

KELLY: We've come a long way, baby, in that respect too. According to the contract we have negotiated with the people at the COGEX Division of GE, their Cognitive Excellence program guarantees the achievement of stipulated minimum scores in social studies—as well as mathematics, sciences, reading and foreign languages—or else the school district gets a proportional rebate according to the recovery clause of the contract.

Let me explain, further, how this works in one area of the social studies; namely, economic education. I use this as an example because I coauthored that section of our textbook series published by the American Venture Press.

LEE: Excuse me, but is that the publisher that is a subsidiary of Upright Oil of New Jersey?

KELLY: Yes, that's right, and I received very valuable assistance from the Education Division people in the Upright Oil Company while I was preparing the manuscript for the series. The whole section on economic education, which is entitled HOBSO—How Our Business System Operates—stresses hands-on experience by the pupils. First, the pupils are involved in a computer-simulated game that deals with the basics of our country's enterprise system. Then, they actually set up a small business in their own classroom in which roles are assigned, capital raised, raw materials purchased, and goods produced and marketed. The products can be small items, such as candy or other food, doll clothing, and handicrafts; but the key point is that this enterprise is actually and legally a subdivision of a local ongoing firm. The parent company assumes whatever losses that may occur or, what is more frequently the case, distributes to the pupil-shareholders whatever profits accrue. The COGEX Division has a standardized before and after instrument to assess the pupils' understanding of such basic economic concepts as supply, demand, price and profit. For those pupils who fail to gain a minimal knowledge of these concepts, there are reinforcement modules they can replay until mastery is attained. Everybody gains. The officials in the local companies are pleased to get the public visibility they receive, as well as deriving a genuine feeling of satisfaction in inducting the young into the basics of our enterprise system. The school administrators are pleased to team up with local companies because it is good public relations and reduces their costs of putting on such a program. Both the teachers and the parents are pleased because the kids are learning good, solid subject-matter content.

TERRY: This all sounds so neat and slick that I hesitate to enter a demurrer. But I will anyway. One of the things I try to teach my students when we discuss any social institution—like the government, the family . . .

LEE: And the economy?

TERRY: . . . the economy—is that they should not only understand the status quo of that institution, but also analyze its shortcomings, drawbacks, or alternatives. As you describe your economic education program, it seems to me that you are preparing—yes, even indoctrinating—your pupils to fit in as smooth cogs in the existing economic machinery.

KELLY: You must remember that these are still elementary school children. We can't introduce too much cognitive dissonance at this age. Besides, we don't want to antagonize those powerful legislators in our state who want to pass a law establishing an Index of Prohibited Topics for the schools—as has already been done in 8 or 10 other states. But your comments raise an even more fundamental question. Do you really think it is the function of the schools to raise serious doubts in students' minds about the very foundations on which our society is built? If you do, then you are a member of a vanishing breed of dreamers.

Even if you persist in promoting such social criticism, your prospects for success don't appear too bright at this time in our history. Since the abortive attempts at serious social reconstruction in the 2010s, we have seen a major reinforcement of the existing social order—especially in our economic system. Even our educational system reflects this. We have more private schools, including those run for profit, than we have ever had in our history. It isn't likely that they are about to sow the seeds of their own destruction.

LEE: I guess I am just an unreconstructed rebel.

KELLY: We do, of course, have other parts of our social studies curriculum that seriously question and criticize the existing order. For example, we have several units that are team taught with our science specialists. These deal critically with global environmental issues. We used the recent catastrophe of the explosion of the liquid gas facilities off the Atlantic coast as a case study. And now with gasoline selling at $10 a gallon, we are reintroducing our units using some of the instructional materials prepared back in the 1970s for historical background and critical comparison.

TERRY: Well, Kelly, we've touched some of the highlights of what's going on at the high school and elementary school level. Lee, what do you see as the state of the subject in the middle schools?

LEE: I intend to begin by giving a brief historical sketch of the development of the idea of the middle school. I want to do this to stress the fact that the middle school grades have been the locale for more educational innovations than anywhere else in K through 12. For example, when our state department of education mandated courses in computer literacy, the middle schools were the first to be fully equipped with the necessary hardware and software. We completed the entire program by 1995, and it was not too soon because that also was the year that the experimental versions of the Global Age units were first tried out.

KELLY: Weren't those the ones that raised a storm of controversy when they were introduced—even to the extent of having a congressional investigation because many thought they undermined our nationalism, patriotism and sovereignty?

LEE: Right you are. The controversy dragged on for several years until the blue ribbon National Investigating Commission on the Social Studies issued its multivolume report in 2005. Fortunately, by that time the social climate in the United States had moderated considerably, so that the majority report not only exonerated the Global Age program but even endorsed it—albeit not without an accompanying bitterly critical minority report. The program probably reached its peak in the schools between 2010 and 2020. But a lot of events had to coalesce to produce this reasonably favorable milieu.

TERRY: Not the least of which was the election of Jane Wysock as president in 2012.

LEE: Yes, that's true. She brought to Washington not only a more enlightened national approach to our permanent underclass but, at the international level, she also greatly widened the perspective of the nation on its world view. Of course, she had help—if you want to call it that—from some catastrophic events. For several years prior to her election there had been a global depression compounded by widespread starvation and scattered revolutions. But perhaps the most sobering event was the detonation of the nuclear devices by the Middle East ultranationalists in 2010.

KELLY: Don't forget her own background. Before her election as governor she was a middle school teacher. That in itself isn't surprising. We have had many teacher-trained politicians. But remember the program she started in her school and how she referred to it so frequently in her low-keyed way? She initiated what she called the first world income tax. What she did was simply to ask her pupils to contribute voluntarily 1 percent of their allowance money to be forwarded to various world relief organizations. The response of her pupils was overwhelming, and soon the program mushroomed nationally and then—through the UNESCO-related schools project—internationally.

LEE: And after she was elected president she introduced her Point One program in her first State of the Union address. Following a long tough congressional battle, the first worldwide income tax law was passed. Many nations followed suit, and there was established the International Revenue Service.

TERRY: Those were pretty heady times for us social studies teachers. We had one of our own in the White House. And what a role model! She took John Kennedy's "Ask not . . ." statement a giant step forward. And before she died just a few years ago, she, like Thomas Jefferson, requested only one simple statement as her epitaph. Hers was: "The founder of the World Income Tax Movement."

LEE: To go back to the middle schools again, I need only list some of the curricular modifications and innovations that they have initiated:

- A participatory democracy program whereby the pupils have a real voice in running their school, electing student aids to assist the administrators and sitting on the faculty curriculum committee.

- Fusing science and social studies in their Planetary Studies courses.
- Establishing direct linkages with their counterpart pupils in Soviet schools and elsewhere through satellite-transmitted television in which pupil-to-pupil exchanges take place through the medium of automatic voice overlay translations.
- Organizing the Junior Humanities Olympics, in which middle school children from all over the world compete with their original works of art, poetry, music and dance.

Unfortunately, the initial enthusiasm for some of these approaches began to fade with the re-emergence of a reactionary wave around 2030. As you all know, we are still in the midst of it. It has been given considerable impetus by the Secular Nationalism movement—which has taken on many elements of a national religion. On the educational front, the rallying cry revolves around the book *Why Johnny Can't Think*. The main thesis of the author is that modern youth cannot think straight on political and ethical matters because the schools have abandoned an emphasis on transmitting essential factual knowledge in favor of studying contemporary social issues, participatory decision making, problem solving, and similar "social slush." The author even suggests that we establish a new category under the Index of Prohibited Topics legislation to include prohibited teaching *methods* such as those just listed.

TERRY: Sounds ominous to me.

LEE: It is. But tomorrow I'm going to urge teachers to meet this challenge head-on, rather than to compromise and accommodate, as we have so often done in the past. We can get moral support from the recently revised NCSS position statement on Freedom to Learn and Freedom to Teach. We can even get financial support for legal fees, if we have to go to court in defense of these freedoms, from the International Civil Defense Fund specifically established to protect civil liberties. The greatest danger we as teachers and citizens now face is not military aggression but the suppression of ideas. It is bad enough if we, as adults, are muzzled. It's even worse to prevent our pupils from the critical examination of social thought. That old 20th-century author who wrote the book *Ideas Are Weapons* was right.

KELLY: I've heard that some social studies teachers in our system have joined the national Committee for Communication, which took its cue from the Committees of Correspondence during the Revolutionary War. The members' avowed purpose is to keep alive and promote the idea of a radical social studies—one that is not afraid to buck the prevailing winds.

LEE: We have already begun the counterattack in our school. The culminating social studies course emphasizes the three ideas of liberty, equality and fraternity. They are presented through a combination of various media and methods we have already talked about here. Some of the related ideas that our pupils explore under liberty are the changing conceptions of freedom and authority;

under equality, the nature of justice and equity; and under fraternity, the responsibilities of humans for each other, and the nature of community—including the growth of a global community.

TERRY: So we agree that all is not yet lost in the social studies. I can't help thinking about what I saw in one of our tele-documentary series, which recently replaced our textbooks in world history. In one of the programs on developments in Europe in the 1980s, we saw Polish people struggling to regain their political independence and even their very existence as a nation. They were singing their national anthem, which begins with the words "Yeszsze Polska nie zginiewa poki mie zyimy." The Bell and Howell AUTOFORTRAN projector flashed on our wall-sized screen the translation, "Poland is not yet dead while we are still living." Somehow or other, I think these words also apply to those of us in social studies.

LEE: Then we end our session tomorrow on the upbeat. Agreed?

INDEX

A

AAA (See American Anthropological Association.)

AAG (See Association of American Geographers.)

Afghanistanis 152

Africa, Project 158

Afro-American 7, 37

Agricultural History 9

AHA See American Historical Association.

Ainu people 151

Albanian 143, 152

Alberta 17, 19, 20

Almond, Gabriel 64

Alperowitz, Gar 7

American Anthropological Association (AAA) 140, 156, 160

American Association of School Administrators 97, 98

American Board of Professional Psychology 169

American Economic Association 97, 102

American Geographical Society 35

American Historical Association (AHA) 5, 10, 16, 19, 21, 22, 48, 154

American Indian Historical Society 18

American Museum of Natural History (New York) 159

American Political Science Association 60, 63

American Psychological Association (APA) 165, 166, 168, 175, 176, 182–186

American Sociological Association 125, 128, 129, 132, 134

anthropology, cultural 141, 142
    physical 139, 141

Anthropology Curriculum Study Project (ACSP) 155, 156, 160

APA See American Psychological Association.

Arab oil embargo 92

archaeology 139, 141–143

Arendt, Hannah 61

Aries, Philippe 8

Aristotle 85

Armenian 143

arms race 121

Army Air Force Training Program 31

artificial intelligence (AI) 171

Asia 7

Asian Studies Inquiry 158

Association of American Geographers (AAG) 29, 33–37, 44, 49, 52, 55, 158

Association of Humanistic Psychology 176

ASTP-Area-Language Program 31

attribution theory 170

Austria 95

B

Bailey, Wilfred C. 155

Bailyn, Bernard 12

Balikci, Asen 155

Balto-Slavic languages (linguistics) 143

BCMA Associates 133

behavioralism in political science 59, 62–69

behaviorism 169–171, 176, 181

Bell, Daniel 62

Benedict, Ruth 140

Berlak, Harold 74

Bloch, Marc 7, 10

Bloom, Benjamin 23, 24

Blumenbach, J. F. 141

Boas, Franz 140, 143

Bogue, Allan G. 9

Boulder, Colorado 175

bourgeosie 113

Brecht, Arnold 62

British Columbia 20

Brookings Institution 101

Bruner, Jerome 23, 24, 105, 155

Burgess, John 60

C

California 19

California, University of (Berkeley) 140

"Cambridge Controversy" (Massachusetts) 90

Cambridge, Massachusetts 151, 155

Cambridge school (England) 8, 85

Canada; Canadian 11, 15, 17–20, 22, 25, 28, 159

Canadian Studies Foundation 18

capitalism 7, 85, 151

cartography 30, 36

Catholics 112

Celtic 143

Chicago, University of 118, 140, 156

Chomsky, Noam 143

citizen action, teaching students 75, 80, 82

civil rights movements 3, 7, 36, 65, 120